W9-CFO-314

The
Great Kanawha
Navigation

The
Great Kanawha
Navigation

EMORY L. KEMP

University of Pittsburgh Press

Published by the University of Pittsburgh Press, Pittsburgh, Pa., 15261
Copyright © 2000, University of Pittsburgh Press
Manufactured in the United States of America
Printed on acid-free paper
10 9 8 7 6 5 4 3 2 1

Library of Congress Cataloging-in-Publication Data
Kemp, Emory Leland.
    The great Kanawha navigation / Emory L. Kemp.
        p. cm.
    Includes bibliographical references and index.
        ISBN 0-8229-4112-0 (cloth : alk. paper)
        1. Kanawha River (W. Va)—Navigation.   2. Inland navigation—West
Virginia.   I. Title.
    HE630.K36 K45 2000
    386'.3'097543—dc21   99-050596

Contents

Foreword

Dr. Emory Kemp has skillfully drawn together technical, historical, and archival materials on the Kanawha Navigation Project and presented them in a book that will be of special interest to historians, industrial archeologists, and engineers, as well as of general interest to the reading public. Beginning with Albert Gallatin's 1808 report on "Internal Improvements," and continuing with the planning of the James River and Kanawha River Canal and the Great American Central Water Line, Dr. Kemp weaves a fascinating story. It incorporates a detailed history of the technology as well as the national, regional, and local politics and economics that influenced the engineering decisions concerning the Kanawha Project.

October 11, 1998, marked the 100-year anniversary of the opening of the Kanawha navigation system—the first river in America completely canalized with wicket dams. After decades of planning in connection with a broad variety of waterway improvements, the first contract for the Kanawha slackwater navigation system was awarded on August 20, 1875, for Lock 5 at Marmet. The original Kanawha navigation system consisted of ten Chanoine wicket dams. The French Chanoine system was selected over other French systems on the basis of cost and suitability for navigation. Construction of the system, repeatedly hampered by delays due to unfavorable weather, shortages of materials, accidents, and labor and legal problems, took twenty-three years to complete.

By the late 1920s, Locks and Dams 4 and 5 were in need of major repair. The Corps of Engineers had completed its nine-foot-channel project on the Ohio River, and there was substantial support for extending the nine-foot channel to the Kanawha navigation system. Beginning in the spring of 1931, the ten Chanoine lock-and-dam complexes were replaced by four high-lift dams—Gallipolis (now Robert C. Byrd), on the Ohio River, and Winfield, Marmet, and London, on the Kanawha.

The transition to a nine-foot channel and high-lift dams required new technologies to permit the replacement of traditional stone construction with modern reinforced concrete. The French Chanoine wicket dams were replaced with the German roller-gate system, and the dam at Marmet became the first in America to use roller gates for navigational purposes. The high-lift dams also made it possible to incorporate hydroelectric generating plants into the new lock-and-dam system.

The Great Kanawha Navigation Study was initiated in 1995 under the auspices of the Huntington (West Virginia) District Cultural Resources Management Program, as part of the environmental studies associated with improvements in Kanawha River navigation. Since 1975 the management of cultural resources has been an important part of the work of Ohio Valley historians and archeologists. The discipline of cultural resources management has developed in response to federal legislation requiring federal agencies "to inventory, to assess the significance of, and to manage cultural resources on public lands." The Huntington District Cultural Resources Management Program was designed to comply with federal legislation protecting cultural resources, and to carry out research in support of these federally mandated objectives. Since its inception in 1975, the Huntington District Cultural Resources Management Program has produced hundreds of technical reports in the areas of prehistoric and historic archeology, industrial archeology, and history. Many of these reports have been made available to scholars and the general public through publication in local, regional, national, and international journals and monographs.

Through his many articles on the Corps of Engineers' flood-control and navigation projects, Dr. Emory Kemp has played a major role in disseminating information regarding the Corps of Engineers' industrial heritage. His articles on West Virginia's covered bridges and historic turnpikes have also provided valuable background information for the interpretation and preservation of historical features at many Huntington District projects.

The University of Pittsburgh has also played a significant role in disseminating information concerning the Huntington District's cultural resources by publishing the results of the district's earliest systematic archeological survey and mitigation project at the Paintsville Reservoir, in eastern Kentucky. Published in the University of Pittsburgh's *Ethnology Monographs* series as volumes 4 and 6, this research provided the baseline data for much of the subsequent archeological research conducted in eastern Kentucky.

The West Virginia University Institute for the History of Technology and Industrial Archaeology and the University of Pittsburgh should be commended for their own valuable contributions to public archaeology and public history.

Robert F. Maslowski, Ph.D.
Archaeologist, U. S. Army Corps of Engineers
Huntington District

Acknowledgments

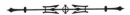

In a large research project stretching over many months, numerous people need to be recognized for their contributions to this history of the Great Kanawha Navigation. The Institute for the History of Technology and Industrial Archaeology is most grateful to the Huntington District of the U.S. Army Corps of Engineers for sponsoring this work, and especially to Dr. Robert Maslowski for his support in all phases of our endeavors.

My colleague, Larry Sypolt, and I ranged far afield in carrying out our research. In Huntington we received generous support from members of the Huntington District Headquarters staff, and from Cora Teel at the Marshall University Archives. Gerald Sutphin of Huntington was most generous in sharing his rich collection on the steamboat era of the Ohio and Great Kanawha Rivers.

"Record Group 77" became our slogan as we perused records at the National Archives Record Center at Suitland, Maryland, Washington D.C., and Philadelphia. Kelly Blake and Dr. Robert Plowman at Philadelphia rallied to our cause and greatly facilitated our research efforts.

Much information in professional journals and official government documents was gleaned from the West Virginia Collection at the Evansdale Library at West Virginia University. Nathan Bender and Harold Forbes deserve our thanks for their knowledgeable assistance as we perused the West Virginia University Archives. In all we collected more than 5,000 sheets of information, which was later sifted and organized by category and date.

The project was divided into two distinct parts. The first featured the wicket dams and locks installed during the nineteenth century, and the second focused on their replacement in the 1930s with roller-gated dams and locks as part of the public-works programs associated with the New Deal. After the research was completed Larry Sypolt prepared a comprehensive nomination for all of the locks and dams for inclusion in the National Register of Historic Places. He also played a pivotal role in this publication by being the "Master of the Footnotes."

Carol Lones and Joellyn Kemp are to be commended for the transformation of rough notes and audio tapes into a final draft. Christine Peyton-Jones handled the layout and title page while John Nicely took large-format photographs as part of project. In the final stages of the preparation, Michael Caplinger and Dr. Janet Kemp handled the editing and assembly of the report with aplomb.

This research first appeared as a report to the Huntington District of the U.S. Army Corps of Engineers. Cynthia Miller and her staff at the University of Pittsburgh Press have transformed it into an attractive scholarly work. The careful editing of Elizabeth Johns created a more concise, unambiguous text, and at the same time a more readable narrative. I am most grateful to Cynthia, Elizabeth, and all others at the Press for bringing this work to fruition.

PART I

CHANOINE WICKET
DAMS AND LOCKS

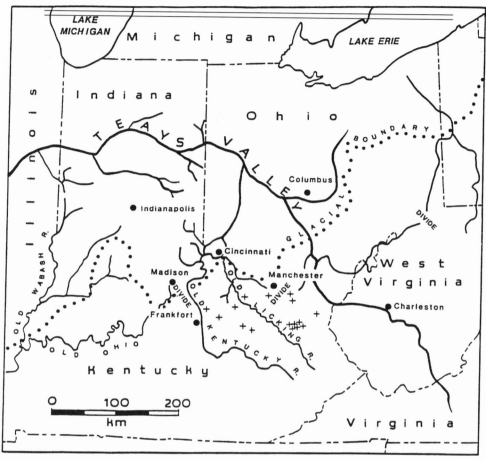

The Teays River and related rivers of the east-central United States. Melhorn and Kempton, eds., *Geology and Hydrogeology of the Teays-Mahomet Bedrock Valley System*, 30.

Introduction:
An Old and Contrary River

From the time of the earliest European settlements in what is now southern West Virginia, the Great Kanawha River has been the principal artery
of commerce, partly because of its singular geology. The geologic prede-
cessor to the Great Kanawha River was the Teays River, an immense drainage system stretching from North Carolina to eastern Illinois and called
more precisely by geologists the Teays-Mahomet River. During the up-
lifting of the land that formed the Appalachian Mountains, the river cut a
path through successive ridges, crossed the more level parts of Ohio and
Indiana, and emptied into the Mississippi drainage basin in Illinois. Given
its source in North Carolina on the eastern seaboard, one might expect
this system to form part of the drainage emptying into the Atlantic Ocean,
but instead it flowed toward the northwest.[1]

The Teays Valley was vulnerable to the glaciation that periodically
blocked much of the midwestern drainage. Thus the Wisconsin Ice Age
(15,000 to 23,000 years ago) diverted the flow, in the process creating the
Ohio River and its dendritic tributaries, such as the Great Kanawha River.
Of all the Ohio River tributaries, only this river follows the general course
of the earlier Teays River through the Appalachian Mountains. There it
has created some of the most spectacular natural scenery in the eastern
United States. Little wonder that its principal tributary, the New River,
which rushes through the gorge from Hinton to Hawks Nest, has been
designated as a natural wild and scenic river by the federal government.

The New River is formed by the confluence of the North Fork and Three Top creeks at Creston, in Ash County, North Carolina, and it flows 284 miles to its confluence with the Gauley River to form the Great Kanawha River. On average, the New River drops 8.2 feet per mile, but the fall in the New River Gorge is more than three times this amount.

The Gauley River has its source in Webster County, West Virginia, at the junction of the North, Middle, and South Forks, and only six miles from the headwaters of the Elk River, a principal tributary of the Great Kanawha River, which the Elk joins at Charleston. The Gauley's entire length is 101 miles. In its first seventy-three miles, it falls 23.4 feet per mile and is only a little less steep at 18.3 feet per mile for the rest of its course. The Gauley River joins the New River at Gauley Bridge to form the Great Kanawha River.[2]

The Great Kanawha River has cut a deep valley through its 99.5 mile course to the Ohio River. The valley varies from a half to one-and-a-half miles in width and from 400 to 1,500 feet deep. The same pattern of erosion is evident in the Great Kanawha River's principal tributaries, such as the Coal, Elk, and Pocatalico, as well as numerous smaller water courses. The Great Kanawha River falls 97.5 feet from Gauley Bridge to its confluence with the Ohio River at Point Pleasant, an average of only 1.02 feet per mile, a rather flat profile compared to the New and Gauley Rivers.

CHAPTER ONE

The Internal Improvements Movement in Virginia

The James River and Kanawha Canal

Albert Gallatin, Secretary of the Treasury, presented a report to Congress in 1808 on internal improvements, which was the first attempt to involve the federal government in the national improvements that were expected to stimulate trade and industrial development. In a larger sense they would also be the instrument for cementing a more perfect union of the former colonies in the new republic.[1]

In the case of Virginia, the vision of connecting the eastern-flowing rivers, which emptied into the Atlantic Ocean, with the Ohio drainage system, first arose not in 1808 but during the colonial period. Until the advent of the railway in America, the internal-improvements movement emphasized canals, natural waterway improvements, and roads. In Virginia, attention first focused on connecting the Potomac and James Rivers with the Ohio River tributaries by means of canals and, later on, through a combination of canals and turnpike roads. The attempt to connect the James and Kanawha by means of a canal was the greatest public work undertaken in Virginia during the nineteenth century. The story, however, begins several decades before the establishment of the Virginia Board of Public Works in 1816. In that early period, around 1750, Governor Spotswood undertook a tour of the Blue Ridge in the company of a survey party. Although there is no evidence of a vision for a canal at that time, one of the governor's companions, the Reverend James Maury, wrote about just such a canal in a 1756 letter to his uncle.[2]

The great proponent of internal improvements was not Governor Spotswood but George Washington, who knew western Virginia well as a result of his tours in 1748, 1753, and 1774. His interests were political, economic, and personal, the latter having to do with the acquisition of large tracts of land. After his tour in 1774, Washington addressed the House of Burgesses about the possibility of a road to the west. When this proposal received only lackluster support, a second bill was submitted, which, after amendment, proposed the development of both the Potomac and the James Rivers. By presenting both schemes simultaneously, Washington sought to conciliate sectional interests in the colony.

After the Revolutionary War, in 1784, Washington made another tour of the trans-Allegheny region to investigate the practicability of opening communication between the headwaters of the rivers running eastward into the Atlantic and those that flow westward into the Ohio. After returning to Mount Vernon, he wrote to Governor Benjamin Harrison, suggesting that "if the falls of the Great Kanawha can be made navigable, it will be found of equal importance to improve the navigation of both the James and Potomac. Upon the whole, the object is, in my estimation, of vast commercial and political importance."[3] It was in the same year, 1784, that Washington became one of the founders of the Potomack Company (later reincorporated as the Chesapeake and Ohio Canal). Sectional interests were conciliated with the formation of the James River Company under Washington's aegis.[4] In fact, he was president of both companies.

Eliot Lacy made the first survey at the falls of the James River at Richmond in 1786, and this was followed by limited river improvements. The management of the waterway was as turbulent as the river it was designed to control, and by the second decade of the nineteenth century it became evident that the James River Company could not meet the growing transportation needs of the Commonwealth of Virginia. A new organization was needed to improve navigation of the river to the mouth of Dunlops Creek and to connect the head of navigation of the Kanawha River with a turnpike road. Equally important was a desire to make the Great Kanawha navigable from the falls just below Gauley Bridge to the Ohio. By an act of the General Assembly of the Commonwealth of Virginia on February 17, 1820, the James River Company ceased operation as a private venture and was transferred to the state.[5] In 1816 the Board of

Public Works had been established to carry out internal improvements in the Commonwealth.

During the period of state control, 1820–1835, the James River Company improved the Great Kanawha River by erecting wing dams to restrict and deepen the channel and sluices to cut through the numerous shoals that stretched fifty-eight miles from Charleston to Point Pleasant. The total cost was $91,766.72.[6]

As the result of accrued deficits and little prospect for the state-owned and -operated canal to complete the waterway to the Ohio River, a new company, the James River and Kanawha Company, was incorporated in March 1832 but not organized until May 1835. This company followed a formula established by the Board of Public Works for turnpike companies, wherein a stock company was established with the Commonwealth purchasing three-fifths of the stock, but only after two-fifths had been subscribed by private investors.[7] The new company continued to pursue the earlier objectives of the state-owned company—a waterway to the Kanawha River.

The new company engaged Judge Benjamin Wright as chief engineer. He was the most prominent canal engineer in the nation at the time, having first established his reputation on the Erie Canal. He was assisted by Daniel Livermore and Charles Ellet, Jr., who was later named chief engineer and served until 1839, when he quarrelled with the company directors and was dismissed.[8] The most difficult part of the project was penetrating the mountains, and although at this stage the company's engineers were sanguine about the early completion of the canal, they decided to connect the partly completed canal with a road to the Great Kanawha River. Thus, in 1836, the James River and Kanawha Company authorized the turnpike road from Covington to the falls of the Great Kanawha, as well as a road extending from the falls to the mouth of the Big Sandy, a total of 208 miles.[9]

As yet undeterred by financial difficulties, the company began work in 1841 on the second or upper division at Lynchburg with an attempt to extend the canal to Buchanan. Following an infusion of funds from the state assembly, the work was completed in November 1851.[10] At that time, the James River Company had completed 160 miles of canal and 37 miles of river slackwater navigation. Instead of a free-flowing river, a series of slackwater pools like a series of stair steps were created behind each lock and dam. The first division cost $39,982 per mile, whereas the most difficult terrain of the second division ran $48,451 per mile.[11]

The next year, work began on the canal beyond Buchanan that was intended to reach Covington. The line was never completed because of financial difficulties. Only 800 feet of a proposed 1,900-foot-long tunnel was excavated; it stands today as a testament to this ill-fated enterprise.

On the eve of the Civil War, the James River and Kanawha Canal Company once again employed Charles Ellet, Jr., this time to study the Great Kanawha River in terms of his plan for improving the navigation of the Ohio and other rivers by means of flood control and low-water augmentation dams and reservoirs. His appointment began in April 1858 at a stipend of $600 per month. On the same canal workmen earned less than a dollar a day. As Lewis reports, it must have been vindication for the company's action in 1839 in terminating Ellet's appointment as chief engineer.[12] By this time, Ellet, who was a leading proponent of long-span suspension bridges, envisioned a grand system of reservoirs and other hydraulic works on the western waters to provide navigation and flood control. Ellet's plan also entailed supplementing traditional levees by building dams on the tributaries of the navigable rivers such as the Great Kanawha and the Ohio.[13]

Not deterred by the financial and social aftermath of the Civil War and the formation of West Virginia, the war-born state, in 1863, the James River and Kanawha Canal Company secured memorials from both states urging the federal government to complete the waterway connecting the James and Kanawha Rivers. Support was garnered from such distant sources as the governor of Kansas as well as from Waitman T. Willey of West Virginia. In his second State of the Union message to Congress in 1870, President Grant specifically supported the James River and Kanawha Canal in his remarks on providing cheap transportation links for the nation.[14] The initiative became known as the Central Water Line.

Although railroads would eventually come to dominate the national transportation network, they were considered to be private enterprises. On the other hand, waterways such as the Erie Canal, Pennsylvania Main Line Canal, and especially the James River and Kanawha Canal were state-supported ventures, and public officials continued to champion them long after they could be justified on financial or technical grounds.

The Central Water Line

Not wishing to approve such a large project without detailed engineering information, Congress passed a law on July 7, 1870, authorizing a survey of the central water route.[15] The survey was undertaken by Major William P. Craighill of the Corps of Engineers, who was to play a prominent role in the construction of the ten locks and dams on the Great Kanawha River during the last decades of the nineteenth century. Craighill's report was submitted to General A. P. Humphries, Chief of Engineers, and thence to the Secretary of War, William W. Belknap, who routed it to the Commerce Committee of Congress in 1871.[16] The report endorsed the concept of providing cheap water-borne transportation to the Ohio River.

More important, Craighill forcefully stated that the project was a feasible engineering proposition. The engineering design called for a summit-level tunnel connecting the Greenbrier River, a tributary of the New River, to the watershed of the eastward-flowing James. The descent from the tunnel elevation to the Great Kanawha was to be accomplished by means of three locks, each with a ten-foot lift. The survey team estimated that an enlarged canal to handle canal boats of several hundred tons could be built from Richmond to the Ohio for $47.6 million. The entire scheme would have provided navigation from Hampton Roads, Virginia, to Point Pleasant, West Virginia, a distance of 1,333 miles.[17]

The plan called for the Great Kanawha to be improved from its mouth to Lyken's Shoals for sluice navigation rather than for locks and dams, but upstream locks and dams would be installed for steamboat navigation as far as Howards Creek. A river navigation could be improved by building wing walls from the river bank, creating a sluice that restricted flow to the main channel. Traffic would be restricted to barges in the summit-level tunnel. The Senate established a select committee in February 1874. After viewing the proposed route, the committee estimated that it would require $55 million to complete, but the valuable route would connect the tidewater at Richmond with 16,000 miles of inland navigation in the Mississippi drainage basin.[18]

It was now the turn of the War Department to study the central water route. An order was issued on January 27, 1874, establishing an ad hoc board that would advise on the practicability of the route and estimate the cost and time needed for construction. The board was made up of distinguished engineers: Col. John Gross Barnard (1815–1882) of the U.S.

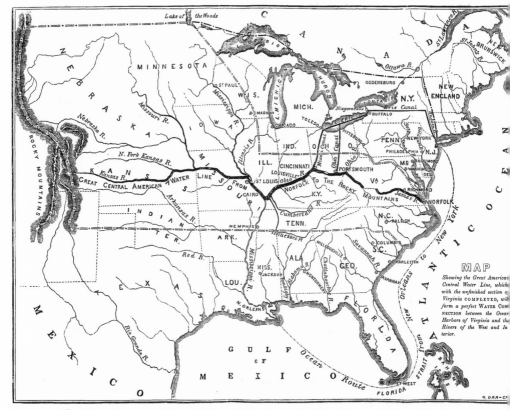

The Great American Central Water Line. Lorraine, *The Central Water-Line from the Ohio River to the Virginia Capes*, fig. 9.

Army Corps of Engineers; Benjamin Henry Latrobe, Jr. (1806–1878), the son of the famous architect, and himself chief engineer of the Baltimore and Ohio Railroad beginning in 1842; Quincy Adams Gillmore (1824–1888), lieutenant colonel of the Corps of Engineers; and Maj. Godfrey Weitzel (1835–1884) of the U.S. Army Corps of Engineers. It must be understood that this report by the blue-ribbon committee was a feasibility study only and not a detailed set of engineering designs. Nevertheless, the report and attached discussions provide valuable insights into the possibilities of an all-water route across the Appalachian Mountains in the Virginias.[19]

To understand better the obstacles facing such a project, the committee set off on an inspection trip in the depths of winter, leaving Richmond on February 5, 1874, by steam yacht to examine the canal route as far as Lynchburg. On the same night, they boarded a Chesapeake and

Ohio Railroad train for Charleston, West Virginia. Because the Kanawha River below Charleston was to be an open river controlled by sluice dams, chutes, and wing dams, it was not deemed necessary to examine the river below the state capital. Beginning on February 10, the party proceeded eastward in a special train, stopping at the location of each of the proposed locks and dams. They spent the night at White Sulphur Springs on Howards Creek, since the proposed west end of the summit-level tunnel was less than three miles away and not far from the confluence of the Greenbrier River. Undeterred by snow, the men proceeded to examine the location of the tunnel and the topography at the summit level. They were, however, unable to undertake a field inspection of the proposed reservoir on Anthony's Creek, a tributary of the Greenbrier River. Because of the poor state of the roads at that time of the year, the inspection party took the train to Lynchburg and thus missed the section of the canal from Buchanan to Lynchburg.

Craighill and Latrobe not only spent the next month in preparing the report but they also visited the Hoosac Tunnel in Massachusetts to secure information on tunnel construction. From there they proceeded to Syracuse and the Erie Canal to study the water consumption associated with the operation of that canal, as well as details of the locks and other hydraulic structures.

To avoid criticism that their report was based upon a superficial reconnaissance, the board consulted all previous surveys as far back as the first one carried out by Major McNeill in 1825–1826. They attempted to verify the data of all previous surveys and combine the information with their field data to serve as the basis of their report.

The James River and Kanawha Canal is a project for connecting the James River at Richmond with the Ohio River at Point Pleasant, by means of a canal and slackwater navigation. The canal to be constructed will have a width of 70 feet at the water line, with a depth of 7 feet; its locks to be 120 feet between the gates and to have a width of chamber of 20 feet. The tonnage of the boats to be used on it will be about 280 tons. The slackwater navigation is to begin at the Greenbrier River, at the end of the canal, and to continue down this, the New, and the Kanawha, to the Ohio River. The locks for this navigation are designed to be 210 feet by 40 feet, with 7 feet depth of water, and to accommodate a barge of 700 tons, or four boats for the enlarged canal.

From Paint Creek Shoals, on the Kanawha, to the Ohio River, it is proposed to improve the navigation by means of open sluice-dams.

To furnish the supply of water for this improvement, it is proposed to construct two reservoirs, the first in the valley of Anthony's Creek, a tributary of the Greenbrier River, and the second in the valley of Meadow River, a tributary of the Gauley River.[20]

The projected work included the enlargement of the existing canal from Richmond to Buchanan, since it was considered by the committee that the lock size in that section was inadequate for the anticipated barge traffic. The next step was to continue construction of the route from Buchanan to the mouth of Fork Run, which had already been located by the James River and Kanawha Company, then locate the canal running up the valley of Fork Run to the summit level, which had been established at 1,700 feet above mean tide level. At this elevation, a tunnel 7.8 miles long would penetrate under Tuckahoe and Katis Mountains. Exiting the tunnel on the west side, the water-borne traffic would enter a slackwater improvement suitable for steam navigation, following the Greenbrier, then the New, and finally the Kanawha River as far downstream as Paint Creek Shoals, where the slackwater system would join the open sluice-dam improvements on the lower Kanawha River and hence join the Ohio.

A benefit-cost analysis by Eduard Lorraine, chief engineer of the James River and Kanawha Canal Company, revealed that the capital required would be an estimated $53 million, but that the projected annual revenues of $8.6 million would be sufficient to undertake construction since the revenues greatly exceeded the 16 percent of the investment thought necessary to retire the indebtedness in a reasonable time.[21]

Each of the board members was given the opportunity to discuss the conclusions of the report, and their remarks provide an unusual insight into the decisions reached by the board. Although the board unanimously endorsed the Central Water Line project, several concerns about the western extension of the canal, including its carrying capacity, were voiced by individual members. Craighill observed, "It could hardly be expected that on all points connected with so vast a project there should be perfect unanimity. Hence, while unanimous in the foregoing, the several members deem that the full exhibition of their several views requires individual expressions of opinion, which will be appended to this."[22]

Further he succinctly stated the case for the Central Water Line: "In the opinion of the board, this route presents extraordinary claims as the measure of relief to the population of the Western States, in furnishing them for their bulky productions cheap transportation in a market, and for fostering the commerce of the United States by developing immense mineral resources now neglected."[23]

With the ringing endorsement of both the Congress and the Corps of Engineers, the James River and Kanawha Company felt that their long-held vision was shortly to become a reality. Yet as an alternative, the James River and Kanawha Company sought authorization to build the Buchanan and Clifton Forge Railway to connect with the Chesapeake and Ohio Railway and tap into the flourishing coal trade from newly opened coal measures in western Virginia and West Virginia.

Despite cost overruns and delays in construction, the building of the great waterway to the Kanawha River below Charleston continued. There were, however, clear signs that the project was beyond the financial resources of the company. Without the support of the federal government, the situation was tenuous at best. The company was attempting to heal its financial wounds when the entire length of the canal along the James River was hit by a severe flood in November 1877, which proved to be ruinous. After much political maneuvering, the company secured a bill authorizing its sale to the Richmond and Allegheny Railway Company, with a stipulation that the railway was required to maintain the canal as a transportation system.[24] It is interesting to note that the same series of events occurred with the Chesapeake and Ohio Canal, which was taken over and operated by the Baltimore and Ohio Railroad until its closure in 1927.

By the 1870s, the long-dreamed-of waterway across the Virginias was deemed to be feasible, both from the engineering and fiscal points of view. However, no benefit-cost analysis could ever justify such a large investment. If one considers the operation of the Pennsylvania Main Line Canal and the Chesapeake and Ohio Canal, by the 1870s it was clear that towpath canals, as opposed to river navigations, would in the long run prove to be financial failures. In fact, both of these improvements were abandoned in the face of competition from the railroads, and no further towpath canals were built following the Civil War. All three systems were trying to surmount the Appalachian Mountains to connect with the western waters. It proved to be an impossible challenge. The Erie Canal was a much more profitable venture since it lay wholly west of the Appalachian Mountains and was a much easier proposition to build and operate. Nevertheless, its successor, the New York Barge Canal, was never the commercial success that its promoters intended. In terms of modern transportation systems, it seems clear that in America only river navigations have formed an important link in the nation's transportation network.

On March 5, 1880, the deed was done and the James River and Kanawha Company was wound up.[25] For nearly a hundred years, the vision of a central waterway, in one form or another, consumed the talents of many, expended the resources of the Commonwealth, and continued as a political issue in the Virginia Assembly. The connection with the Ohio River was indeed made, but with steel rails. A poignant image of the victory of the railway was the laying of the rails on the canal towpath along the James. Across the mountains, the abandonment of the central waterway scheme meant that all water-borne commerce below the falls of the Great Kanawha River would be inexorably tied to the Ohio River system, with the Kanawha navigation forming a feeder to the Ohio River slackwater system.

CHAPTER TWO

A View from the Western Waters

Many had anticipated that the Central Water Line would be a large public work symbolic of the reconstruction in the South. The overly ambitious project, however, foundered in financial and engineering difficulties. Instead, the Kanawha became one of the tributaries feeding waterborne traffic westward into the Ohio-Mississippi system. The lack of a direct connection with the Atlantic tidewater did not prevent the Great Kanawha River navigation from becoming a highly profitable venture and a vital link in the movement of commercial traffic on the western waters. As they planned improvements to the Kanawha through a series of locks and dams, Corps of Engineers personnel had the Central Water Line in mind. They proposed a system of twelve locks and dams, the first of which would have provided for traffic above the falls of the Kanawha as part of the Central Water Line system. This lock and dam was never built, and the twelfth lock at the mouth of the Kanawha River also became unnecessary because of improvements on the Ohio River.

Much has been written about the exploration and improvement of the Ohio for commercial traffic. Literature and art are replete with the romance of the Ohio River during the nineteenth century. Heroic figures such as Corps of Engineers officers Colonel Steven Harriman Long and Captain Henry M. Schreve were heavily involved over a number of years in building hydraulic works in the Ohio River to improve navigation. The Great Kanawha River has received less attention, despite the fact that it was the first canalized river in the nation.[1]

Early industrial activity stimulated these improvements. By the end of the eighteenth century, salt produced in the Kanawha Valley became the first market commodity shipped both east and west. Without a waterway to the east and before the coming of the Chesapeake and Ohio railway, the movement of salt to the east and the importation of consumer goods from the more settled parts of tidewater Virginia used the only means available, the limited roads.

The salt industry was closely linked to the exploitation of abundant gas and oil reserves in the valley. In fact, the technology developed to extract brine from wells was used in the oil fields in Pennsylvania and West Virginia at mid-century, after oil was found to lie along the great anticline farther to the north. The salt industry can also lay claim to being the progenitor of the highly developed chemical industry in the Kanawha Valley. Both of these basic industries, together with timber, benefited from navigation on the river starting with the earliest days of European settlement.

Apparently the first settler came in 1774, but the salt industry dates to 1795, when Joseph Ruffner purchased a 502-acre site from John Dickinson.[2] The property included salt marshes. By 1797 Elisha Brook leased the Ruffner property and proceeded to produce salt by boiling brine in iron kettles. By 1815 there were fifty-two furnaces producing more than 2,300 bushels of salt a day. The market seemed to be insatiable, the only restriction being an adequate transportation system to haul this bulk cargo. The roads were mere trails, and during periods of low water there were numerous shoals and sandbars in the river.

The first shipment of salt on the river was in 1808. Shallow-draft log rafts and canoes were used to carry the salt, which was packed into tubs, boxes, and barrels. These vessels were soon replaced by roughly constructed flatboats, which increased in size over time. Some eventually measured as much as 160 feet in length, and were capable of carrying more than 1,800 barrels of salt. The traffic, however, was all one way. After the downstream voyage, the boats were dismantled and the lumber was sold.

By 1817 coal was employed instead of wood to evaporate brine in salt production, and thus began both the coal industry in the Kanawha Valley and shipment of coal on the river. A year earlier, the shallow draft boat *Eliza* inaugurated steam navigation on the Kanawha. After that date, river trips increased with each decade. Most of the traffic was, however, in flat boats carrying salt and other commodities in barrels downstream. By 1870 salt production had risen to 1.7 million bushels per year.[3]

In 1875, however, only three mines exported coal to markets outside the state. At the same time, the lumber industry was benefiting from a booming market along the Ohio River. This industry continued to be a notable feature of transportation on the river and was one of the primary factors in the adoption of movable dams. By the second decade of the twentieth century, however, most of the timber resources in the valley had been cut over, removing one of the reasons for unrestricted waterways.

Because there were multiple possibilities for commercial development, only perfunctory efforts were made to improve navigation on the Kanawha by the Commonwealth of Virginia prior to 1820, when it acquired ownership of the James River Company. Regarding the Kanawha River, the 1820 act stated:

That, if the James River Company shall, on or before the fifteenth day of March next, assent to the provisions of this act . . . then shall this act immediately be in force; and shall hereafter be considered a compact between the commonwealth and the said company; subject, however, . . . to such change and modifications as the legislature may think proper to make; Provided that no such change or modification shall be made as will take from the James River Company their right to the dividents . . . allowed them by this act.[4]

The following year, the Virginia Assembly again instructed the James River Company to undertake the following work regarding the navigation on the Kanawha River:

Whereas it is the opinion of the General Assembly, that the coal trade on the James [River], and the salt trade on the Great Kanawha [River], ought to be fostered and encouraged; and it being represented that the tolls to be received by the James River Company on those articles, when certain improvements in the navigation of those rivers shall have been made as provided for by the act entitled, "an act to amend the act, entitled, an act for clearing and improving the navigation of James [River], and for uniting the eastern and western waters, by the James and Kanawha rivers," may be found to be burthensome on both or one of those articles; and whereas it is expedient at this time to provide a remedy for such evil, should it, on experience, be found to arise;

1. Be it therefore enacted, That, until the improvements contemplated by the above recited act, shall be completed, and the stock issued by the company for loans of money, shall be purchased in, as provided for by said act, or otherwise redeemed, the tolls on those articles respectively, shall not be less than one cent per

bushel; but that it shall be lawful for the said company, from time to time, as to them it may seem meet and expedient, and until it shall otherwise be regulated by law, to graduate the same respectively, by raising or lowering the said tolls, so that the same be not less than one, nor more than two cents per bushel.[5]

Several years later, in the Virginia Act of 1829, the commissioners of the Kanawha road and navigation were authorized to complete improvements in the river up to the termination of the turnpike from Covington.

The state improvements fostered the steamboat trade on the river, and provided more reliable navigation for commercial traffic, although shipping was still subject to the vagaries of the river, with cycles of freshet and low water continually repeating themselves. Nevertheless, regular steam-packet service was available between Charleston and ports on the Ohio as early as 1829. Sutphin has documented many of the passenger steamers in service on the river as well as ship-building activities in the valley, including on tributaries of the Kanawha.[6]

River improvements began in 1829 and involved the removal of snags and boulders, dredging at sand bars, and the building of wing dams to restrict the channel. (These induce a scouring action in the stream that cuts a deeper channel.) The most dramatic operation was blasting and excavating chutes through the various shoals. At Red House and else-where, these shoals were formed by rock ledges across the river. Channel improvements, including the use of dredges and snag boats, were a con-tinuous drain on the resources of the Commonwealth, which had spent $91,766 on channel improvements by 1830s.[7] Despite the state's commit-ment to navigation on the Great Kanawha River, the sluice navigation was inadequate and unreliable for the increasing traffic.

At mid-century, sectionalist controversies arose when citizens in west-ern Virginia thought they were being short-changed in state funding for transportation systems as a consequence of internal improvements in the Piedmont and Tidewater regions of Virginia. Representatives of the coal industry in the Kanawha Valley joined the fray, claiming that river im-provements were inadequate. In 1855, the coal operators held a meeting and sent a petition to Richmond demanding action. The General Assem-bly responded by authorizing the James River and Kanawha Company to issue bonds for river improvements.[8] Investors, however, were hesitant to subscribe, and few bonds were sold. To placate the disgruntled river op-erators, the General Assembly established the Kanawha Board in 1858, giving it responsibility for navigation on the river. In the same year, Charles Ellet, Jr., produced his reservoir plan at the behest of the company, and the board proceeded to upgrade the existing system by widening the chutes to allow larger coal and lumber flatboats to cross the shoals.[9]

But the coal operators' project of having the Commonwealth improve navigation on the Kanawha River suffered a serious blow in 1861, the year of a severe flood as well as the firing on Fort Sumter that ushered in the Civil War. The flood destroyed the wooden locks and dams on the Guyandotte River and badly damaged the Coal River slackwater navigation. These two feeder systems had been cheaply built and required constant maintenance, so that they were not cost effective. The war itself brought further destruction of the river works and vessels by both sides in the conflict.[10]

In 1863 the newly formed state of West Virginia reestablished the Kanawha Board, giving it responsibility for river improvements and at the same time authorizing it to collect tolls from vessels and, if necessary, to issue bonds for improvement projects.[11]

With interest growing in the Central Water Line, and with the understanding that it could only be completed under the aegis of the federal government, a slackwater navigation scheme for the Kanawha River gained increasing support. The first federal funds were appropriated on March 3, 1873, a modest grant of only $25,000 that was followed in the next year by an equal amount for channel improvement. With such meager funds, the Corps of Engineers, in cooperation with the Kanawha Board, applied the money to improving the existing system rather than starting construction of locks and dams. Significantly, this was the beginning of the federal government's involvement in the Kanawha River navigation.[12] In an act of the West Virginia legislature on March 10, 1881, the river navigation was offered to the federal government in the following statement:

The Board of Public Works is authorized and directed on behalf of the state of West Virginia to turn over and surrender to the United States Government, the full control of the Kanawha River, with all its improvements heretofore made by the state or the state of Virginia so soon as the United States Government shall agree to take charge and control of said river and when that has been accomplished, the Kanawha Board shall close up its business in the shortest practical time by collecting all debts due it and selling its property of all kinds and out of the proceeds therefore paying its legal indebtedness as of the date of such transfer.[13]

This transfer and the reduction of indebtedness was not finally accomplished until 1883. As a result of the Federal Waterways Improvement Act of 1824, the U.S. Army Corps of Engineers assumed the responsibility for navigation of the Ohio and other rivers. Thus, the Secretary of War oversaw all Ohio River navigation improvements. When the Kanawha River, a tributary of the Ohio River, was transferred to the federal government it became the responsibility of the Secretary of War. However, the Secretary noted, in a letter of March 10, 1882, to the governor of West Virginia, that the executive department was not permitted to accept control of the Great Kanawha River nor extend its jurisdiction over the waterway beyond what had already been authorized.[14] With the elimination of the indebtedness, however, jurisdiction over the river was finally transferred to the federal government, and construction of a series of ten dams and associated locks got underway. This project would secure complete human control of the hydraulics of the river as well as improve transportation to such an extent that it would become a highly profitable transportation artery for Kanawha Valley industries. Indeed, it is still the most highly profitable tributary of the Ohio-Mississippi system.

In the Secretary of War's 1873 report to Congress, a detailed treatise prepared by Eduard Lorraine, chief engineer for the James River and Kanawha Canal Company, provided the basis for proposed improvements on the Great Kanawha River.[15] In preparing his recommendation, the author referred to the survey work made by E. H. Gill in 1838 and Charles B. Fisk's report of 1855. As an experienced canal engineer, Fisk had been involved not only on the James River and Kanawha Canal but also with the Chesapeake and Ohio Canals and others. It was Fisk who proposed the sluice navigation system below Charleston in his 1855 report. The Secretary's report to Congress also used Ellet's report of 1858, as well as his survey report of 1872. Ellet outlined two different approaches to the problem of improving navigation on the Great Kanawha River to handle the increasing coal trade.

The first plan, based upon free navigation channels, projected the construction of low dams from either bank of the river, leaving an opening in the dam sufficiently wide and deep to pass steamboats, barges made up into tows, and rafts. Taking up Ellet's reservoir idea, the open-dam improvement scheme depended upon a reservoir on the Meadow River to provide sufficient capacity for a channel at least six-and-a-half-feet deep during periods of low water. This open-dam system below Charleston was featured in earlier reports of the Central Water Line. Lorraine estimated the cost of this open-channel improvement at $1.9 million.[16]

The alternative design projected locks and dams all along the length of the river, from the falls of the Kanawha to its mouth at Point Pleasant. It appears that this was the first published recommendation for locks and dams, which were estimated to cost $2.9 million. In the same report to Congress, an estimate for a single lock and dam was prefaced by this comment: "The following estimate, then, is based upon an open-dam improvement from the mouth of the river to the foot of Paint Creek Shoal, and from that point up to the Great Falls a lock and dam improvement, the locks to be 240 feet long and 40 feet wide, with 7 feet depth of water."[17]

Addison Scott, the appointed resident engineer for the Corps of Engineers, and W. P. Craighill submitted a plan in 1874, which served as the basis for subsequent appropriation of funds, and for construction of ten locks and dams under the authorization of March 3, 1875. After conferring with the Kanawha Board, Scott selected the Paint Creek Shoals for the first lock and dam, estimating it would cost $224,000 for a stone lock and a timber-crib dam, and $261,000 for a stone lock and dam. Significantly, Maj. Thomas Brown of Charleston, who was very familiar with the coal trade in the valley, stated:

It is now generally conceded that the development of the Great Kanawha coal field is dependent on the locking and damming of the Great Kanawha River.

Of the companies organized in the past twenty years on the Kanawha, Elk, and Coal rivers to mine and ship coal, most have proven unprofitable to the stockholders, and many have altogether ceased operations; and this result is attributable to the deficiency of the navigation facilities of the Great Kanawha River.

The money thus unprofitably expended in the last twenty years will, in the aggregate, amount to about $4,000,000.[18]

The momentum for a river system completely controlled by locks and dams grew from this time. The original system was planned to consist of twelve locks and dams and to form the eastern part of the great Central Water Line system, as well as providing shipping for the coal trade down river.

The transportation companies on the river utilized barges secured together in large tows powered by stern-wheel steamboats. With sufficient water in a river, this was an efficient means of transporting bulk cargo. Both the Kanawha and Ohio Rivers, however, often suffered from insufficient water for navigation, while channels would regularly be blocked with ice in the winter. Freshets posed special dangers to navigation. What the barge operators wanted was an open-river system that was improved with hydraulic works such as wing dams, but one that would not impede navigation. The conventional lock and fixed dam would require tows to be broken apart at each lock and sent through in sections, only to be joined together again for the trip to the next lock, where the procedure would be repeated. For this reason, transportation companies on the Ohio were very much opposed to a lock-and-dam system. A solution was at hand in terms of the French movable dam, which would provide, under conditions of sufficient water, open river navigation while catering to traffic by traditional slackwater navigation at lower stages of the river.

CHAPTER THREE

Movable Dams

The French movable dams were seen as a system that would permit open navigation on the Ohio and Kanawha while at the same time extending the navigation season by providing a slackwater system analogous to a series of steps from one pool level to another. By the 1870s it was clear to the Corps of Engineers that the development of sluice navigation, even with reservoirs on non-navigable tributaries, would not sustain the increasing coal traffic, both in terms of the numbers of tows plying the Kanawha River and the size of the individual tows and lumber rafts. The tows consisted of numerous barges lashed together and pushed by a sternwheel boat (inappropriately called a tow boat). With rivermen clamoring for navigation improvements, the Corps of Engineers was commissioned in 1872 to make a report on the French movable dams. It was prepared by Godfrey Weitzel and William E. Merrill, submitted to the Chief of Engineers, and forwarded to the Secretary of War for publication in 1875.[1] A detailed summary of this French technology occupied eighty-three pages in the Secretary of War's reply to the congressional mandate on the subject. An addendum to the Secretary's report included two articles translated from the *Annales des Ponts et Chaussées* providing further engineering details.[2]

The movable dam system is composed of distinct parts. An iron framework supporting baffles, wickets, or needles is mounted on a fixed foundation below the depth of the navigable channel. Both the baffles and the framework were designed to be disassembled and lowered on top of the fixed foundation constructed of stone or concrete. Flanking the movable

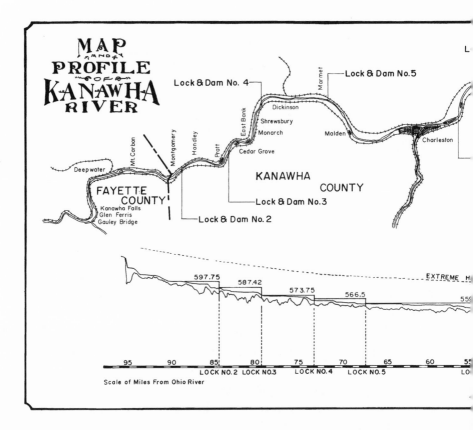

MAP *AND* PROFILE *OF* KANAWHA RIVER

Lock & Dam No. 4

Marmet — Lock & Dam No.5

Dickinson

Shrewsbury

Monarch

Malden

Charleston

Cedar Grove

East Bank

Pratt

Handley

Montgomery

Mt. Carbon

Deepwater

KANAWHA COUNTY

FAYETTE COUNTY

Kanawha Falls
Glen Ferris
Gauley Bridge

Lock & Dam No.3

Lock & Dam No. 2

597.75   587.42   573.75   566.5   55

EXTREME H

95   90   85   80   75   70   65   60   55
LOCK NO.2 LOCK NO.3   LOCK NO.4   LOCK NO.5   LO

Scale of Miles From Ohio River

dam, the so-called navigational pass was a fixed crest weir with a movable framework mounted on top to maintain the pool level when both the dam and the weir were raised, while at the other end of the pass a conventional pound lock with miter gates was provided. Thus, under favorable water levels, vessels could move freely over the navigational pass. In low water, the dam and weir could be raised to provide a slackwater system with vessels using the lock to pass from one slackwater level to another.

The movable dam has an ancient lineage. Staunches and flash locks dating from the Middle Ages permitted the passage of vessels through mill dams. The typical English staunch was like a portcullis with a gate that could be raised by a winch positioned on an overhead framework, allowing vessels to pass in both directions. An alternative was the flash lock, in which an opening in the dam could be closed by a series of needles closely spaced and resting on a framework.[3] These types of hydraulic works

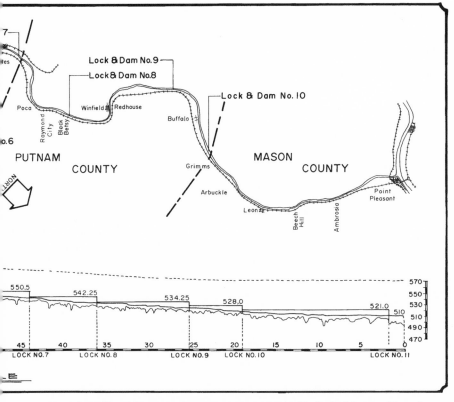

Map and profile of the Kanawha River. West Virginia Geological Survey, *Kanawha County* (Charleston: West Virginia Geological Survey, 1914), 32–33.

not only provide a means for vessels to pass over or through mill dams, but when they are opened a flood of water is released, floating vessels downstream on an artificial tide. Needless to say, working vessels upstream posed considerable difficulties with such a single lock or gate system, in contrast to a conventional pound lock, with upper and lower gates.

Hazard and White, of Philadelphia, invented the bear-trap gate on the Lehigh navigation to enhance the movement of anthracite coal to the Philadelphia market. The first bear-trap gate was completed in 1819, and a dozen more were put in operation the following year.[4] This marks the beginning of the modern use of movable dams for navigation purposes. After a period of neglect, interest was revived in connection with the canalization of the Ohio River. Bear-trap dams were used sparingly and could not be readily adapted to the wide openings needed to accommodate large rafts or multiple barge tows. Nevertheless, they were employed to improve the performance of the movable dam and lock system on the

Ohio. The first application, located at Davis Island just below Pittsburgh, was completed in 1885.[5] Bear-trap gates provided an efficient method of moving debris and particularly ice downstream. Several modifications to the original Hazard and White bear traps are attributed to Thomas Parker; Robert A. Lang is credited with developing yet another alternative. Parker patented his device in 1887, whereas Lang secured his patent in 1890.

A wooden-gated Parker bear-trap dam was built on the Mussel Shoals Canal in Tennessee in 1892, with an opening of 40 feet and a vertical height of 8½ feet. Shortly thereafter, in 1896, a steel-framed bear-trap gate was installed on the Louisville and Portland Canal with an opening of 40 feet and a height of 15 feet 3½ inches. The Lang bear-trap gate was represented at three locations on the headwaters of the Mississippi River in Minnesota in 1895. The largest of these had an opening of 40 feet and a height of 13 feet. All were constructed of wood. The largest bear-trap gate ever constructed was for the Chicago drainage canal. Used for flushing and regulating purposes, it had a clear opening of 160 feet and a height of 17 feet. The steel gate, the largest ever constructed in the country, was completed in 1898, the same year the Kanawha system was opened for traffic.[6]

Flashing of staunches was an annual ritual on the Yonne River in France, which arose in the Massif Central and reached its confluence with the Seine at Montereau. For more than four hundred years, logs were rolled into the river at various points, filling the river from bank to bank. When the flow in the river was adequate, the staunches were opened sequentially and the great flotage surged down the Yonne from Clamency to the Seine and thence to Paris.

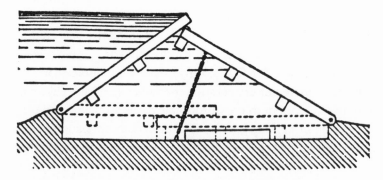

Bear-trap gate, Davis Island. Wegmann, *The Design and Construction of Dams,* 192.

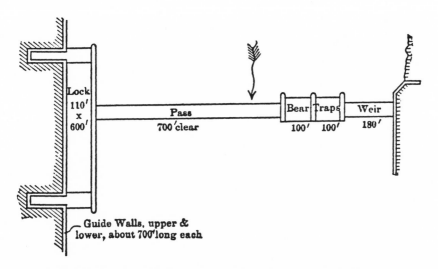

Typical Ohio River lock and dam, showing Chanoine wickets installed on the pass and weir and a pair of bear-trap dams. The rolling lock gates are featured. Thomas and Watt, *The Improvement of Rivers*, 596.

As early as 1858, the French experimented with the bear trap and installed such a weir at Laneuville-au-Pont on the Marne River. This structure had an opening of 29 feet 6 inches. Water could be let in at the top and bottom levels through a pair of culverts. An adjustment in the flow in the culverts would cause the dam to collapse automatically. Apparently this installation was not well constructed, and it discouraged the French engineers of the Ponts et Chaussées from further application.[7]

Besides the bear-trap movable gate, the French invented four other types: (1) frame or needle weirs (*barrage à fermettes,* or *barrage à aiguilles*); (2) movable shutter weirs (*barrage à hausses mobiles*); (3) drum weirs (*barrage à tambour*); and (4) pontoon weirs (*barrage à ponton*).[8] The French entry into the field of movable dams resulted from the need to widen chutes in six dams to permit the passage of rafts and large tows. The French dominated the movable-dam field with many ingenious devices. In every case the engineers were associated with the national Ponts et Chaussées agency. The French tradition was to identify the engineers associated with movable-dam technology by last name only. Through exhaustive research several of their first names have been discovered, but others are still unknown.

Frame or Needle Weirs

In 1834 the Poirée needle dam was first constructed at Basseville, where the Nivernais Canal crosses the Yonne River at the same level. The interesting engineering problem was to maintain the level of the river at a height sufficient for navigation and yet open to leave the original channel of the stream free for the passage of flashes of water carrying rafts and logs downstream. A flash-lock system on the Yonne provided Charles Antoine François Poirée with his idea. These passes were similar to the British flash locks, and to close them a beam providing support for a series of six-foot-long wooden battens or needles was swung from one pier to the other. The project in which Poirée first used this system consisted of five of these openings set side by side with the horizontal beam supported on piers. The first step was to replace the masonry piers with a series of iron trestles parallel to the flow of the stream; these supported a series of needles, thus forming a barrage. The system could be disassembled by removing the needles and pivoting the trestles so that they would fall sideways on top of the foundation. Because of their similarity to roof trusses, they were called *fermettes* (little trestles) in the French literature.[9]

Following the erection of the first Poirée movable dam at Basseville, Poirée's design was quickly modified by other French engineers. A similar dam was erected at Decize in 1836 with an opening of 328 feet, supported on trestles 6.2 feet high and 3.3 feet apart. The following year a similar dam was constructed at Epineau on the Yonne. Numerous other movable dams using the Poirée system were built not only in France but as far away as Russia. For example, Janicki, an engineer on the Moscow River, reported very favorably on this system of movable dams.[10] The French Poirée system was not used, however, on either the Ohio or the Kanawha River. Its first American application was at the end of the century, when the dam on the Big Sandy River, a tributary of the Ohio, was built in 1896 and opened for traffic in 1897. The work was designed and supervised by Benjamin F. Thomas, who presented a detailed paper on the subject in 1898.[11] The Big Sandy River separates West Virginia and Kentucky, and the Thomas Dam at Louisa, Kentucky, was designated Number 3. The original design consisted of a 130-foot-wide pass with a 13-foot head over the sill and a weir opening of 140 feet with a 7-foot

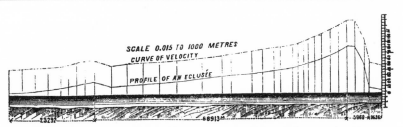

FIG. 1. — Form of an *éclusée* or flash. Curve showing its velocity at each point.

BASSEVILLE BARRAGE.

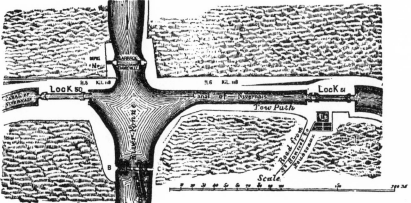

FIG. 2. — Plan of the crossing of the Yonne River, by the Nivernais Canal at Basseville.

FIG. 3. — Elevation of the Basseville barrage, showing half the barrage closed with the fermettes raised, and the other half open, with the fermettes lowered.

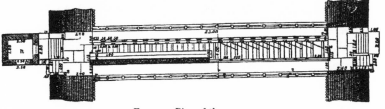

FIG. 4. — Plan of the same.

Poirée needle dam at Basseville, France. Watson, "River Improvements in France, Including a Description of Poirée's System of Movable Dams," 340.

---

height over the weir sill. In both cases, the trestles were spaced at 4-foot centers. After a decade of service, the corrosion of the trestles was so severe that the entire system was replaced. Construction was undertaken in 1907 and 1908, with the needle system being replaced by Chanoine wickets.

The sole survivor of the needle system in the United States is the Bonnet Carré Spillway on the Mississippi River just above New Orleans.[12] The spillway is regulated by a series of needles to divert flood waters from the Mississippi into Lake Pontchartrain and thence to the Gulf of Mexico, thus reducing flooding in the New Orleans area. Various objections were voiced regarding the original Poirée movable dam. The needles did not form a watertight barrier unless some additional device was installed, such as a batten between the needles, and this greatly increased the difficulty of assembling and disassembling the structure. The dams' installation and removal was labor intensive and could be quite dangerous under high water conditions. In order for the needles to be maneuvered manually, they had to be rather thin, making them apt to break and to be lost. Further, if the water rose above the footbridge, it became impossible to maneuver the dam at all. This latter difficulty could be overcome by using a maneuver boat for removing the needles. Large needles on the Bonnet Carré Spillway are placed in position or removed with a rail-mounted overhead crane. Because of these objections, several modifications were proposed following the introduction of the original needle dam. Auguste Boulé replaced the needles with a series of panels. His design was successfully tried at Port-à-l'Anglais and recommended for installation at Port-à-Villez.[13] It appeared that Caméré first used his design, which is rather reminiscent of a roll-up garage door, at Port-à-Villez, in the period 1876–1880.[14]

While the design was never as popular as the Chanoine wicket dam, notable examples of the Boulé shutter dam were featured at the falls of the Ohio, New York State Barge Canal, and on the Trinity River in Texas. Apparently the sole example of the Caméré dam in North America is still in operation at Saint Andrews, Manitoba.

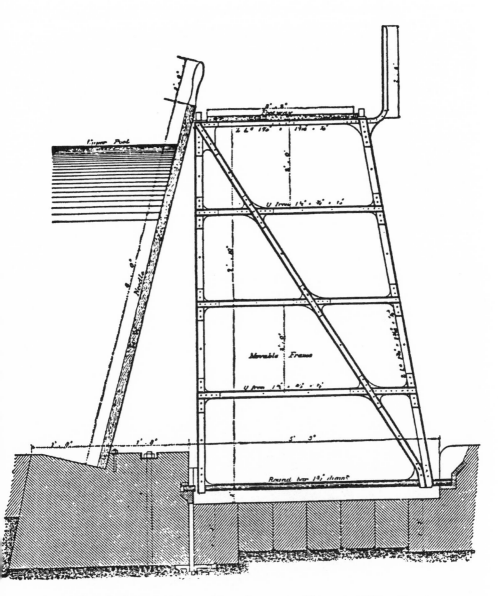

Sector of needle dam on the lower Seine prior to 1880. Thomas and Watt, *The Improvement of Rivers*, 562.

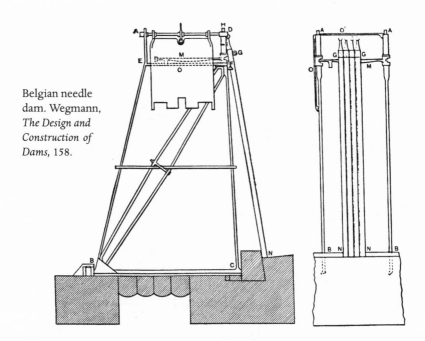

Belgian needle dam. Wegmann, *The Design and Construction of Dams*, 158.

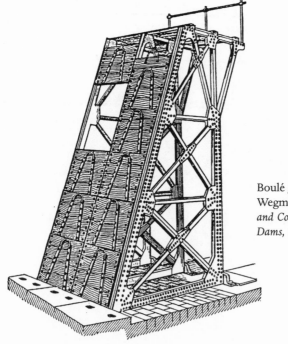

Boulé gate. Wegmann, *The Design and Construction of Dams*, 162.

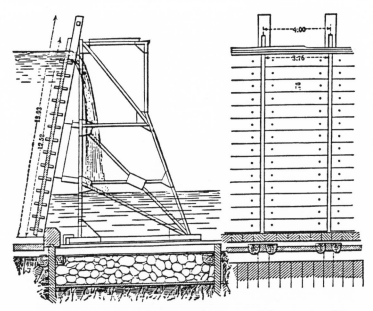

Boulé gates in Moscow dams. Wegmann, *The Design and Construction of Dams*, 163.

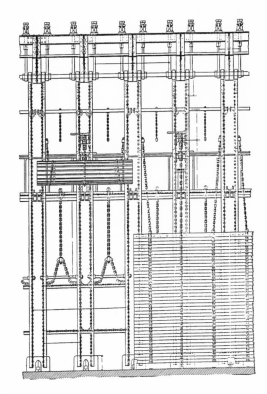

Caméré curtain dam. Wegmann, *The Design and Construction of Dams*, 164.

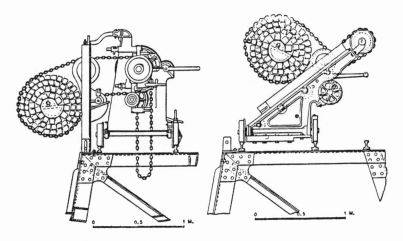

Caméré curtain in rolled-up position. Wegmann, *The Design and Construction of Dams*, 166.

Movable Shutter Weirs

The Chanoine wicket dam became the design chosen by the Corps of Engineers for use on both the Ohio and the Kanawha Rivers. The Chanoine wicket was not, however, the first nor the only movable dam developed by the French. The movable shutter dam, or weir, employing a gate turning on a horizontal axis at the bottom of the shutter, was used as early as the late eighteenth century on the River Orb in France. Later, engineer Thénard used this system between 1832 and 1837 on the River Isle.[15] The movable weir resembles, in principle, the bear trap described above, with the prop taking the place of the lower gate. Thénard intended to modify this system, but he retired and the work was taken up by the French engineer Jacques Chanoine, who was involved with the early Poirée needle dams. In 1850 Chanoine erected a shutter dam at Courbeton that was really a combination of the Poirée and the Thénard shutter gate. This design was not suitable for anything but low head weirs. To obtain a shutter system suitable for navigational passes, further development was clearly needed.

This Chanoine did in 1852 with a weir erected at Conflans-sur-Seine. The pivot point was moved above the bottom of the shutter to a location approximately a third of the way up; this was the center of pressure for water acting against the shutter. This design created a self-acting weir that would collapse when the water reached the height where it could

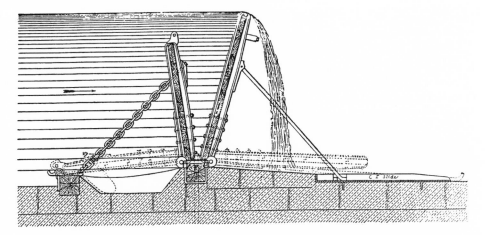

Thénard shutter dam. Wegmann, *The Design and Construction of Dams*, 174.

rotate the shutter. In the closed position, the shutter was supported by a strong wrought-iron prop at an angle of forty-five degrees to the horizontal; its lower end rested in a cast-iron shoe having a quick-release device. This prop could be withdrawn sideways, dropping the entire shutter on top of the foundation. In reverse order, the shutter was raised by a winch positioned on a barge or a foot bridge, by means of a chain attached to its lower edge. To ease erection, the shutter was kept in a horizontal position. As soon as the shutter and prop were in position, water pressure was used to rotate the shutter vertically. A number of such shutters could be erected side by side to create quite wide navigational passes or even to serve as a control device on top of the adjacent weir.

The first movable dam of this type was completed in 1858. It had a navigable pass of 114½ feet and was composed of twenty-nine shutters 7 feet 9 inches in height and 3 feet 7 inches wide.[16] This system was so successful that it was widely applied in France by 1870. At Port-à-l'Anglais, a movable shutter and weir, together with a conventional lock, were constructed in 1863–1864.[17] By 1869, however, it became necessary to provide a much larger navigational pass. A channel was cut 115 feet in width, and movable shutters were placed across the channel retaining water to a height of 13½ feet above the sill. It was this configuration that attracted the U.S. Army Corps of Engineers during their inspection of French movable dams and resulted ultimately in their application not only at Davis Island on the Ohio River but for the entire set of movable dams on the Kanawha.[18]

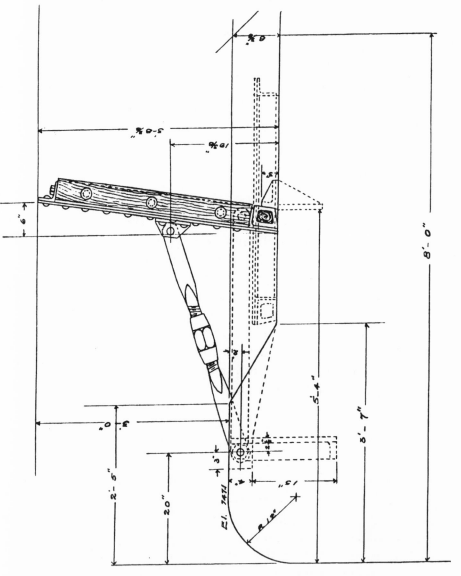

Betwa movable dam as used on the Monongahela River. U.S. Army Corps of Engineers, Pittsburgh District Archives.

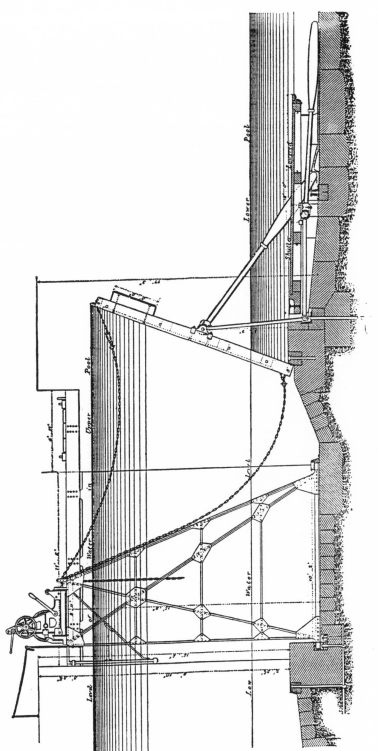

Chanoine shutter-dam for navigable pass at Port à l'Anglais on the upper Seine, constructed in 1870. Wegmann, *The Design and Construction of Dams*, 176.

Drum Weirs

Drum weirs, another type of movable dam investigated by the Corps of Engineers, were invented by the French engineer Desfontaines. They featured linked paddles revolving inside a drum. The paddles were worked by the action of water on the lower paddle as it was let in from the upper pool through conduits into the dam. Water could be directed above or below the lower paddle, depending on whether the weirs were to be closed or opened. The first movable dams of this type were erected on the Marne in 1857; between 1861 and 1867 nine more movable drum dams were constructed on the river.[19]

Hiram Martin Chittenden of the Corps of Engineers modified the French dam for installation at Locks and Dams 2 and 3 on the Monongahela River. Because their proclivity to collect debris caused them to malfunction, they were not utilized elsewhere. Searching for a more suitable movable dam, engineer officers of the Corps of Engineers ex-

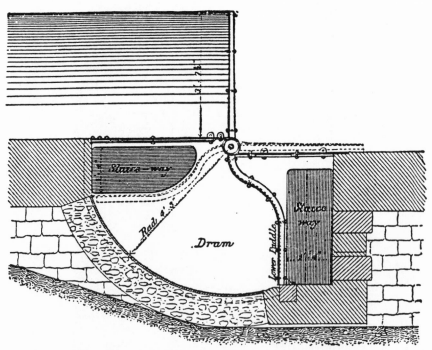

Desfontaines drum dam. Thomas and Watt, *The Improvement of Rivers*, 647.

perimented with a design used by the British Royal Engineers on the Betwa Dam in India. This device was itself a modification of the Thénard shutter without the counter leaf. These self-acting wickets were installed on Dams 1 and 5 on the Monongahela River as an experiment. At one-third the cost of the drum dam, they were an attractive alternative, but they failed to perform well in navigable waterways such as the Monongahela River since they were easily tripped by tow-boat wakes and by drifting ice. Neither condition was encountered in India.

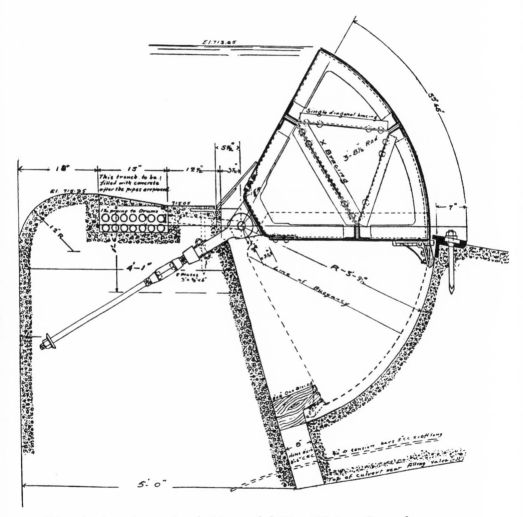

Chittenden drum dam used on the Monongahela River. U.S. Army Corps of Engineers, Pittsburgh District Archives.

Pontoon Weirs

The final type of movable dam was the pontoon weir invented by engineer Krantz in 1868. When the weir is open, the pontoon lies flat on the foundation conduit with the shutter resting on top. The gate is closed by hydraulic action. When the lower sluice gates are shut and the upper ones open, the pontoon rises in the conduit, revolving on its end and raising the shutter with it. As designed, the pontoon flotation force was thought to be sufficient to overcome the resistance of the water and the friction of the moving parts. At Port-à-Villez on the Seine, a pontoon movable dam was erected but never put into operation since experiments conducted at another site showed that there was insufficient water pressure to raise the pontoon without the water level at the foot of the dam being reduced to unacceptably low levels.[20] This type of dam was reported by the Corps of Engineers but never seriously considered, and it was never applied in American practice.

With a rich field to select from, the American engineers chose the Chanoine shutter wicket as the most appropriate movable dam type for use on the Ohio and Kanawha Rivers.

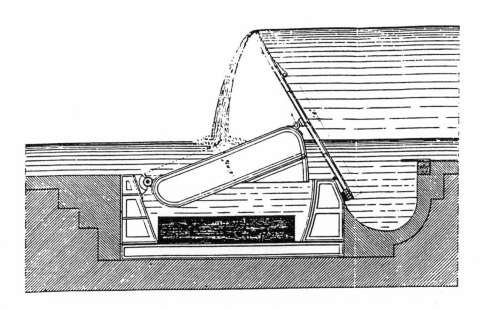

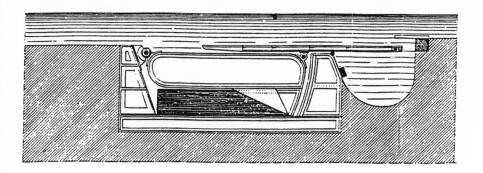

Krantz pontoon wicket gate. Wegmann, *The Design and Construction of Dams*, 182.

CHAPTER FOUR

The First Kanawha Locks and Dams

The Engineers

The Kanawha River improvement, under construction for more than two decades, was completed in 1898. Many engineers were involved in the design and construction of this great public work, together with civilian building contractors and of course the legion of anonymous workmen. The contractors are known only in a corporate sense on the basis of available official documents. In contrast, biographical information is readily available on the military engineers involved in the project, together with details of the career of Addison Scott, the only senior civilian engineer in a position of leadership.[1] Addison Scott emerges as the leading engineer; he was engaged throughout the project as the resident or assistant engineer. Although not an Army officer, he was often referred to as Captain.

Scott was born on February 20, 1843, in Dryden, New York, the son of a farmer. During his boyhood, he worked on his father's farm and attended the local school. Beginning around 1859, he attended Ithaca Academy, where he studied, among other subjects, mathematics and land surveying. During his years as a student at the academy, he also taught school.

In 1866, at the age of twenty-three, he joined a survey of the upper Mississippi under the direction of Maj. G. K. Warren, who was a distinguished Civil War veteran holding the rank of brevet brigadier general. Scott's appointment ended as winter approached in the fall of 1866, and

Addison M. Scott. Addison Moffet Scott Collection, James E. Morrow Library, Marshall University, Huntington, W.V.

he returned to his studies at Ithaca Academy. Later he made the difficult decision to leave the academy and join Warren as an assistant engineer on the improvement of navigation on the upper Mississippi. It was to be the beginning of a career devoted entirely to the Corps of Engineers and river navigation. His most important assignment was as assistant engineer under Warren to supervise the construction of a combined rail and highway bridge across the Mississippi River at Rock Island–Davenport. He remained on the project until it was finished in 1873.

Warren was transferred to Newport, Rhode Island, in 1873 and offered Scott a position on his staff. In that year, however, the federal government began its improvement of the Great Kanawha River. Declining Warren's offer, Scott was employed from the beginning of this project till three years after its completion in 1898. Details of Scott's career appear in an undated deposition in connection with a dispute on a cofferdam. James A. Tanner interrogated Addison Scott as a witness:

Q.: Mr. Scott, how long have you been Civil Engineer, and where have you worked in that capacity?

A.: All of my life since leaving school I have been employed as Civil Engineer, serving as Assistant in the Corps of Engineers. I have been so employed all the time since 1867. I was first in the Mississippi, and afterwards in the Kanawha River improvement.

Q.: How long have you been engaged in working upon the Kanawha River improvement?

A.: Since the Summer of 1873, now a little over 28 years.

Q.: And during that 28 years you have been the Resident Engineer in charge of the supervision of the work.

A.: All the time except about 6½ years beginning in August 1876 to Feb., 1883; between those dates I was the principal assistant engineer on the work under Resident Engineers; first under Lieutenant Turtle of the Corps of Engineers, and after that under Captain Ruffner, of the Corps of Engineers. Since February 1883 I have been Resident Engineer in local charge of the work under different Engineer officers who have had their offices either at Baltimore or Cincinnati.

Q.: Did you ever spend any time in the investigation of river improvement construction in any foreign Country or Countries?

A.: In the fall of 1880 I made a trip to Europe, was gone about three months, and spent the greater part of my time in examining movable dams in France and Belgium.[2]

After the completion of the Kanawha River project, Craighill, whom Scott had served, wrote in 1899: "To him alone is due, more than any other person, the success of this work. I say what I know, and it gives me sincere pleasure thus to bear record to the merit of a most faithful and deserving man."[3]

From the district office of the Corps of Engineers in Baltimore, William Price Craighill oversaw the project from initial surveys and designs dating from 1870 until he was appointed Chief of Engineers in 1895. A native Virginian, he was born July 1, 1833 at Charles Town, Virginia (West Virginia after 1863). After graduating second in his class at West Point in 1853, he received a commission in the Corps of Engineers and engaged in construction work at Fort Delaware. He returned to West Point as professor of engineering just before the outbreak of the Civil War. Toward the end of this conflict, he was assigned as superintendent for the Baltimore harbor defenses and remained in Baltimore for the next three decades, until he was appointed Chief of Engineers by President Grover Cleveland. Two years later he retired and died at his birthplace on January 18, 1909.[4]

For his leadership, vision, and professional activities, William Emery Merrill earned the sobriquet "father of the Ohio River improvement."

Col. William P. Craighill. Division of Culture, Archives, and History, photography file, Charleston, W.V.

Born in Wisconsin in 1837, Merrill graduated at the head of his class in 1859 from West Point, just in time to serve with distinction during the Civil War. It was not until 1870 that the military phase of his career ended, the latter part of which he devoted to river and harbor work for the Corps of Engineers. In fact, he more than any other engineer promoted and oversaw the canalization project of the Ohio River. He was involved in the early surveys of the Central Water Line and kept an active interest in the Kanawha River improvement, until his death in 1891.

Merrill fostered the idea of locks and movable dams on the Ohio. Facing considerable opposition from many sources, he succeeded in securing a congressional appropriation for the first lock and movable dam on the Ohio River at Davis Island. The appropriation was received in 1879, but work was not completed until 1885, long after Locks and Dams 3, 4, and 5 had been in operation on the Kanawha River.

With the Davis Island lock and movable dam serving as a prototype, and given the success of the first three such structures on the Kanawha, the canalization of the entire Ohio was undertaken. This huge project was not completed until 1929, long after Merrill's death.[5] Merrill and Godfrey Weitzel prepared a lengthy report on the adaptation of the French movable dam for use on the Ohio River.[6] It can be considered the basic engineering document on the subject published at the time in America.

Godfrey Weitzel's career paralleled that of Merrill in many respects. Born in Cincinnati in 1835, the son of German emigrants, Weitzel graduated from the U.S. Military Academy second in his class in 1855, four years ahead of Merrill. He too had a distinguished Civil War record. After Lee's surrender and a short tour of duty in Texas, he returned in 1866 as a major in the Corps of Engineers, spending the rest of his career in public works. Perhaps his most important projects were the locks at Sault Sainte Marie in Michigan, the Stannard Lighthouse on Lake Superior, and, farther south, the Louisville and Portland Canal skirting the falls of the Ohio at Louisville, Kentucky. He reached the rank of lieutenant colonel in 1882 and died two years later in Philadelphia.[7]

A generation younger than Merrill and Weitzel, William Murray Black was born in 1855 in Lancaster, Pennsylvania, and graduated from West Point first in his class in 1877. Prior to service in the Spanish American War, he worked as a junior officer on the Kanawha project. Following the war with Spain, he is credited with the provision of a comprehensive sanitary scheme for Havana, Cuba. As Chief of Engineers from 1916 to 1919, he was involved in mobilizing, training, and finally discharging a greatly expanded wartime Corps of Engineers, which saw service in France as well as America. After the war he was retired; he died in Washington, D.C., in 1933.[8]

A native of Charleston, West Virginia, Ernest Howard Ruffner was a scion of the family who had been pioneers in the Kanawha Valley salt industry. Ruffner graduated from the U.S. Military Academy in the class of 1867 and served as a civil engineer on the Ohio and Kanawha Rivers during his career with the Corps of Engineers. He was born in Kentucky, retired as colonel in 1909, and died at the age of ninety-two in Cincinnati in 1937. He was noted as a strict disciplinarian and a no-nonsense leader who served in a number of capacities during his career with the Corps of Engineers.[9]

Thomas Turtle was a classmate of Ruffner in the U.S. Military Academy class of 1867. During his short lifetime, he served not only on the Ohio and Kanawha Rivers but also in the office of the Chief of Engineers from 1890 to 1894. He died in the District of Columbia in 1894 at age 50, having attained the rank of major in the Corps of Engineers.[10]

Unlike the military engineers, whose biographies were maintained at the Military Academy and in government documents, the civilian engineers employed at one time or another on the project are little known, apart from Addison Scott. Among this group was W. H. Hutton, who served with Craighill on the original Central Water Line survey and report; and Benjamin Thomas, who is credited with the idea of the needle dam on the Big Sandy River, the invention of a Thomas hurter (that is, *heurtoir*, a prop to support the movable dam wickets), and the publication of a lengthy paper on movable dams.[11]

These were the men who formed the leadership cadre, in one way or another, throughout the early surveys, planning, design, and construction of the ten locks and fixed and movable dams on the Great Kanawha River.

Project Organization

Given that he had worked for General Warren on the Mississippi River project, it was not surprising that Merrill invited Scott to be his assistant on the Kanawha project, which was approved by Congress in 1873. The following year, Merrill transferred the administration of the project to William Price Craighill. It was a logical move since Craighill had been responsible for the James River and Kanawha Canal survey and was thoroughly familiar with the Kanawha and its tributaries. In the same year, 1874, Craighill and his assistant, Lieutenant Thomas Turtle, finished the survey of the Central Water Line, which remained under active consideration for several decades.[12]

Thomas Turtle as a military engineer, and Addison Scott as a civil engineer, were responsible in the field for the Kanawha project from 1876 to 1880. Turtle's tour of duty on the Kanawha would probably have been longer if he had not precipitated a political storm. Specifically, he was accused of hiring Democrats and former rebels. He denied the charge, but influential West Virginia Republicans appealed to President Rutherford B. Hayes to take action, which he did. Unknown to Turtle, he had fired one of the president's relatives! Craighill was forced to transfer him elsewhere in the Corps of Engineers; he was replaced, briefly for the next year, by Lt. William M. Black, later Chief of Engineers.

In turn, Capt. Ernest H. Ruffner superseded Black. Black apparently found it difficult to work with Ruffner, who had a reputation for an inflexible and arbitrary leadership style. Black was transferred to the Davis Island lock and movable dam project on the upper Ohio River.

Scott, who was highly thought of, not only by Craighill and others in the Corps of Engineers but by local business concerns and shipping operators on the Kanawha River, also clashed with Ruffner and offered his resignation. As a result of rising protest, oversight of the project was transferred to the Baltimore district office under the direct supervision of Craighill, who immediately rehired Scott. Thus, Craighill and Scott, the career military engineering officer and the civil engineer, formed the celebrated team that oversaw the Kanawha project, with Scott in Charleston and Craighill in Baltimore until 1895. In that year, Craighill was named Chief of Engineers and the Baltimore office was filled by Col. Peter Hains. The entire project was finished and opened for traffic in 1898, but Scott continued to serve in the Charleston office until 1901. In another reorganization, the Kanawha navigation project was transferred from Baltimore to the division office in Cincinnati, under the command of Col. Ernest M. Ruffner. Apparently, the altercation between Scott and Ruffner had not been forgotten by the latter. No sooner was the project transferred to Cincinnati than Ruffner attempted to transfer Scott from the Charleston office. Scott refused and was accused of insubordination and discharged. Having invested wisely in local business and real estate, Scott enjoyed a long retirement until his death in 1927.[13]

Construction Begins

All was in place by 1873 to begin the complete channelization of the Great Kanawha River below the falls by a series of slackwater pools, to be formed by twelve locks and associated French-style movable dams and weirs. The dozen locks and dams would not only provide a far superior navigation for shipping bulk cargoes to the Ohio River but also form an essential link of the anticipated Central Water Line.

In a letter to Craighill in August 1874, Scott proposed improvements to the open-channel navigation, including such details as riprap walls at Cabin Creek and Elk Shoals, and riprap dams at Elk Shoals and Ten Mile Island.[14] Additional work included improving the chute at Elk Shoal and removing the remaining obstructions in the channel. Much was accomplished with the first federal appropriation, but in the long view it was really a maintenance project for an obsolete open-channel system that was incapable of providing navigation suitable for exploiting the rich raw materials, particularly coal, in the Kanawha Valley.

The situation had scarcely improved according to Fisk's earlier report of 1855, quoting Lorraine's report, which stated: "Two months in the year are lost from dry weather; one half month from the presence of ice; one month, boats can run of 3-foot draught; three and a half months, boats can run of 4 to 6 foot draught; five months, boats can run of 6-foot draught and upward."[15]

Lorraine reported to Congress that the estimated cost of an improved open-channel navigation with wing walls and other devices was $1.9 million, compared to an estimate of $2.9 million for a system of locks and dams throughout the river below the falls.[16] Following Lorraine's report, the conclusions of an 1872 survey of the New River by Craighill and his associates, N. H. Hutton and C. R. Boyd, indicated that the grand vision of a Central Water Line was still very much alive.[17]

Earlier, in anticipation of improvements to be undertaken on the Ohio River and some of its navigable tributaries, the Corps of Engineers empaneled a board of engineers to examine the feasibility of using movable dams on the Ohio and other rivers. Their comprehensive 131-page report, accompanied by 112 figures, served as the basis for the adoption and design of the locks and dams subsequently built on the Great Kanawha River.[18] This work was further supplemented by Thomas in a survey completed in 1883. The Thomas study was published by the American Society of Civil Engineers in 1898, on the occasion of the completion of the needle dam he had overseen on the Big Sandy River near Louisa, Kentucky.[19]

With its prior investigations of the river and knowledge of movable dams, the Corps of Engineers was ready to begin the project with the preparation of contract drawings and specifications. An appropriation was anticipated following passage of the River and Harbor Act on March 3, 1873.[20] Authorization by Congress does not necessarily mean that an appropriation will be following for any project, but subsequent acts of Congress over the next quarter of a century did provide the necessary funds in small increments. With the first appropriation, money was available for the building of locks and dams at sites 4 and 5. D. M. and C. P. Dull succeeded in receiving the contract for Lock 5 at Brownstown (later Marmet) on August 20, 1875. Charles McGafferty and Company were low bidders on the Cabin Creek Shoal site, No. 4, and were awarded a contract on October 15, 1875. A third contract for the construction of a navigable pass adjacent to Lock 5 was awarded to Schultz and Jolliffe on March 28, 1876.[21] It should be noted that at each of the lock and dam sites, contracts for the construction of the lock were let first. This would allow the lock to be used for navigation at suitable stages of the river while the dam and overflow weir were under construction.

Craighill anticipated a new appropriation early in 1876 so the additional work could be initiated—namely, the dam and navigation pass at Dam 4, as well as the lock and dam at site No. 3. Congress's lateness in acting meant that the beginning of the next phase was delayed until 1877.

In all large public works there are commonly delays caused by weather,

Lock and Dam 5, Kanawha River, under construction, 1881. "Lock and Dam No. 5, near Brownstown, WV, of Great Kanawha River Improvement." *The Virginias: A Mining, Industrial and Scientific Journal* 2 (August 1881): 108.

Lock No. 5 in foreground with Marmet locks and dam under construction, July 1932. U.S. Army Corps of Engineers, Huntington District Archives.

material shortages, labor problems, accidents, or even legal matters. The project to construct ten locks and dams on the Great Kanawha River was no exception. In the case of Lock 5, for example, the contract was delayed because the government had failed to gain title to the land. Thus, the contract was delayed until September 12 and preliminary site work not begun until September 16. Following dredging of the lock site, the cofferdam was begun on October 7, 1875, and not finished until January. Scott noted that the work was delayed because of high water, although he felt the contractor could have expedited the work. In any event, the cofferdam was not pumped out until June 11, 1876. But it was not well founded, and a leak emerged that necessitated letting water into the cofferdam, plugging the leak with puddled clay, and then pumping the water out again. By June 18 a twelve-foot rise in the river stopped all work. It was reported that the contractor would be ready to begin the foundation work inside the cofferdam in July.[22]

While work was underway at the site, the quarrymen had prepared 1,824 cubic yards of stone and the sawyers 49,356 board feet of timber. Nevertheless, Scott stated in his report that he was very annoyed at the delays in the work. This was, however, not the case of the contract for the movable part of the dam. Schultz and Jolliffe, who commenced work in April, were reported to be "progressing in an encouraging manner."[23]

At Lock 4 work began in October after the contract was awarded and continued at the quarry until January 1876, when all operations stopped because of the contractor's "lack of men to go on." It appears there was a strike, and nothing more was done until May 12. At the time of preparation of the annual report in midsummer, Scott reported that fair progress was being made on the stone work. However, the dredging of the lock was delayed at the end of May because of an explosion in the dredge's boiler, and then by a rise of water in the river.[24]

Significant technical details were provided at the time by William R. Hutton, a civil engineer. With the Central Water Line still a viable project in 1876, Hutton reported that the three upper dams would be of the fixed-crest type because the greater slope of the river above the Paint Creek Shoals would have made the operation of movable dams "inexpedient," since they would have to be operated in consort with each other. Because they were linked by fairly short slackwater pools, dropping the wicket at one pass only meant that insufficient water would occur at the next dam upstream. With fixed dams, the minimum pool elevation was assured at each dam.

Most important, in his report Hutton championed the Chanoine wicket dam over the Desfontaines system of movable dams solely on the basis of cost.[25] This opinion coincided with others as to the most suitable type of French design to be undertaken for navigation. The Chanoine wicket was adopted not only on the Kanawha but throughout the Ohio River improvement. In later stages of movable-dam construction, American modifications were introduced in the form of modified hurters to designs by Thomas and Pasqueau. All other details remained true to the original Chanoine system.[26]

Whereas the movable dam was a totally new innovation in America, the design of the locks followed tradition. A description provided by Hutton serves as a prototype for the ten locks built over a quarter of a century. Hutton states, "As a type of the low lock and movable dam, a description is introduced of No. 5, at Brownstown, some 8 miles above

Charleston, now under construction. The lock, which is 361 feet in total length, 300 feet between hollow quoins, and 50 feet in clear width, is designed to pass at one lockage 4 coal-barges of the dimensions usual on the Ohio and Kanawha Rivers; that is, 130 feet long, 24 feet wide, and drawing 6 feet of water. It is placed in the river as near to its left bank as practicable."[27]

Hutton further states that the dam, which is at right angles to the lock, is 460 feet long and joins the riverside lock wall at the lower abutment. The dams were divided into a pass and a weir. Typically, the pass was at least 250 feet wide to allow unimpeded river traffic. Built at a higher elevation, the weirs with their movable Chanoine wickets controlled pool levels behind the dam.

In a departure from the usual lock design, the upper and lower miter sills were built at the same level so that if both sets of gates were open, the locks would serve as an extension of the pass when the river was at a suitable level for open navigation. Departing from established tradition, the miter sills were laid up in stone and faced with wood, whereas the floor was cast in concrete and covered with wooden planks.

The ashlar masonry of the quoins, miter sills, and angles, and random stone courses of the walls and other structures, were all laid up in hydraulic cement mortar. The heavy timber lock gates featured cast-iron wickets at the bottom to regulate water in the lock. The details of a typical lock are illustrated in a drawing and supplemented by series of photographs.

The 1879 construction season resulted in excellent progress at all three work sites, Nos. 3, 4, and 5. Locks and Dams 4 and 5 were essentially finished and usable while Lock and Dam 3 was "well forward."[28] The only official complaint concerned the timber, which was said to be unsatisfactory in quality as well as severely delayed in delivery. The legal steps necessary to acquire land for Locks and Dams 6 and 7 had been slow but were nearing an end. Pressure was mounting from the coal industry to undertake work at site No. 2, the farthest upstream of the system. Efforts were made to acquire land at Cannelton, but the owner resisted, necessitating a search for a new location farther downstream that would still provide suitable slackwater for the coal interests. At the same time, properties at sites 6 and 7 were acquired through condemnation proceedings, a common occurrence.

By 1880, with five years of construction experience, the estimated

Installation of trestles and wickets. "Lock and Dam No. 5, near Brownstown, WV, of Great Kanawha River Improvement." *The Virginias: A Mining, Industrial and Scientific Journal* 2 (August 1881): 117.

cost of each lock and dam was $350,000. As of June 4, 1880, appropriations awarded amounted to $1.14 million, including $200,000 for the current year.[29] The engineers felt that in order for proper progress to be made, it was necessary to begin work on a new site each year, resulting in an appropriation for the cost of one new lock and dam. A revised estimate showed that $2.4 million would be required to complete all ten locks and dams.[30] With the imminent completion of Locks and Dams 4 and 5, Craighill proposed an act of Congress to provide for their operation, maintenance, and repair by the federal government.[31]

Although Locks and Dams 4 and 5 would be opened for traffic in 1880, the annual report of Lt. Thomas Turtle noted that the contractors of both dams had failed to live up to their contracts and work was undertaken by hired labor under the supervision of the Corps of Engineers.[32] These locks and dams were open in late 1880, followed by Lock and Dam 3 two years later. During construction of Lock and Dam 3, various interests sought to have either Lock and Dam 2 or 7 undertaken as the next phase of the project. At the same time, Capt. E. H. Ruffner, unable to

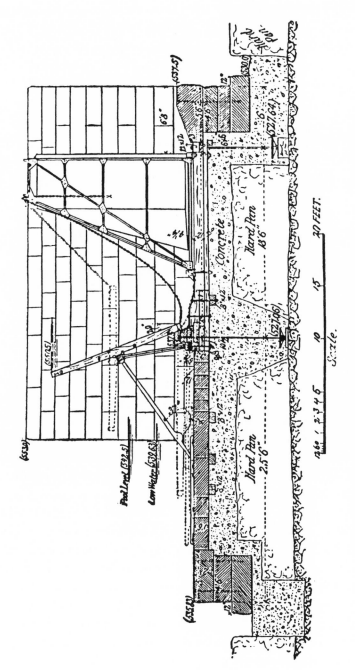

Section of the navigation pass of the Kanawha River. Wegmann, *The Design and Construction of Dams*, 180.

secure property at the proposed site of Lock and Dam 2, received permission to relocate it downstream. Ruffner raised the question of the possible deleterious effects of the new location of Lock and Dam 2 on the operation of Lock 3.[33] The delay in locating Lock 2 led to a petition from other coal operators to begin Lock and Dam 6. Craighill assured them that the alternate site would prove satisfactory, suggesting that Ruffner's concern may have been associated with a large mass of dredge materials below Dam 3.[34]

By August 22, 1882, the Corps of Engineers had approved the disposition of $200,000 appropriated by Congress, stipulating that work begin on Lock 2 as soon as the property was secure, and also requiring the continuation of work on Lock 6. Operating funds for Locks 3, 4, and 5, which were already open for traffic, were to be taken from the appropriation.[35] Craighill authorized Ruffner to prepare plans and specifications for Lock and Dam 2. He justified his decision to build Lock and Dam 2 first because the Chief of Engineers had previously approved it. The decision stood and resulted in Lock 2 being completed more than a decade before Lock and Dam 7.[36] As late as July 28, Theodore Wright, president of the Winifrede Coal Company, unsuccessfully urged the Corps of Engineers to give preference to No. 7 rather than No. 2 in the construction sequence.[37]

The pattern of delays continued with regard to Lock and Dam 6. The Corps of Engineers granted an extension to the contractor, Harris and Black, from November 4, 1880, to November 30, 1882. They had clearly not completed the contract on Lock 6 when, in June 1883, they petitioned the Corps of Engineers for a partial payment of $10,000, which was refused.[38]

Construction Materials

Natural cement had been closely associated with the building of canals in Britain, Europe, and America. By the use of a suitable cement rock, a hydraulic cement could be produced that would set under water and in its hardened form was waterproof. The secret was to find limestone with an argillaceous component of approximately 33 percent, which, when calcined, ground, and combined with water, formed a chain of di- and tricalcium silicates, which, unlike lime mortar, possessed a waterproof component.[39] Canvass White is credited with the discovery of cement rock in America, leading to its production first on the Erie Canal and then on nearly every subsequent canal in America. One of the most famous natural cements was produced under the name Rosendale cement. In the case of the Corps of Engineers, it was the standard referred to in their specifications. On the Chesapeake and Ohio Canal, eleven natural cement mills distributed along the waterway supplied cement for locks and dams. In turn, the canal later provided a cheap means of transporting the cement to markets in Washington, D.C., and elsewhere. It was a synergistic joint venture.

In 1824 Joseph Aspdin of Leeds, England, produced hydraulic cement using blended materials, and because the concrete produced from this cement had the appearance of a highly regarded limestone on the Isle of Portland, it was promoted as Portland cement. The first Portland cement manufactured in the United States was produced by David Saylor at Coplay, Pennsylvania, beginning in 1871. It was quickly recognized as superior to natural cement in uniformity and strength. The Corps of Engineers put its stamp of approval on the new material when it specified Portland cement for the South Pass jetties at the mouth of the Mississippi River.

By carefully selecting both the calcareous (that is, limestone, or even oyster shells) and the argillaceous materials (for example, clay, slate, shale) and firing the mixture at much higher temperatures than used in natural cement production, approximately 2,700 degrees Fahrenheit, one could obtain a superior cement. There were, however, several disadvantages in using it as the binder in mortar. Portland cement mortar was much harder and stronger than lime mortar, but its very strength and hardness caused brickwork or even stone to crack when the structure moved, whereas natural cement mortar had much more "give" and in many respects was more appropriate for mortar. Portland cement, however, produced a more durable and stronger concrete.[40]

In the case of hydraulic masonry structures, Captain Turtle was concerned that Portland cement mortar was more porous than natural cement and would cause leaks. He reasoned that much less Portland cement would be needed to obtain a specified strength, and hence result in a more porous material, because with a stronger cement-paste less binder and more sand could be used for a given mortar mix. Basing his opinion on earlier French practice, Turtle preferred the natural cement.[41]

The records do not reveal when the possibility of using Portland cement in the Great Kanawha Navigation was first discussed. In reply to Craighill's letter on the subject dated January 3, 1883, the Chief of Engineers, Brigadier General Horatio G. Wright, authorized him to purchase British or European Portland cement if he wished.[42]

Craighill explored the possibility of importing Portland cement. The S. L. Merchant and Company quotation indicated that imported cement cost $1.72 per 300-pound barrel, whereas a similar weight of Rosendale cement would be $1.02 per barrel. Merchant's letter, dated February 13, 1883, was the basis for the reply by Captain Turtle stating his reservations about using Portland cement in lock walls and recommending the use of Rosendale cement.[43] Shortly after the use of imported Portland cement was approved, specifications and drawings were issued for the construction of a movable dam and control weir adjoining Lock 6, already under construction. The section on cement in the specifications indicated that all of this material would be supplied to the contractor by the Corps of Engineers.[44] Extensive research has failed to reveal if, in fact, Portland cement was used on subsequent contracts.

Not only was the quality and price of cement a concern, but also the strength and durability of the stone supplied by the contractor. Lt. Col. Quincy Adams Gillmore, an 1849 West Point graduate well known for his research and publications on engineering materials, conducted tests on local sandstone.[45] The results are typical of the quality-control tests used throughout the navigation project. Concrete's strength at this time rarely exceeded 3,000 pounds per square inch (psi) compressive stress, while the weakest stone could withstand more than four times that amount.[46] Reflecting on twenty-eight years' experience on the project, Scott, in an interrogatory conducted as part of a law case, testified:

Q.: Did you not consider it a fact as to the details of the availability of the stone, that as practical stone men, that they were better able to determine questions as they arose then [sic] yourself?

A.: I will say that was true in the case of Sam Campbell, and Mr. Myers, who were practical stone cutters and stone men, and who were undoubtedly better judges of the stone then I was, but I do not think, it was true of any of the other men, and don't think so yet, though I think, they were all pretty good stone men, as good as you ordinarily get on that kind of work. The fact of the business is it was a very difficult matter to inspect the Sattis stone after the quarry "got to missing so badly." I myself could not always tell about the stone until after they commenced to cut it. After they had begun to cut a stone I could always form a very good conclusion in regard to it, but I could not always do it before Myers and Campbell could. They were excellent judges of the stone. After a cutter had commenced to point a stone, and you noticed the way it cut, and examined the spalls that came off, a man that had experience with it, as I had, could tell the good stone from the bad, and which stone was proper for face work. I acknowledge that we made mistakes some times and let in stone that ought not to have gone in, and there were no doubt some pieces of stone rejected that were good, but we were using our best judgement.[47]

All of the iron components were specified. The requirements read in part:

Wrought iron will be good, tough, refined iron, capable of being bent cold to ninety degrees and straightened without breaking, free from all flaws and defects. Flat, square and round bars will be out of wind, straight and of correct dimensions. Rivets of best rivet iron. Forgings to be executed in the best and most workmanlike manner, free from all defects, bad welds and bad workmanship, and neatly finished. Threads of all screws to be accurately and cleanly cut by machinery. Heads, nuts and threads to be of standard proportions. . . . Rivetting to be done in the best manner. All rivets to be put in hot and to entirely fill the holes; abutting joints to be true and the edges neatly dressed; the holes to be accurately spaced and exactly opposite.

Cast iron shall be of strong, tough, re-melted gray iron, of homogeneous texture, capable of being filed, cut, drilled or chipped. Gearing to be of the best charcoal iron that can be obtained for the purpose, to be approved by the Engineer. Castings to be well made, well shaped, smooth, free from scoria, cracks, flaws, airholes and other defects. . . . Castings will conform closely in form and dimensions to the drawings, and will be thoroughly cleaned and the lumps removed. They shall weigh not less than ninety-five per cent of the caluclated weight.[48]

Since the iron work was manufactured off site, separate specifications were prepared, the earliest of which appeared in 1877.[49] Other specifications were prepared regarding the fabrication of iron lock gates and associated fittings. The metal framework for a movable dam or weir was really a series of small trestles (called *fermettes* in French), and they could routinely be produced by fabricating shops, especially bridge companies.

Construction Continues

In March 1882, the Corps of Engineers empaneled a board of engineer officers to examine Locks and Dams 4 and 5, then in operation, and to report on the adaptability of the French movable-dam inventions to navigation systems in America.[50] Dams 4 and 5 were the first movable dams erected anywhere in North America. In particular, the board of engineers commented favorably on Lock and Dam 5 and the ongoing installation of Pasqueau hurters in place of similar Chanoine designs. Pasqueau hurters, the props that held up the wickets, were being installed in half of Dam 5, but it would be another year before hurters could be placed in Dam 6. For this reason the board deferred judgment until these hurters and associated tripping beams were tested in practice. Another recommendation submitted by the board of engineers concerned the problem of bank erosion caused by the construction of Lock and Dam 3. The board also addressed the problem of water releases from the proposed alternate location of Lock and Dam 2, which would have an adverse effect on Lock and Dam 3, the next downstream lock location. They recommended that the planned fifteen-foot height of Dam 2 be reduced to twelve feet to eliminate the problem.

In a curious recommendation, the Board of Engineers also suggested that Lock 2 be increased in size to match Lock 6 (that is, from 50 × 271 feet to 55 × 313 feet). Considering that there were intermediate smaller locks already in operation, increasing the size of the lock upstream did not make much sense, although the narrow lock was to cause a great inconvenience to shipping in the upper reaches of the Kanawha, as we will see. Lock 6 and all of the remaining locks lower down had chamber sizes of 55 × 313 feet. These first locks were designed to accommodate four barges 24 feet wide by 130 feet long. But the newer barges were 26 feet wide, precluding a pair locking through side by side.

At the time the board was formed, Craighill wrote to Scott that the river and harbor bill had failed in Congress, necessitating a revision in the distribution of funds on hand, which amounted to $229,000. Nevertheless, plans and specifications for Lock 2 received a first review by Turtle in preparation for advertising for bids.[51]

In a confidential letter dated March 29, 1884, Craighill asked Scott to prepare the "necessary papers" required to widen Lock 2 by two feet. He urged Scott to keep the matter private, since he planned to submit the estimate to the Chief of Engineers and "he may refuse to do."[52] Within a fortnight, Craighill decided to drop the issue. Thus, the design dimensions of Lock 2 were the same size as Locks 3, 4, and 5. In addition, "the change in head and tail at Lock 5, desired by Mr. Wright, will not be made and the subject of increasing the width of Lock 2 will not be reopened."[53] The work proceeded with additional contracts being let for Dam 6 in August and December 1884.[54]

It was not only the size of the locks and the width of the navigation passes but also the height of bridges crossing the Great Kanawha River that were of concern to the engineers. There was no simple solution to the problem of clearance, with the result that a study considered the river stages and the height of pilot houses and stacks on the largest steam-powered tows and packets. Because of the flat profile of the Kanawha, the backwater of the Ohio reached far upriver and thus had a strong influence on the Kanawha's stages, especially high water. For this reason it was felt that greater clearance should be provided at the lower reaches of the river. Scott recommended:

All considered my own judgment in regard to limitation for heights of channel spans would be: for all bridges between the mouth of the river and the head of Knobshoal at least 90 feet; between the head of Knobshoal and the head of Red House Shoal at least 85 feet; between the head of the Red House Shoal and the mouth of Coal River at least 82 feet; between the Mouth of Coal and the mouth of Elk River at least 78 feet; between the mouth of Elk River and the head of proposed slackwater navigation at least 75 feet - All above local low water measured to the *lowest part of span*.[55]

For excessively high stages of the river, Scott assumed the steamboats would have hinged funnels, allowing their height to be reduced to the level of the top of the pilot house. He claimed that river stages required the lowering of the funnels on an average of only one day a year. The channel width was also a concern. Scott, replying to Turtle, stated that the clear span between bridge piers should be "materially" wider than the navigation passes because the bridge piers would not have guide walls for large rafts and wide tows using the passes in times of high water. A century later, there are still incidents of vessels striking bridge piers with disastrous results.

Shortly before the Scott report on bridge clearances, Craighill announced to Scott that the last contract for finishing Lock and Dam 2 had been awarded to Strong and Son.[56] It would, however, be nearly two years before the work at this site would be completed.

At the end of the 1884 federal fiscal year, Scott forwarded a progress report on Lock 2 and Dam 6, as well as on the operations of Locks and Dams 3, 4, and 5, which were already in service.[57]

Construction on Lock 2 began in June 1883. The year was taken with excavating, dredging, opening stone quarries, and building a large coffer-dam in which work on the lock could be done "in the dry." The cofferdam was 478 feet long and it paralleled the channel, with perpendicular arms extending to the shore. The upper arm was 102 feet long and the lower one 120 feet. Scott provides a clear picture of the construction techniques employed at the time for large hydraulic structures. The entire cofferdam was made of a series of linked timber cribs sunk to solid rock. These cribs were not unlike a traditional log cabin. The cribs at this site averaged 22 feet in height with approximately 13 feet below water. In an effort to stabilize the cofferdam, the cribs were filled with coarse gravel and large stones placed by dredges. The outside wall of the cofferdam was "banked with clay" to provide a waterproof seal. The amount of material used in the temporary structure was quite impressive.[58]

In the case of Lock 6, pumping began on May 31, and the de-watering was complete by June 5. Pumping continued to keep the excavation dry until the whole operation was overwhelmed by a freshet that increased the river level by twelve feet. By the end of June the water was still too high to permit work. At the time of the flood, the first stone was set on the foundation and work had been progressing well on the bottom course, which rested on bedrock fourteen feet below the low-water mark.[59] Although the progress of lock and dam construction varied with each of the ten sites, the above description is typical for the entire project.

In the previous year, the movable dams were in the raised position for 189 days at Lock and Dam 4 and 153 days at Lock and Dam 5. Despite some difficulties in operating the Chanoine wickets, the traffic through each of these locks was impressive. For instance, the following tally comes from records kept at Lock 4:

Number of steamers locked during the year	994
Number of coal barges and other craft	603
Total number of lockages, all kinds	1,031
Coal down through the navigation pass [bushels]	2,829,500
Coal down through the lock [bushels]	2,439,150
Steamers through the navigation pass	1,170
Coal barges and other craft through the navigation pass	706
Rainfall during the year (inches)	40.10[60]

Even though the wickets were down somewhat less than six months, the bushels of coal through the navigation pass were slightly greater than the amount through the lock. Successful operation of the lock and dam pleased not only the rivermen but also the engineers.

The Pasqueau hurters proved themselves at Lock and Dam 5 to such an extent that these fittings were installed at both the pass and control weir on Dam 6.

Plans for the foundation of Lock and Dam 6 were greatly modified because the underwater timbers, weir sills, and cribs at the earlier Locks and Dams 4 and 5 were beginning to rot, so that masonry with an iron sill was substituted. Thus, Locks and Dams 4 and 5 were the only ones with extensive timber work in the passes and weirs. In the 1930s the deterioration of these two earliest locks finally required the replacement of the entire set of up-river locks (that is, Locks and Dams 2 through 6) with more modern structures.

There was often a hiatus between the authorization of a project and the receipt of funds sufficient to continue the work efficiently and on schedule. The appropriation for July 1884 was a case in point. The miserly $15,000 appropriated was quite insufficient to carry on construction of the locks and dams.[61] Thus it was decided, in conjunction with local interests, to invest the money in ice piers. Ice not only restricted navigation on both the Great Kanawha and Ohio Rivers but could also damage vessels. Building ice piers on each bank of the river, near its confluence with the Ohio, created a harbor of refuge during the winter. Half the funds were to be obtained from the Kanawha project and the other half from the Ohio River appropriation.

Scott provided a progress report on work at each site. At Lock 2, the contractor, Frank Hefright, made good progress thanks in part to very favorable weather from July to the end of December 1884. He was well ahead of schedule for a September 15, 1885, deadline. A second contract to complete the lock was awarded to Strong and Son of Cleveland in the amount of $68,139.50.[62] By October 1886 Craighill sent a sharply worded letter to Strong and Son regarding progress at Lock 2. Although claiming to find the prospect disagreeable, he threatened to take legal action.[63] At the same time a contract was let to Harold and McDonald in the amount of $102,060.50 for the foundation, pier, and abutment of Dam 6, and to O. A. and W. T. Thayer, who were named to supply the iron work for the foundations of the dam for a bid price of $2,196.00.[64]

With the completion of Locks and Dams 2 through 6, the original scheme of the Central Water Line would be realized, with slackwater controlling the river above Charleston and open navigation below. There was, however, exceptionally low water during the boating season of 1886, which limited the river traffic. The following comments appeared in the annual report:

Coal-boat navigation on the Ohio from Point Pleasant down was suspended by ice forty-two days during the year. The Kanawha was obstructed by ice about ten days. After making allowance for suspension by ice, it appears that if the Great Kanawha had been slackwatered to its mouth Kanawha coal could have been shipped down the Ohio on one hundred and eighty days during the year instead of on but seventy-three days, a consideration of great importance, not only to Kanawha, but to the lower Ohio and Mississippi valley, so materially interested in a greater and more regular supply of coal.

There are, at present writing (October 10), fully 350 barges loaded with coal in the river, the greater part of which has been loaded from two to four months waiting a rise. There has not been shipping water in the Kanawha below the dams since June 6, while our Point Pleasant record shows the Ohio, from there down, to have been at and above 6 feet on fifty-nine days since that date.[65]

Completing the Kanawha Improvement:
Building Locks and Dams 7–11

The proponents of the Central Water Line envisaged a canal and river slackwater system from Richmond to Charleston. Below Charleston the Great Kanawha was to be improved for open navigation by means of wing walls, dredging, and chutes cut into numerous shoals. This seemed to be the most cost-effective solution and one that was compatible with traffic on the uncontrolled Ohio River. The last decade of the nineteenth century, however, saw the conversion of the lower reaches of the Kanawha into a slackwater system by the construction of Locks and Dams 7, 8, 9, 10, and 11, while open navigation was provided at other stages of the river by lowering the wickets in the navigational passes at each dam. As a result, the Kanawha became the first fully controlled river navigation in the nation.

The team of Craighill and Scott broke asunder in 1889, when the colonel's responsibility for the Kanawha project was passed to Capt. Thomas Turtle. Craighill remained a supervising engineer for Maryland, Delaware, North Carolina, Virginia, and West Virginia until 1895, when he was appointed Chief of Engineers by President Grover Cleveland.[66]

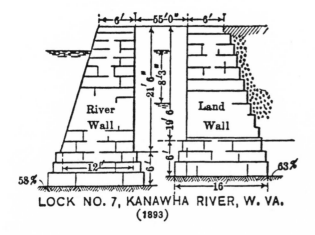

LOCK NO. 7, KANAWHA RIVER, W. VA.
(1893)

Cross-section of Lock 7, 1893. Thomas and Watt, *The Improvement of Rivers*, plate 45a.

During this period, his correspondence indicates that he was still active in decision making on the Kanawha from his office in Baltimore. Turtle's involvement was first manifest regarding land to be acquired so that the contracts could be let for building Lock 8.[67] Scott received the contract on August 29, 1889.[68]

In 1889 Craighill had declined to make a decision on a petition from Carkin, Stickney, and Cram for contract modifications, citing his imminent departure. A year later, however, he sent a cautionary letter to the contractor stating the contract must be completed in 1890 and he would not grant an extension. By midyear it was clear that the lock would not be finished, but because of the "extraordinary frequency, height and duration of freshets" the colonel granted an extension until November 1, 1891.[69]

In a series of letters to Scott, Craighill authorized the use of the Scott hurter as a modification of the earlier Chanoine and Pasqueau devices—but only on the Kanawha project, and only on the basis that, as a government employee, Scott would not be compensated. The usually taciturn Craighill wrote, "I would be very glad to see your heurter used elsewhere and that you should receive a reward for your invention."[70]

Munford and Reynolds were awarded the contract for Dam 7 in June 1891, while in May the contract with C. I. McDonald, engaged in building Lock and Dam 8, was extended to November 22, 1891. The colonel was clearly anxious about delays in the contract for Locks and Dams 7 and 8. He wished Scott to convey his concern to the contractor with a

View inside the cofferdam for navigation pass and center pier, Lock and Dam 9. Collection of G. W. Sutphin, Huntington, W.V.

Wickets and part of the service bridge, Lock and Dam 9, 1896. Collection of G. W. Sutphin, Huntington, W.V.

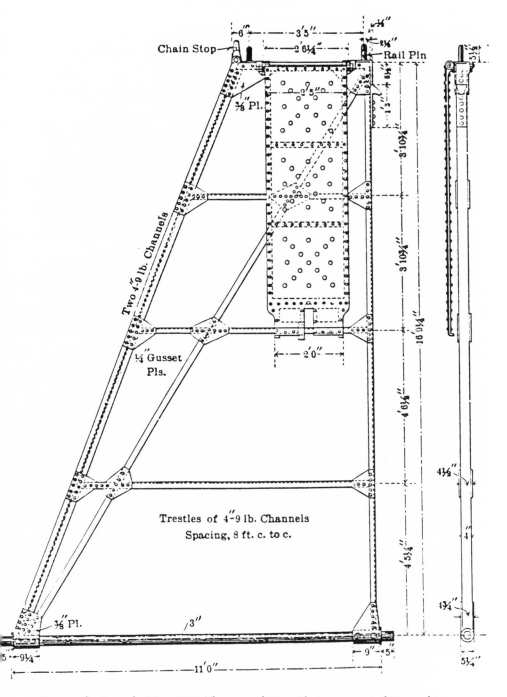

Pass trestle, Kanawha River, 1896. Thomas and Watt, *The Improvement of Rivers,* plate 63.

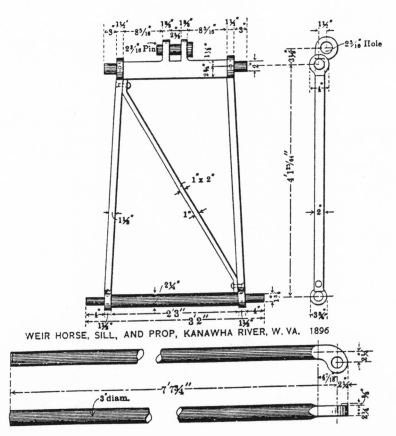

WEIR HORSE, SILL, AND PROP, KANAWHA RIVER, W. VA. 1896

Details of weir horse, sill, and prop, Kanawha River, 1896. Thomas and Watt, *The Improvement of Rivers,* plate 64.

proviso that failure to complete on time would involve them in "much" expense. If the situation was not rectified, he would make other arrangements to complete the contracts. Since hired labor was previously used, this is clearly what Craighill is alluding to. He was less threatening with Carkin, Stickney, and Cram when he agreed to yet another extension, to December 31, 1891, and relented on the Dam 7 contract by extending it to December 31, 1892.[71]

(Opposite) Wooden wicket passes on Kanawha and Ohio Rivers, 1880–1900. Thomas and Watt, *The Improvement of Rivers,* plate 60.

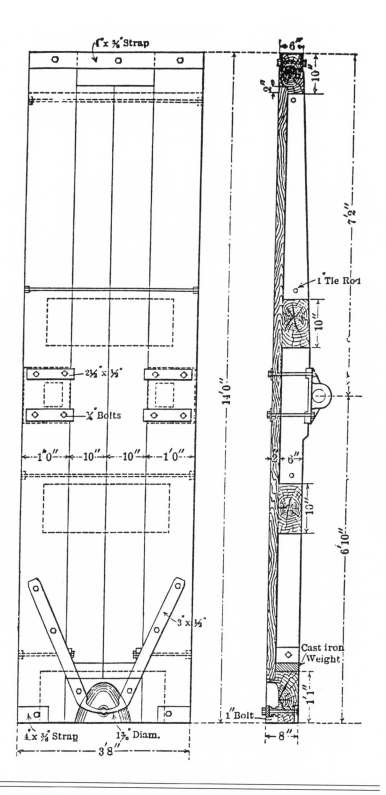

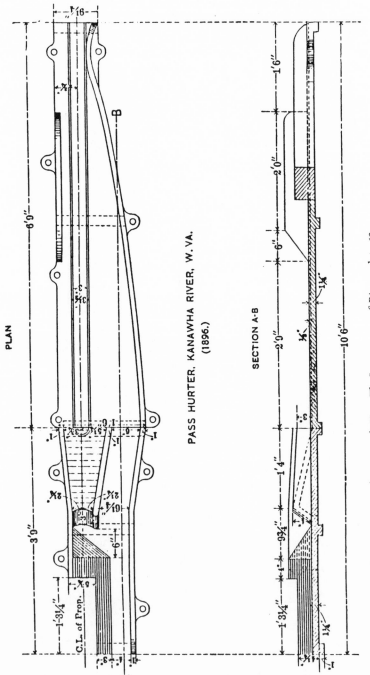

PLAN

PASS HURTER. KANAWHA RIVER, W. VA.
(1896.)

SECTION A-B

Pass hurter, Kanawha River, 1896. Thomas and Watt, *The Improvement of Rivers*, plate 62.

The World's Columbian Exhibition

The year 1892 was also the date scheduled for the opening of the World's Columbian Exhibition in Chicago, although because of various difficulties it was not opened until 1893. To showcase the Corps of Engineers' involvement in large public works, the Great Kanawha Improvement was selected as a subject for public display. This involved preparing a full-size model of the Scott hurter and a typical Chanoine wicket. Brig. Gen. Thomas L. Casey, Chief of Enginers, ordered that

Officers of the Corps of Engineers will submit lists of such articles, models, materials, plans, drawings, photographs, etc. as they can furnish for the worlds [sic] Columbian Exhibition illustrative of the duties and operations of the Corps of Engineers and will report as to,

    I. Amount of space required indoors and in the open air
    II. Motive power, if any required
    III. Number of employees required for the care of the proposed exhibits
    IV. Probable cost of exhibit and care of same

This information will be transmitted in time to reach this office not later than September 19, 1890 and is not expected to embrace complete details.[72]

Craighill responded by offering a model of Dam 6, which apparently was in Scott's office as part of the proposed exhibition. At the end of 1890, Capt. W. L. Marshall (later the Chief of Engineers) informed Craighill that funds had been secured for the exhibition. He added:

Colonel, I have thought that as a scale and object lessen [sic] in connection with your models, that it would be a good thing to set up outside and in front of the W.D. exhibit, say two wickets and foundation of one of your movable dams and say three trestles (two of them with bridge and one down) full size as used in the work.

Have you the extra iron parts of such wickets and trestles?

Please let me know your opinion as to the advisability of setting up full size trestles and wickets for movable dams.[73]

In January 1892 Craighill informed Scott that the sum of seven hundred dollars was available for the expenses of the Kanawha exhibit at Chicago, from which they paid for photos, models, and other materials for the exhibition.[74]

Despite its delay in opening, the Columbian Exhibition was a great success by all accounts and clearly did showcase the role of the Corps of Engineers in large public works concerned with navigable waterways.

The Work Continues

While the Columbian Exhibition showcased the work of the Corps of Engineers, work was still in progress on the remaining locks and dams. Not content with the extension Craighill had authorized, Carkin, Stickney, and Cram lodged a strong protest regarding the stonework on Lock 7. It appears that the Corps of Engineers inspectors were demanding a much higher standard of masonry than the contractor believed the specifications called for. Craighill had visited the site and commented that he had never had dealings with contractors who had given so little personal attention to their work as Carkin, Stickney, and Cram did; but for the time being the matter remained unresolved.[75]

At the same time, all was not well at Lock and Dam 8, and the contractor there, C. I. McDonald, was chastised for failing to make satisfactory progress.[76] The contractor responded to Craighill, "I am somewhat surprised to receive yours of the second instant. I am st. [sic] stating that it appears that I am not trying or caring to finish my contract on Lock, in the extended time. You can rest assured that I have been, and am now, and shall continue to exert every effort to finish the Lock contract in the extended time."[77]

As the new year of 1892 got underway, a new completion schedule for Locks and Dams 7 and 8 was established. Specifically, Locks 7 and 8 were to be finished by February 1, 1892, while Dams 7 and 8 were to be finished by December 31, 1892.[78] The new year also marked the beginning of design work on Lock 9 and the location of the site for Lock and Dam 10.[79] Craighill wrote to Scott in August, "I've just returned from a visit to Washington. General Casey and the Secretary of War were both absent, but I have good reason to believe that the one-contractor business is dead so far as the Kanawha is concerned. I will ask you to proceed with the specifications of Lock and Dam 9, excluding iron and gates. We will strike while the iron is hot."[80]

Craighill continues by saying, "Then take up 10 and 11 successfully in the same way and try to have each ready at least as soon as the title is approved by the Attorney General." The usually taciturn and business-like Craighill ended his letter to Scott on a note of levity: "I hope you are having a good time. I wish I could."

Clearly Craighill found the delays troubling since he was pressing hard to have the entire system completed in two or three years. Regarding

Locks and Dams 7 and 8, Craighill advised Scott: "Please write to the contractors of 7 and 8 in my name at an early date and, calling attention to the date of completion of their contracts, December 31, 1892, state that I expect to visit the works about the 21st or 22nd. If completion is not to be expected in 1892 I would wish to know the reason why. I do not purpose to recommend any further extension except for the best reasons. Non-extension means forfeiture of retained percenta and further payment."[81]

Despite the holidays, Scott brought the specifications for Lock and Dam 11 with him to Baltimore for a December 28 meeting. Three days later, Craighill extended the contract for Locks and Dams 7 and 8 to June 1, 1893, noting that it would be without expense to the contractors.[82] The petition for an extension cited high water as the justification.

Locks and Dams 7 and 8 had been under construction for about four years. Contractors began No. 7 in the spring of 1889, closely followed by No. 8 in the autumn of the same year; both were finally completed and put into operation on October 10, 1893.[83]

Wickets, hurters, and lock gates represented the most visible aspect of any lock and dam. These movable parts were let under separate contracts to iron-fabricating firms and then erected on site by hired labor under the supervision of the engineers. The Fred J. Myers Manufacturing Company received the contract for Locks and Dams 7 and 8 in June 1892, with delivery scheduled for September 1894.[84] The largest contract, however, was let to Youngstown Bridge Company. Craighill confided in Scott regarding the "Youngstown people" in a January 7, 1895, letter: "They seem inclined to be troublesome and we must give them no loopholes to crawl through."[85]

Events would prove Craighill quite perceptive in his judgment. The contract, dated October 16, 1894, called for 635,000 pounds of wrought iron and steel, 49,000 pounds of driftbolts, and 337,000 pounds of cast iron.[86] A supplementary contract, for movable iron parts on the weirs, was consummated on December 16, 1895.[87] Following Youngstown Bridge's request for an extension in February 1896, an argument ensued between Colonel Hains of the Corps of Engineers and the company over wages for the government inspector.[88] Replying to the company's request, Hains stated, "the contract stipulates that should the time for completion of a contract be extended all expenses for inspections shall be deducted from the payments due or to become due to the contractor."[89] Despite the apparent firmness of the Corps of Engineers, the contractor eventually received an extension to November 30, 1896, with no deduction in the contract price.[90] Then, not content with the first extension, Youngstown Bridge Company requested an additional three-month extension, which prompted the following blunt reply from Scott: "It is to the interest of the United States to grant the extension of time asked for and it is respectfully recommended that it be done. The contractors have no good excuse, so far known to this office, for not completing the work within the agreed time. They have delayed the work in the shops at different times, materially, in order to get on with other contracts."[91]

The contract was not completed until May 1896, but in the meantime work continued on the supplementary contract let February 15, 1896, for the iron work for all three weirs. This work included 311,000 pounds of wrought iron, 21,343 pounds of driftbolt, and 244,000 pounds of casting. The contract was completed in April 1897.[92]

The year 1896 also saw considerable progress on the last three locks and dams. Zimmerman, Truax, and Sheridan received the contract for Locks and Dams 9 and 10 on May 23, 1893, and began site work the following June.[93]

At Lock and Dam 11, work began with a contract to Thomas Munford dated June 1, 1893.[94] Continuing an established pattern, the contract was extended from November 13, 1896, to a completion date of December 31, 1897.[95] Thus, despite earlier predictions, it was clear by this time that the entire project would not be completed until the end of 1898.

The contracts for the final three locks and dams precipitated a lively debate between contractors and the Corps of Engineers regarding completion dates, but in no case does it appear that any of the contractors requested additional funds. The usual claim was based upon high water, which prevented the contractors from pursuing the work. In the case of Zimmerman, Truax, and Sheridan, a more stressful situation developed regarding the matter of "Sattes" stone. This stone was rejected for use during 1896, but had been earlier employed, apparently with implied approval by the Corps of Engineers, since no complaint was forthcoming

---

(*Opposite, top*) Lock and Dam 11 during construction, showing trestle and wickets installed, 1898. The trestle is being raised. Collection of G. W. Sutphin, Huntington, W.V.

(*Opposite, bottom*) Lock and Dam 11 during construction, showing erected trestle and one wicket on the "swing," 1898. Collection of G. W. Sutphin, Huntington, W.V.

from 1893 until March 1895. An abstract of a six-page report produced by the contractor explained:

Inability to get stone that would be accepted by the engineers. The quarries from which the Government Engineers, as well as ourselves, expected to get our supply, in which we had placed an extensive plant for quarrying, conveying and loading stone and which at first proved entirely satisfactory and acceptable, finally failed to hold up to the returned standard and stone being condemned, we were forced in consequence, at great trouble and expense and after many failures and much delay, to obtain stone elsewhere.[96]

To bolster these arguments, the company sent, under separate cover, two six-inch-cube samples of the Sattes stone.[97] Earlier this contractor had submitted a separate letter making a plea for an extension because of the vagaries of the weather.

It was not only Zimmerman and Company badgering the Corps of Engineers but also Thomas Munford, who held the contract for Lock and Dam 11. At the beginning of his contract, Munford set the stage for later requests for time extensions by noting that the plans had changed, reducing the cofferdam height. This in turn reduced the protection afforded the men working in the cofferdam. The company argued that the cofferdam would be over-topped more frequently causing delays: "The change consists in reducing the height (of the cofferdam) two feet which you can readily see is equivalent to raising the water which we have to contend with a like height, thereby possibly reducing considerably the time we will be enabled to work in the cofferdam."[98]

At the end of 1897, Munford's request for an extension was granted, from a deadline of December 31, 1897, to December 30, 1898.[99] Less than a month before the system was opened for river traffic, he requested another extension on a supplementary contract dated March 24, 1898, extended until October 30, 1898, in order to complete riprap work on Dam 11. The request was recommended by Scott and apparently approved. Thus, certain small items such as this did not prevent the lock system from being opened on October 11, 1898.[100]

With a few minor details still outstanding, such as the riprap at Dam

(*Opposite, top*) Lock and Dam 11 during construction with trestle and all but one wicket raised, 1898. The tow-supported cable tramway supplied materials to the site during construction. Collection of G. W. Sutphin, Huntington, W.V.

(*Opposite, bottom*) Lock and Dam 11 during construction showing the installation of a lock gate, 1898. Collection of G. W. Sutphin, Huntington, W.V.

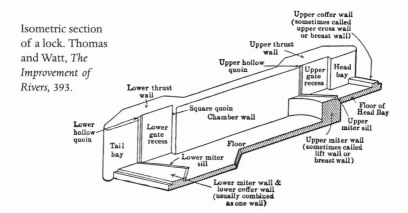

Isometric section of a lock. Thomas and Watt, *The Improvement of Rivers*, 393.

Upper coffer wall (sometimes called upper cross wall or breast wall)

Upper thrust wall

Upper hollow quoin

Upper gate recess

Head bay

Lower thrust wall

Floor of Head Bay

Upper miter sill

Square quoin

Chamber wall

Upper miter wall (sometimes called lift wall or breast wall)

Lower hollow quoin

Lower gate recess

Floor

Tail bay

Lower miter sill

Lower miter wall & lower coffer wall (usually combined as one wall)

11, the great work that had taken twenty-three years to complete was opened for traffic on October 11, 1898.[101] Not only were there delays in completing the work, but the cost overruns increased the final amount appropriated to $4.2 million. This includes $50,000 spent for channel improvements before any construction began on the movable locks and dams system. Completion dates and lock sizes for the entire project mark the

KANAWHA RIVER, WEST VIRGINIA.

No.	Location.	Miles from mouth.	Completed.	Lift, Feet.	Lock. Built of	Lock. Built on	Dam. Total Gross Length.	Weir. Composed of	Weir. Length, Feet.	Pass. Composed of	Pass. Length, Feet.	Cost of Works.
2	Montgomery, W. Va. ..	85.2	1887	10.3	Stone	Rock	524	} Fixed dams				{ $353,60•
3	Paint Creek..........	80.0	1882	13.7	"	"	564.5					490,00•
4	Coalburg............	73.7	1880	7.2	"	"	468	Ch. wkts.	210	Ch. wkts.	248	275,00•
5	Marmet.............	67.7	1880	7.5	"	"	529	"	265	"	250	275,00•
6	Charleston (4 miles distant)...............	54.5	1886	8.5	"	"	568	"	310	"	248	337,60•
7	St. Albans...........	44.2	1893	8.2	"	"	574	"	316	"	248	341,20•
8	Winfield............	36.0	1893	8.0	"	"	550	"	292	"	248	281,90•
9	Fraziers Bottom......	25.2	1898	6.2	"	"	542	"	284	"	248	315,00•
10	Buffalo.............	18.7	1898	7.0	"	"	542	"	284	"	248	290,00•
11	Point Pleasant........	1.7	1898	10.	"	Hardpan	678	"	364	"	304	650,00•

The chambers of Locks 2, 3, 4, and 5 are 50 feet in width and 271 to 274 feet in available length. The remaining locks are 55 feet in width and 313 feet in available length. The least channel depth is 6 feet. All t movable dams are operated from service bridges.

Data on Kanawha River locks and dams. Thomas and Watt, *The Improvement of Rivers*, 691.

Data Concerning Locks and Dams in KANAWHA RIVER, W. VA.

(Furnished the Survey by Thos. E. Jeffers, U. S. Engineer, Charleston, W. Va.)

LOCKS									DAMS										
							Tide reference.						Length of wickets.		Tide reference				
No. of Lock.	Miles from mouth.	1879 Low water.	Clear Width.	Available length.	Length over all.	Length between quoins	Miter sill.	Top of wall.	Style.	Length of pass.	Length of Weir.	Height of pass trestle.	Pass.	Weir.	Pass sill.	Weir sill.	Upper pool.	Normal lift.	When finished.
			Feet.	Feet.	Feet.	Feet.				Feet	Feet	Ft. In.	Ft. In.	Ft. In.				Feet	
2.	84½	585.46	50	271	377	308	578.75	609.75	Fixed	...	...	.. ...	.. ...	.. ...	......	......	597.75	10.33	1887
3.	79½	571.32	50	272	381	312	566.75	596.75	"	...	...	.. ...	.. ...	.. ...	......	......	587.42	13.67	1882
4.	73¼	564.44	50	274	365	300	559.75	579.75	Movable	248	210	16 2¼	13 9	6 3½	561	567.75	573.75	7.25	1880
5.	07¼	556.22	50	274	365	300	552.50	572.50	"	250	265.5	17 ½	13 10	5 3	553.50	561.50	566.50	7.50	1880
6.	54	548.64	55	313	410.5	342	543.75	565.50	"	248	310	16.8½	13 5½	7 7	546.50	552	559	8.50	1886
7.	44	539.63	55	313	411	342	535.50	555.50	"	248	316	16 9¼	14 ⅛	9 2 5-32	537.50	542	550.50	8.25	1898
8.	36	531.27	55	313	411	342	526	547.25	"	248	292	16 9¼	14 ⅛	9 2 5-32	529.25	533.75	542.25	8	1893
9.	25¼	523.64	55	313	411	342	520.50	539.50	"	248	284	16 9¾	14 ⅛	9 2 5-32	521.25	525.75	534.25	6.25	1898
10.	19	517.41	55	313	411	342	514	533	"	248	284	16 9¼	14 ⅛	9 2 5-32	515	519.50	528	7	1898
11.	1¾	510.08	55	313	411	342	504	526	"	304	364	16 9¼	14 ⅛	9 2 5-32	508	512.50	521	10.93	1898

NOTE: Upper miter sill: Lock No. 2=589.75; Lock No. 3=576.75. Top of wall at head of Lock No. 3=601.25. Elevations are 3.855 Lower than U. S. Geological Survey.

Additional data on Kanawha River locks and dams. West Virginia Geological Survey, *Kanawha County* (Wheeling: Wheeling News Lithograph Co., 1914).

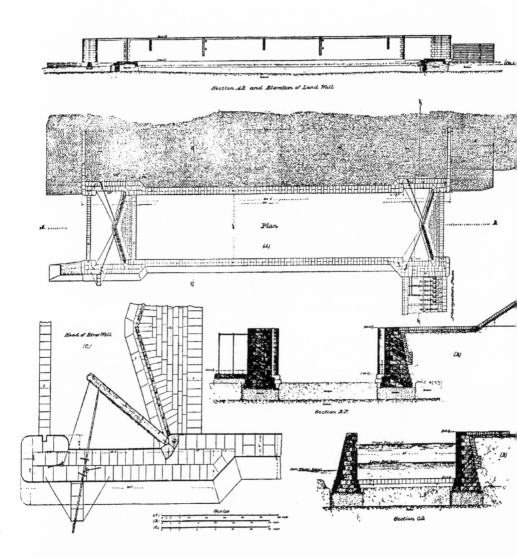

General plan and details of Lock 7, Kanawha River. Thomas and Watt, *The Improvement of Rivers*, 401.

progress over a twenty-three year period. The total cost amounted to $4,208,200. The summary of congressional appropriations includes the initial $50,000 for channel improvements, resulting in a net of $4,158,200, a figure remarkably close to the $4,153,000 estimated by Scott in 1876, twenty-two years earlier.[102] This is a testament to the fiscal control and comprehensive supervision that characterized the entire project. Many hands, from humble laborers to engineer officers and civilian contractors, were responsible for the success of this major public work. It is, however, the team of Craighill and Scott who should be celebrated before all others.

The Charleston *Daily Gazette* of October 22, 1898, hailed the completion of the Kanawha River project with the following editorial comments:

The great value of the improvement, by the government, of the Kanawha river, is splendidly illustrated at this time.

Today, 150 barges of coal, containing two and one-fourth millions of bushels, are in the Point Pleasant basin, and about to leave for the Cincinnati, Louisville and other lower river markets. This coal all comes from the Kanawha collieries, and will find a ready market below.

Our chief competitor for this trade is Pittsburg—and this is where one valuable advantage comes in. Our coal can go out when the Ohio river has six feet of water from Point Pleasant to Cincinnati, while Pittsburg must await a good sized rise in the river, a regular coal boat freshet, all the way up to that city. . . .

Our last lock was only quite recently completed, and this will be the first shipment from the lower pool. After looking anxiously forward to this event for more than twenty-five years, and patiently laboring for it in season and out of season during all that time, our coal men naturally feel good over this excellent piece of fortune now realized. And the whole business community are interested in, and rejoice over, this event. Our business men, professional men, manufacturers, and all, have loyally pulled together in behalf of this enterprise.[103]

As we have noted, William Craighill rose to be Chief of Engineers in 1895 and effectively left the project at that point. In 1901 the Corps of Engineers, in an attempt to decentralize some of its actions, established divisions that oversaw the work of several districts. In an ironic reversal of history, Col. Ernest M. Ruffner was appointed as the division engineer at Cincinnati in charge of the Great Kanawha project and other public works. Colonel Ruffner had not forgotten his controversy with Addison Scott a quarter-century earlier. He now ordered Scott to be transferred from the Kanawha office, and the latter refused, threatening to resign. Ruffner was in a position to discharge Scott, a civilian employee, on a claim of insubordination. This effectively ended Scott's involvement with the project.

In 1891, while the project was still underway, Scott wrote an article strongly promoting the improvement of the Kanawha in terms of its expected benefits to commerce and economic development. In it he compared the shipment of coal by rail and water over the previous decade: "The comparative slight falling off in the river shipment between 1889 1890 was mainly, if not altogether, due to a difference in the market at Cincinnati, Louisville, &c., in the two years. The shipment by river for the last six months indicates that the output for the twelve months ending June, 1891, will be likely to exceed any previous year."[104]

Even before the system was complete, with only the upper five locks and dams in operation, the increase in coal shipments was nearly three-fold, and only slightly less than the amount shipped by rail. The first five locks and dams, Nos. 2 through 6, were the only elements of the idea of the Central Water Line that were put into operation. The construction of locks and a dam at the falls would provide navigation upstream to Gauley Bridge and perhaps beyond. These were never built.

CHAPTER FIVE

Operations for More Than
Two Decades

In a confidential report prepared in 1926, the expenditures for construction, operation, and maintenance of the Kanawha system were estimated. Construction cost approximately $4,072,100, while operating expenses from 1880 to 1926 amounted to $3,047,100, giving a total of $7,119,200. The report declared the direct saving to shippers using the navigation system exceeded this total figure by $8,249,000, or approximately $15.4 million.[1] By 1926, however, the savings were about equal to the operating and maintenance costs if the capital invested in the system were not figured into the total. Coal continued to represent the vast majority of tonnage shipped on the river, although sand and gravel, logs, and packet steamboats also benefited from the improvement. The typical downstream tow consisted of six loaded wooden barges and a fuel flat to supply the steam tow. The number of barges varied from six to ten depending upon the stage of the river. When the movable wickets were down, and on rises with a head of three feet or more, a smaller number of barges could be pushed upstream because turbulence and eddies near the dams made it difficult to enter the lock. Often barges were damaged and time was lost as operators sought to maneuver a tow into a lock under these conditions.[2]

The most sustained complaints about the lock-and-dam system concerned the operations of Lock and Dam 11. Rivermen experienced more delays and interruption there than at any of the other locks on the river. They had a valid claim since it appeared that the channel, at that location

Lock 4, Kanawha River, with sternwheeler in chamber. "View of Lock and Dam No. 4, near Coalberg, WV, of Great Kanawha River Improvement." *The Virginias: A Mining, Industrial and Scientific Journal* 2 (July 1881): 104.

near the mouth of the river, had a depth of fourteen to sixteen feet and a considerable width before the intrusion of this lock and dam. A large sandbar, about seven feet high, was a notable feature of the river at that location. The situation differed greatly after the dam was put into operation. The pass, positioned in the middle of the dam, was dropped only in high water to provide open river navigation. When, however, river stages were not high enough for open navigation, the slackwater pool behind the dam was maintained by letting water out over the weir, being controlled by shorter wickets and a higher elevation than the pass wickets and dam crest. The weir was located at the end of the dam. In the case of Lock and Dam 11, the large sandbar was eroded away when water was released over the weir, and the sand settled out in the channel.[3]

This was not the only problem. The rivermen claimed the dam was not sufficiently high to provide a six-foot depth immediately below Lock 10. Elsewhere such a problem might have been solved most economically by dredging, but here the rocky bottom of the river was very near the six-foot channel bottom. Frequently, tows risked grounding in an attempt to push through sand accumulating on the bottom, knowing full well that bedrock was near the draft of the barges.

Maneuvering Chanoine wickets at locks and dam under flood conditions. U.S. Army Corps of Engineers, Huntington District Archives.

Another problem resulted from the canalization of the Ohio to a nine-foot depth, three feet deeper than the Kanawha channel. Thus, when there was even a moderate rise in the Ohio, typically nine to nine-and-a-half feet, wickets on Dam 11 would trip and lower the pool behind the dam to the same level as the river below. This often made the depth below Lock 10 three feet or less, effectively shutting off navigation in the Kanawha River.

River traffic, however, continued using the movable dam system until the 1930s, but there was clearly a need to increase the channel depth to nine feet to be compatible with the Ohio River. Assuming that funds were available, the engineering question was whether to increase the height of the ten Kanawha locks and dams or build a new series of locks and demolish the existing system in its entirety. In reply to many complaints about the operation of the locks and dams, Thomas E. Jeffries, assistant engineer, remarked:

> I think as a rule we are prone to remember the faults and forget the virtues, and steamboat people are not exceptions to this rule. If a steamboat is delayed, or

sticks anywhere in the river, it is always remembered, but the general good service that is given is soon forgotten and never considered when expensive work is asked for. I do not wish, however, to deny that there has been trouble to tows of loaded barges in No. 11 pool, and that this trouble has been increased by the construction of Dam No. 26 and is likely to be further increased when Dam No. 25 is built, as when the bear traps at the latter dam are lowered to let out surplus water they will produce a rise that will cause trouble at Dam No. 11, Kanawha River, more frequently perhaps and to a greater extent than at present, as it will probably be found more difficult to counteract this increased height by bleeding Dam No. 26 than it is now.[4]

In the same memorandum, Jeffries considered, in some detail, what it would take to rectify the system by raising the height of No. 11, but he did not attempt to estimate the cost.

Problems with the operation of Lock and Dam 11 surfaced as early as 1907, in a pair of letters written in reply to inquiries from the Wheeling office of the Corps of Engineers.[5] Jeffries provided details of river stages and the tripping of the wickets at Dam 11, as well as attempts at dredging to alleviate the problem.

An additional problem surfaced during low water. Industries located along the river, and indeed the city of Charleston, depended upon the river for their water supply. Both complained that there was insufficient water in the pool for their operations.[6] Telegrams from the Chief of Engineers, William M. Black, to the district office are vivid reminders that the series of locks and dams not only operated as a navigational system but served other clients for whom a dependable source of water was essential.

Black's first telegram, addressed to Colonel Stickle in Wheeling, West Virginia, was dated December 12, 1917:

FEDERAL FUEL ADMINISTRATION REPORTS MINES MADE IDLE AND REDUCTION ONE HUNDRED THOUSAND TONS COAL PRODUCTION DUE TO VIRGINIAN POWER CO POWER PLANT BEING MADE IDLE BY LOWERING WICKETS DAM FOUR KANAWHA RIVER PLEASE INVESTIGATE AND TAKE PROMPT ACTION TO COOPERATE IN IMPROVING SITUATION WIRE ACTION TAKEN.

A second telegram addressed to Stickle and dated December 13, 1917, added:

MR MORGAN CHAIRMAN PUBLIC SERVICE COMMISSION CHARLESTON WESTVA HAS WIRED SECRETARY WAR QUOTE CHARLESTON WITHOUT WATER RESULT OF GOVERN-MENT ENGINEERS LOWERING WICKETS LOCK SW KANAWHA RIVER LOWER WATERS BE-

LOW INTAKE PIPE CITY WATER WORKS WHICH CANNOT BE LOWERED DISASTROUS FIRE LAST NIGHT WITHOUT FIRE PROTECTION DOMESTIC SITUATION SERIOUS WILL YOU NOT ONCE ORDER ENGINEERS TO RAISE DAM AT LOCK SIX UNQUOTE TAKE SUCH ACTION AS IS PRACTICABLE TO RELIEVE SITUATION AND WIRE PRMPTLY WHAT STEPS YOU CONSIDER ADVISABLE AND STEPS BEING TAKEN.[7]

Not long after the opening of the locks and dams, Maj. E. H. Ruffner published a notice to all concerned about the operation of the system in an attempt to bring order to what were still largely unregulated operations.[8] The primary concern was the frequent requests by coal-boat operators to contiunue the old practice of "flashing" the movable dams. This created a rise in the river of several feet that carried barges downstream on an artificial tide. Major Ruffner was concerned about possible damage to vessels and properties if this practice were not carefully regulated. He indicated that the practice would continue only if the operators organized so that they could speak with one voice. Another concern was steam packets, whose captains requested increased depth during low water on upstream journeys. This was done by opening a dam farther upstream, thus raising the downstream pools. The "flashing" of coal tows and other manipulations of the movable dams continued at least into 1917 and undoubtedly until the end of the movable dam period.[9]

Surveys and Plans

With the introduction of the nine-foot-deep channel on the Ohio and difficulties operating Lock and Dam 11 because of the backwater created by the Ohio River, serious study was given to improvements on the Kanawha. In 1913, in the course of preparing a report, Lt. Col. W. E. Craighill, son of William Price Craighill, studied a number of alternatives. These included employing smaller barges on the Great Kanawha River, with a transfer point for larger barges at the confluence of the Kanawha and Ohio Rivers, as well as the development of combined water and rail transportation. Craighill and his two colleagues concluded that the advantages accruing from a greater navigational depth had to be compared to the disruption to navigation over the many years it would take to raise each of the ten locks and dams. Thus, they concluded that any improvement scheme was "unworthy" of the investment by the federal government.[10]

Two important insights are expressed in this report, which formed the basis for a totally different way to increase traffic on the Kanawha River. The Army engineers studied stream flow gauges for sixteen years and concluded that the present movable dams were available for open river navigation nearly half the year, or 181 days, on average. If, however, the locks and dams were to be raised to operate a nine-foot channel, the passes would be open for only 59 days a year. This was the beginning of a concept of non-navigable gated dams constructed in fewer numbers and at different locations than the eight movable and two fixed-crest dams of the original system.

As noted earlier, the original design called for twelve locks and dams, which were later reduced to ten by the elimination of No. 1 near the falls and No. 12 at the mouth of the river. Even with the difficulties experienced with Lock and Dam 11, no plans appeared either to increase the height of No. 11 or to build Lock and Dam 12. With the completion of the ten locks and dams and the opening of the system for navigation, there was renewed interest in providing access to the pool above the falls of the Kanawha. In 1900 Addison Scott wrote to Captain H. F. Hodges in the division office in Cincinnati suggesting a survey of the river from Lock and Dam 2 to the falls.[11] In the recommendation, Scott noted that this portion of the river had never been surveyed except for a line of levels. In view of the possibility of an appropriation for building additional locks and dams above the No. 2 backwater, Scott suggested, a modest investment would procure the information needed for preliminary planning, including cost estimates. Hodges replied that there was no authorization for such a survey since the existing project no longer contemplated the construction of Lock and Dam 1.[12] Nevertheless, Hodges wrote to the Chief of Engineers through the division engineer requesting such a survey.[13] There the matter rested for two years.

Interest was rekindled with the passage on June 3, 1902, of the Rivers and Harbors Act, which authorized a survey but not the construction of Lock and Dam 1. Thomas Jefferies undertook the survey in the summer of 1903. He found the field work very difficult because, as he states: "With 3 1/2 feet of water on the Falls gage, the river at both Loup Creek and Long Shoals was exceedingly rough and swift, causing much labor with a drag line, wading and pushing, to get the skiff over the shoals. The waves in Loup Creek Shoals, in places, seemed to be three feet high, and it was only along the shore that a boat could be kept afloat. The trees, brush, briars, and large stone along the bank will make the survey hard and te-

dious work, prolonging the time and increasing the cost above my antici-
pations."[14]

The delay meant more time in the field than the anticipated fortnight
at a cost of $600. Jeffries also reported that the lodging for his team at $1
per night was unacceptably high![15] The cost of the survey was doubled to
$1,200, and Jeffries' report was also delayed. In fact, it was not submitted
until November 7, 1903.[16] It concluded that, with a pool elevation of 618
feet, there would be approximately 3,000 feet of excavation at the upper
end of Long Shoal that would have to be deepened, requiring 120,000
cubic yards of excavation in hard rock. The alternative of raising the pool
level was not acceptable because it would reduce the power on the turbines of the William Willson Aluminum Company. One of the primary
objectives of this proposed construction would be to enhance power production at the falls, not reduce it, and provide cheap transportation in the
slackwater behind the falls.

Appropriations were not forthcoming, and so Lock and Dam 1 was
never built. The power plant dating from this era is still in operation at
the Great Falls of the Kanawha.

World War I and Beyond

The storm clouds of war that had broken across Europe in 1914 had extended to the United States by 1917. Virtually all civil works of the Corps
of Engineers came to a standstill, including planning for such projects as
the Kanawha navigation improvement. Under the leadership of Maj. Gen.
William M. Black, Chief of Engineers, more than 300,000 men were
mobilized for engineering duty in the Great War. America's role was brief
but pivotal in securing the Armistice. Having rapidly expanded during
the war, the Corps of Engineers was faced with demobilizing this force
of men during 1919 and returning to its peacetime activities, especially
large public works on the western waters.[17]

One of the largest of these schemes involved the complete canalization of the Ohio River from Pittsburgh to Cairo, Illinois, by a system of
locks and movable wicket dams. Davis Island, site of the first such lock
and dam in 1885, served as a prototype.[18] It was not until 1905, when
Congress authorized a feasibility study for the Ohio River under the direction of Daniel W. Lockwood, that momentum developed for canaliz-
ing the entire river system. The Lockwood report recommended a slack-

water navigation extending nearly a thousand miles over the entire length of the river at a cost of $63 million. With presidential and congressional support, the canalization was authorized in 1910, with an estimated completion date of 1922. As approved, the system consisted of fifty-four locks and dams with a minimum nine-foot channel throughout its entire length.[19]

Although authorized, the appropriations were not forthcoming at a rate that would insure completion by 1922. Like similar undertakings, the project stagnated during the First World War. Nevertheless, the Ohio slackwater system was upgraded to a nine-foot channel depth, whereas the Kanawha River slackwater had smaller locks and a draft of only six feet. The Ohio system greatly influenced engineers of the day in their decision to repair, modify, or replace Locks and Dams 4 and 5 above Charleston on the Kanawha.

To facilitate the decision-making process, the River and Harbor Acts of 1922 and 1927 directed the Corps of Engineers to undertake a study and make recommendations regarding Locks and Dams 4 and 5.[20] In the 1880s, the capital of the war-born state, West Virginia, had been moved from Wheeling to Charleston.[21] The move took place on steamboats on the Ohio and Kanawha Rivers. In a similar fashion in 1922, the Corps reorganized its district and moved the Wheeling office, together with all its impedimenta and staff, to Huntington, which was strategically located on the Ohio River and close to the Kanawha River. The Kanawha study was the first large project undertaken in the new Huntington office. Early in 1926, the district engineer, Harry M. Trippe, who was in charge of the survey, submitted his report with a recommendation that Dams 2 through 5, on the upper reaches of the river above Charleston, be replaced by two much-higher, gated dams with larger locks of the so-called "Monongahela" size, or 55 by 360 feet.[22]

Because the five locks below Charleston had only a six-foot draft, some Army engineers favored maintaining the six-foot channel depth. There were, however, shipping interests in the valley and others with a vision of a nine-foot channel to be compatible with the Ohio River improvements, which were not finished until 1929. A lobbying group, the Kanawha Valley Improvement Association, founded in 1926, put pressure on Washington for the nine-foot depth and a channel width of at least two hundred feet. This group had in mind the construction of several more locks and dams to replace the five downstream movable dams stretching from Charleston to Point Pleasant.[23]

The promoters of the nine-foot channel and reduced number of locks were quite aware that the decision to upgrade the system would rest upon a convincing economic argument. The decade before the Great War saw a steady million tons of coal shipped on the Kanawha, although the total production continued to increase, indicating that more and more coal was being shipped on the railways. (See Table 5.1.) It appeared that the limited size of the locks and the six-foot channel restricted trade, giving an advantage to railway interests, particularly the system of hauling coal on the rails to Huntington and transferring it into larger Ohio River barges for the trip downstream.

During the war, the products of the German chemical industry, a world leader, had become unavailable, providing an opportunity for indigenous industries to develop. The Kanawha Valley possessed a long tradition of chemical production based upon salt, abundant raw materials, and energy, not only from coal but also from natural gas and oil. The valley's proximity to efficient rail and river transportation made it a ideal location. During the war the government also located an ordinance works at South Charleston and a huge explosives plant at Nitro, farther downstream. This latter industry was built without any preexisting infrastructure, and it included the creation of an entire prefabricated town, appro-

TABLE 5.1. **Comparison of Coal Shipments by River and Rail** *(in bushels)*

Year ending	Shipments by river	Shipments by railroad	Total
June 30, 1881	9,628,696	6,631,660	16,260,356
June 1, 1883	15,370,458	13,290,255	28,660,713
" 1884	18,421,084	12,059,172	30,480,256
" 1885	17,812,323	12,972,217	30,784,540
" 1886	17,861,613	13,953,745	31,815,358
" 1887	23,233,374	19,160,896	42,394,270
" 1888	20,100,625	20,962,686	41,063,311
" 1889	26,921,788	22,031,121	48,952,909
" 1890	24,161,554	27,433,425	51,594,979

Source: Addison M. Scott, "Coal: Commerce and Development on the Great Kanawha Valley, the Cheapest Transportation Known." Pamphlet published by the Charleston (W.Va.) *Daily Gazette,* 1891, 1–9.

priately named Nitro. Adding to the chemical industries' bulk shipments on the river, several oil refineries transported their liquids in closed barges to various ports along the Ohio River and its tributaries.[24] With the prospect of a greater variety of products and increased tonnage, promoters of the nine-foot channel felt they had a compelling argument for construction of entirely new and larger locks and dams. Victory was theirs with the passage of the River and Harbor Act of July 3, 1930, which authorized the construction of two new high-lift locks and dams with a nine-foot channel, eliminating Locks and Dams 2, 3, 4, and 5: "The replacement of Locks and Dams Nos. 2 to 5, inclusive, was provided for by the River and Harbor Act of 3 July 1930, which further provided that any dredging in the section of river above Charleston should be prosecuted with a view to obtaining a depth of 9 feet and a width of 200 feet."[25]

With the new locks and dams located away from the original structures, navigation would be uninterrupted during the construction of these new structures. Portions of the original movable-dam system thus remained in operation for a few more years. The River and Harbor Act of 1930 marked the beginning of a new system of non-navigable dams with gated crests, based upon a new technology imported from Germany. Thus, the French system gave way to German innovations that found their first application in America on the Kanawha River.

PART II

ROLLER GATED DAMS AND LOCKS

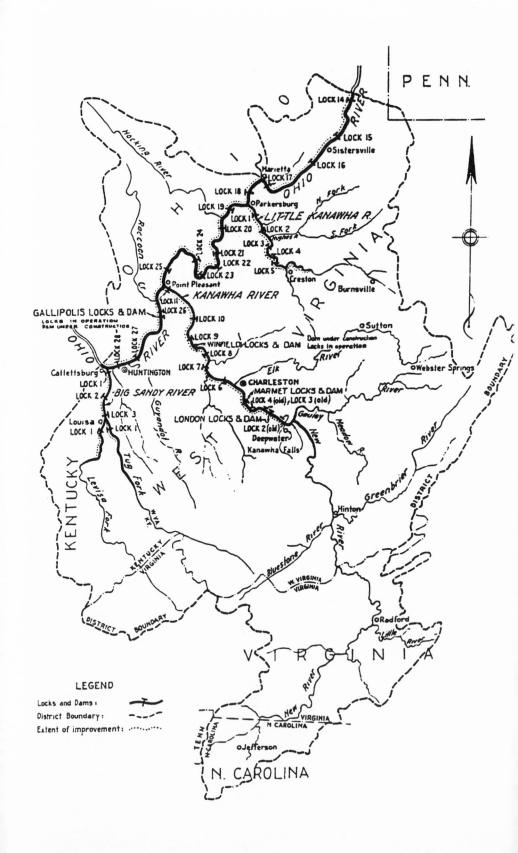

PENN.

LOCK 14

OHIO RIVER

LOCK 15
Sistersville
LOCK 16

Marietta
LOCK 17

LOCK 18

Parkersburg
N. Fork
LOCK 19

LOCK 1
LITTLE KANAWHA R.
LOCK 24
LOCK 20
LOCK 2
S. Fork

LOCK 3
Hughes R.
LOCK 21
LOCK 4
LOCK 22

LOCK 25
LOCK 5
Creston
LOCK 23
Burnsville

Point Pleasant
KANAWHA RIVER

LOCK 11
LOCK 26
Sutton

GALLIPOLIS LOCKS & DAM
LOCKS IN OPERATION
DAM UNDER CONSTRUCTION
LOCK 10

LOCK 27
LOCK 9
Dam under construction
Locks in operation
LOCK 28
WINFIELD LOCKS & DAM
River
LOCK 8
Webster Springs

OHIO
RIVER
LOCK 7
Elk

Catlettsburg
HUNTINGTON
LOCK 6
CHARLESTON
River
LOCK 1
MARMET LOCKS & DAM
BIG SANDY RIVER
LOCK 4 (old), LOCK 3 (old)
LOCK 2

LONDON LOCKS & DAM
Gauley
LOCK 3
LOCK 2 (old)
Louisa
LOCK 1
LOCK 1
Deepwater
New
Kanawha Falls

Guyandol R.

KENTUCKY

Tug Fork

WEST

WVA.
KY.
Greenbrier River

Levisa Fork

Hinton
DISTRICT
BOUNDARY

KENTUCKY
VIRGINIA

Bluestone River
New River
W. VIRGINIA
VIRGINIA

DISTRICT BOUNDARY

Radford
Little River

VIRGINIA

New River

TENN
N. CAROLINA
VIRGINIA
N. CAROLINA

Jefferson

N. CAROLINA

LEGEND

Locks and Dams :
District Boundary :
Extent of improvement :

Introduction:
The Prelude to a New
Navigation System

Engineers of the Huntington District had become concerned during the late 1920s with the deteriorating condition of Locks and Dams 4 and 5. They were the oldest in the Kanawha system, having been completed in 1880, and the dams used a traditional wood-crib structure lacking in durability. Expensive rehabilitation work would be necessary to keep the navigation above Charleston in operation. Another, far better, proposal emerged in the late 1920s, as the Corps completed its nine-foot channel project on the Ohio River to deepen the Kanawha navigation channel to the same depth as the Ohio's.

On February 17, 1928, the Chief of Engineers recommended to the Secretary of War that Locks and Dams 2, 3, 4, and 5 be replaced with two new locks and dams.[1] In place of the single locks, the report recommended double locks 56 feet by 360 feet with a 21-foot lift. These locks would accommodate a 9-foot channel, and the pools would be dredged to this depth. The Corps estimated that the cost would be $3.6 million.[2] Later that year, on July 17, 1928, the division engineer advised modifying the

(Opposite) Map of Great Kanawha, Ohio River, and tributaries with locations of the original wicket locks and dams and the roller gate replacements. "Engineering Projects in the Huntington Engineer District" (Plate 1), Jan. 1937; RG 77, Entry 111 Bulkies, File 7245-164/1, National Archives and Records Admin. (NARA), Washington, D.C.

proposal to increase the lift to 30 feet at each of the locks. The Chief of Engineers studied the recommendation because the increased elevations in the pools behind the locks would involve considerable flooding of heavily industrialized areas.

There was substantial local and political support for improving the entire Kanawha River to a nine-foot channel. House Document 190 provided a useful compromise in that the deteriorating locks could be replaced by two locks and dams above Charleston, eliminating the problem perceived by the Army engineers, while at the same time they could be part of a future nine-foot channel project.[3] With the prospect of a rivers and harbors act, various parties lent their support to a nine-foot channel to be compatible with the Ohio River. On January 31, 1930, Ernest M. Merrill, president of the Kanawha Valley Improvement Association, submitted a resolution to Representative S. Wallace Dempsey, chairman of the Committee on Rivers and Harbors of the U.S. Congress. Not only did Merrill lend his support to the nine-foot channel project, but he proposed model legislation.[4] The governor of West Virginia added his support when he telegraphed Maj. Gen. Lytle Brown, Chief of Engineers, urging that a special report on the project below Charleston be supplied in time for consideration in the current session of Congress.[5]

Adding his voice to the clamor for river improvement, George E. Sutherland, president of the West Virginia Sand and Gravel Company, graphically described to the district engineer, Lt. Col. E. D. Ardery, the difficulties of negotiating Lock 10. He concluded: "I cannot help but blame a part of this delay on the man in charge of Lock No. 10. However, I suppose a large part of it is due to the present system of locks and dams in the Great Kanawha River, but it is certainly conclusive evidence as to why the river is not more generally used especially by manufacturing industries in the Great Kanawha Valley who must have some reasonable assurance of prompt delivery of both their inbound and outbound freight."[6]

A month later, Congressman J. A. Hughes, of West Virginia's fourth district, urged the Assistant Chief of Engineers to expedite the report on the stretch of river below Charleston so that the Committee on Rivers and Harbors could have it in time for a bill.[7] Merrill had been following the status of the lower-river report and also urged Gen. Lytle Brown to transmit the report to Congress as soon as possible.[8] The great push to include the entire river in an omnibus bill depended on approval of the survey below Lock and Dam 5. The senior member of the Board of Engineers for Rivers and Harbors, Brig. Gen. Herbert Deakyne, wrote to the Chief of Engineers on March 11, 1930, informing him: "While the Board is of the opinion that the needs of commerce and navigation require a 9 foot improvement in the Kanawha River, it is unable, with the information thus far presented to make the necessary studies of the engineering features on which to base a definite recommendation."[9] The very next day the Chief of Engineers, Lytle Brown, wrote to Senator David A. Reed indicating that he had not received a copy of the report, but he would be glad to share it with Reed at his convenience.[10]

With preliminary studies in hand, Colonel Spalding was anxious to get the upper Kanawha River Project under way as soon as possible. He telegrammed the district engineer that he would arrive in Huntington on Thursday, from Louisville, to discuss in detail the plans for improvement of the Kanawha above Charleston and the matter of expediting the beginning of the work, when and if Congress should act. He also wished to discuss detailed plans for expediting the work below Charleston.[11]

In anticipation of the War Department Appropriation Act, Lieutenant Colonel Daley, on direction from the Chief of Engineers, wrote to the division engineer in St. Louis indicating that he expected an appropriation of $55 million, of which 12.5 percent would be reserved for contingencies.[12] He directed the district engineer to submit recommendations for allotments not later than May 21, 1930, in order that these allotments could be made promptly following the passage of the act whose passage was expected before June 15.

The visit of Lt. Col. George A. Spalding was reported in the May 2 issue of the *Montgomery News*.[13] In the article, it was noted that the House of Representatives had passed a General Rivers and Harbors Appropriation Bill that included $3 million for improving the river from Montgomery to Charleston. A confirmation was printed in the same newspaper article to the effect that the Corps of Engineers was supporting improvement of the river below Charleston, but was engaged in working out the details before the report was finally submitted. The War Department Appropriation Act of May 28, 1930, approved the overall appropriation of $55 million expected by the Corps of Engineers. It was not, however, until July 3, 1930, that Congress adopted a modification of the project for the improvement of the Kanawha River.[14] This provided for the replacement of Locks 2, 3, 4, and 5 with two locks and dams of larger dimensions, the location and design of which would be determined by the Chief of Engineers after detailed surveys and explorations had been made. At this stage, Lytle Brown wrote to the Secretary of War asking for $25,000 from the contingency fund of the Rivers and Harbors Act of July 3, 1930, in order to expedite the work.[15] The district engineer, Col. E. D. Ardery, announced in the *Montgomery News* of August 15 that work would begin on the project very soon, with bids to be received on August 19 for core borings in the vicinity of the proposed sites for both of the new locks and dams.[16] In this same announcement, he mentioned that the engineering plans were being worked out at the division offices in St. Louis.

Not everyone was happy with the proposed sites.[17] Several formal protests were made to the district engineer on behalf of the C&O Railway, the Kanawha County Road Department, and other interests. The railway felt that the increased pool level would saturate the fill under its tracks. The gas company was concerned that their lines would be under water, and the county road engineer complained that certain roads would be covered with water. It appears that these protests were simply formalities, lodged so that later claims could be made against the Corps of Engineers if necessary.[18] It was noted that the amount appropriated for both locks and dams was $3.6 million.[19]

Not content that the appropriations for construction of the two locks and dams had been authorized, C. Paul Heavener, chairman of the Drought Committee for Kanawha County, sent a resolution to President Herbert Hoover on September 12, 1930, urging that work begin at the earliest possible date, in order to alleviate unemployment and improve the economic base for industries in the valley.[20] In a memorandum to the Secretary of War, Gen. Lytle Brown summarized the current situation with regard to the Kanawha Navigation.[21] The act authorized only the construction of the Marmet and London locks and dams and did not provide funds for the improvements below Charleston.[22]

Plans were well under way for the dam and locks, together with a hydroelectric power station to be constructed on the left bank of the dam. The Chief of Engineers assured the Secretary of War that it would be possible to enter into a contract for constructing the first dam during the coming year. It was noted that authorization for developing plans below

Charleston were directed by Congress in the River and Harbor Act of January 21, 1927. He did not anticipate the final report until the coming winter.[23]

Following public discussion and further engineering studies, the district engineer, Maj. Fred W. Herman, Jr., provided a status report to the Chief of Engineers indicating that the location of the locks and dams had been determined. The Marmet double locks were originally intended to be built at the same location as the old Lock 5, completed in 1880, but the site was moved slightly upstream because it was considered impossible to build the new locks and dam and keep navigation open in the upper pools. The proposed new location was referred to as the Marmet site. The upper site, which was originally proposed and incorporated in House Document 190, was found to be insufficient to provide nine-foot depths without raising the pool level to such an extent that low and flat land would be flooded, not only on the Kanawha but on the Paint Creek tributary.[24] Thus, the new site was called the London site, and was upstream from that originally proposed.

Although there was a consideration of a 27-foot lift at London, and only 24 feet at Marmet, it was recommended that locks and dams at both locations should be identical, providing a standardization in the gates and other features. Thus, pool elevations were awaiting final engineering designs. It was also noted that the successful improvement of the Monongahela River Navigation had allowed a great increase in the amount of coal transported to Pittsburgh and farther down the Ohio River. Thus, the decision was made to provide twin Monongahela-type locks, 55 feet by 360 feet, rather than yield to navigation interests who were pushing for a single 720-foot-long lock. The Corps' justification was that the shorter locks offered only slightly decreased facilities for passing the longer tows than would be the case for one longer lock. Twin locks would allow one to be closed for maintenance purposes. The argument has not proven to be the case with greatly increased size of tows and tonnage moved through the Kanawha system.[25]

It was clear that a decision on the movable gates had not been made. Studies of roller gates and vertical-lift Stoney gates were underway. The S. Morgan Smith Company, which was the licensee for the Maschinenfabrik Augsburg-Nurnberg (MAN, the well-known German firm), forwarded the roller-gate design to the division engineer in St. Louis, on

February 10, 1931, and presented a preliminary price for supplying roller gates for both the Rock Island Lock and Dam and the Marmet Locks and Dam. In the case of the Marmet lock, their preliminary price was $349,410, including freight. That was based on an estimate of 3.8 million pounds of steel for a gate 100 feet long and 26 feet in diameter.[26]

The district engineer estimated that the cost for both dams would be in the neighborhood of $5 million. He recommended twin locks at each of the sites and advised that these locks be constructed immediately so that navigation could continue while the dams and their movable gates were constructed. He said he was sending plans and specification for the locks at Marmet under separate cover. Those for London would be forthcoming in a month's time.[27]

In response to Colonel Spalding's urging that the project be expedited, the Army engineers issued specifications on January 7, 1931, for the building of the landside Marmet lock. Bids were to be opened a month later on February 6.[28] Before we continue with the history of the construction of Marmet and London locks and dams, it will be helpful to examine the engineering design and analysis to understand what went on behind the scenes in developing the contract drawings and specifications.

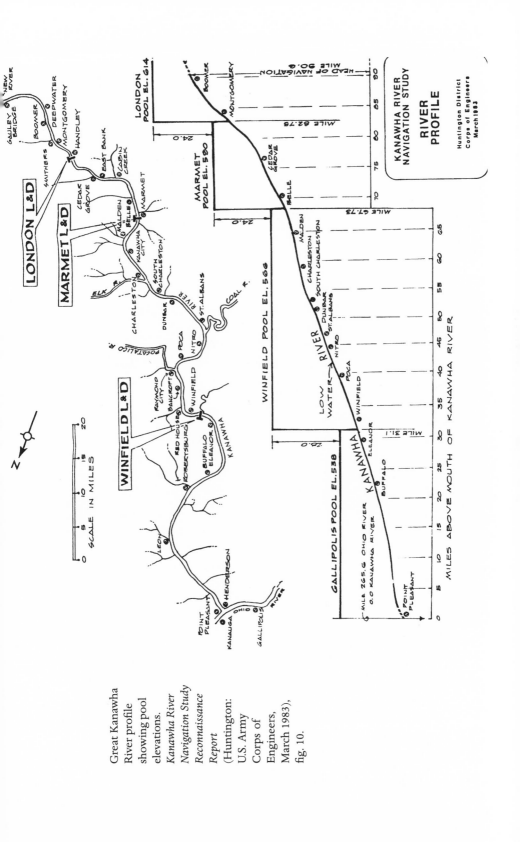

Great Kanawha
River profile
showing pool
elevations.
*Kanawha River
Navigation Study
Reconnaissance
Report*
(Huntington:
U.S. Army
Corps of
Engineers,
March 1983),
fig. 10.

CHAPTER SIX

Design of the Locks and Dams

Gate Design

The first set of locks and dams on the Kanawha, as well as the four constructed in the 1930s, adopted foreign designs for movable structures to be mounted on top of fixed-crest dams. In the first case, it was the French Chanoine wicket; in the second, it was the German roller-gate system licensed to the Dravo Corporation in Pittsburgh, Pennsylvania. Thus, the Corps of Engineers did not have a direct role in the conception or design of these movable systems. Its role was to adapt these systems to traditional construction techniques perfected by the Corps over a number of years.

The adoption of the nine-foot channel for the Ohio River system and subsequently for the Great Kanawha Navigation posed a series of engineering possibilities and limitations. For instance, replacing the ten locks and dams with three high-lift locks and dams would create a pool of sufficient depth to make hydroelectric power generation feasible. This aspect of the history of the Great Kanawha Navigation will be examined later.

Moving from a six-foot channel depth to nine feet lengthened the period when the river could accept open navigation. With less than two months, on average, it was deemed inappropriate to upgrade the open-navigation system using the Chanoine or other wicket designs, although such wicket dams could theoretically be used for heads in excess of twenty feet. ("Head" is an engineering term for a measure of hydraulic pressure, which increases with depth.) In practice, these heights were not feasible because of the greatly increased size of the wickets and supporting framework. Even with relatively low heads, such dams required skilled operators, and at the best of times they were dangerous for personnel. Thus, non-navigable movable dams were proposed. In this system, all river traffic would, of necessity, pass through locks provided at the dams. That being the case, it would seem that a fixed-crest dam could serve the situation in the most efficient manner. A system of gated dams was, however, the best solution since gates could be opened to pass flotsam, ice, and, most important, freshets, which would cause flooding in the pools behind the dam unless released by opening the gates. Thus, the Army engineers considered non-navigable movable dams with various gate designs. These included the sector or Tainter gate, vertical-lift gate with or without Stoney rollers, and the German roller gate.

The vertical lift gate has an ancient origin, but it was given a modern form by the Irish engineer Francis G. G. Stoney (1837–1897).[1] He developed a flat steel gate moving on a train of rollers in vertical grooves in the piers. Apparently, the first application of a Stoney gate occurred around 1875. The first large gates, however, were not installed until 1883, for the drainage work for Lough Erne in Northern Ireland. A notable example in America is the set of 119 rectangular sliding gates at 36 feet on center used to control pool levels on the Keokuk Dam (1910–1913) on the Mississippi River.

Hydraulic pressures on such flat gates limited the width of the opening, since a flat plate is not as efficient as a curved surface in sustaining water pressures. Given the need to maximize the openings between the piers, it is not surprising that the Stoney gate was not adapted by the Corps of Engineers at any of their later movable dams associated with the Upper Mississippi nine-foot-channel project. The Stoney gate valve did, however, find wide application as a valve in navigation locks where it controlled the filling and emptying of the chambers. Except for the locks at Gallipolis, Stoney valves were installed in the locks on the Great Kanawha Navigation (1930–1938) and are still in use.

Just as the bear-trap gates on the Lehigh Navigation are an original American invention, the sector gate, at least in its modern form, appears to be an early American contribution to hydraulic engineering.[2] The credit goes to Captain Marshall Lewis, who applied for a patent based upon improvements in the sector gate, not claiming it as an original invention.[3]

His patent application of 1827 described a semicircular sector gate of iron. Because sector gates are simple and economic devices for controlling water passing over weirs and dams, it is not surprising that many improvements evolved in the basic design.

An interesting case developed in 1840–1841, and resulted in legal action when similar patents by George Hildreth and George Heath were contested.[4] More significant for this study, the 1856 design by François Poirée of a sector gate in connection with his movable dam projects did not find wide application because it could not be easily utilized for open navigation on French rivers.[5] At about the same time as the invention of the Stoney gate, circa 1880, Thomas Parker and Jeremiah B. Tainter developed a gate for use in the lumber industry for controlling water levels in mill reservoirs. Not only did the gates control these levels but, equally important, they passed ice and other debris as necessary. It was a highly successful design, so it is not surprising that the Tainter gate patent of 1880 was assigned to the Corps of Engineers, which purchased the rights.[6]

In cross section, the Tainter gate is a pie-shaped structure with the upstream surface the sector of a long cylinder. In early designs, the gates were operated by a crane mounted on a service bridge over the gates. During the 1930s electrically driven chain-hoist machinery was applied on the Upper Mississippi Valley nine-foot-channel project. Since the gates could be raised smoothly out of the water, lifting gear had only to raise the dead load of the gate and not also work against water pressure. With electric-drive machinery the gates could be raised simultaneously if needed, an improvement over a crane lifting one gate at a time.

Nevertheless, in their earliest form, Tainter gates were restricted to openings only up to thirty-five feet and not the hundred feet required by the Corps of Engineers. Their reliability was also questioned.[7] Under the circumstances, it is not surprising that roller gates were given preference over Tainter gates at the time of construction of the lock and dams on the Great Kanawha River and the Gallipolis locks and dam. On the Upper Mississippi, a mixed system of Tainter and roller gates was used until construction of Lock and Dam 24, where only the Tainter gates were used.[8] The mixed system in all of the earlier dams on the Upper Mississippi used only three or four passes with hundred-foot-long roller gates. The rest of the dam was controlled by Tainter gates. Hydraulic studies indicated that three or four roller gates in the main channel could pass the necessary ice, flotsam, and freshets. While not all hydraulic engineers supported this mixed system, the twenty-two sites on the Upper Mississippi have functioned satisfactorily for more than half a century.

Many improvements were made to the basic Tainter gate design during the construction of the nine-foot Upper Mississippi project. It was found that raising the gates to pass flows of ice, whether they were Tainter or roller gates, required lifting them entirely clear of the water, whereas in normal operations the water escaped under the gate to control the slackwater elevation. But the fully raised gates quickly lowered the pool levels to unacceptable elevations for navigation and natural habitat. Such large quantities of water passing over the crest also caused significant scour downstream, for those locks and dams were not founded directly on rock. One solution was to design a submersible gate that could be lowered enough to pass the ice and then be raised to normal pool level. The depth below pool level for these submerged gates ranged from four to eight feet, but at these greater depths erosion was a recurring problem. Therefore, the depth of the gate pit was usually restricted to four to six feet.

The first submersible Tainter gates had only steel plates on the water face and varied little from the nonsubmersible type. Subsequently, elliptical and arch gates were developed with plating on both sides and improved internal framing utilizing the steel skin as part of the structure. These improvements allowed gates to be erected with spans up to eighty feet.

Dam 24, designed in 1937 and constructed during 1938–1939, featured Tainter gates only.[9] This site represented the latest development in sector-gate design and the triumph of the Tainter gate over the roller gate. The Great Kanawha Navigation and Upper Mississippi nine-foot-channel projects represented the flourishing period for roller gates. After the end of the decade 1927–1937, the roller gate was not used by the Corps of Engineers in lock-and-dam projects. Thus, the use of roller gates exclusively on the Great Kanawha Navigation and the Gallipolis locks and dam represent highly significant examples during the heyday of roller-gate technology in America.

An international engineering conference was held in St. Louis, in 1904. In a session on national waterways, K. E. Hilgard presented a paper on rolling dams, which were an entirely new concept for American engineers concerned with movable dams.[10] The originator and patentee of the design, Max Carstanjen, was the chief engineer of the Gustavburg

Bridge Works near Mainz, Germany. This firm was a branch of the Maschinenfabrik Augsburg-Nurnberg, well known by the acronym MAN.

The first roller dam was erected in 1901–1902 at Schweinfurt in Germany.[11] By 1928, 250 such dams were recorded as having been built.[12] The majority, 140, were in Germany, but a significant number, 24, had been constructed in the United States. The first application of the roller-gate dam in America was not by the Corps of Engineers but by private and public agencies in the Pacific Northwest. The Washington Water Power Company used three roller gates to control pool levels at a dam on Long Lake near Spokane.[13] This work was completed in 1914 and utilized gates 65 feet long. Two years later, in 1916, the U.S. Bureau of Reclamation built seven roller gates measuring 70 feet wide and 15 feet in diameter, for an irrigation dam on the Grand River near Palisade, Colorado. This project established the basic American design for roller gates, which developed during World War I because of a prohibition against German proprietary designs and products. A Bureau of Reclamation engineer, Frank Teichman, reworked the MAN patent drawings, and the Riter-Conley Manufacturing Company of Pittsburgh fabricated the gates.[14] The Bureau of Reclamation design was used with little modification by the Corps of Engineers on Mississippi Dam 15, designed many years later in 1931. It was the first such gate used on a Corps project.[15]

The first roller dam designs consisted of a hollow, riveted, watertight drum resembling a boiler. Spanning between piers, the drum closes the dam when resting on top of the masonry or concrete crest. As the roller gate is raised, water flows over the crest of the dam and underneath the drum. The drum diameter, together with a projecting apron, is a measure of the height of water retained behind the drum. Special devices are needed for sealing out water in the space between the crest and the dam and the ends of the drum, and reducing to a minimum any leakage that might occur. This is in marked contrast to the earlier Chanoine and Poirée dams, which were well known for leaks between the wickets or needles. With a rise in river levels, the roller gate can be raised with a chain or wire rope drive. The tube is fitted at one end with a large circumferential gear wheel, which engages a gear rack mounted in recesses in the pier. The system requires a long structural member capable of resisting both torsion during raising and lowering, and bending and shear resulting from high water pressures. Because a circular tube or drum is ideal to resist

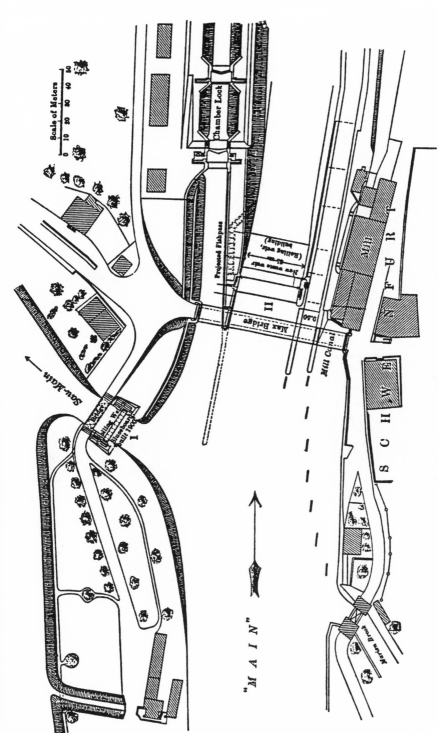

Site plan of original Schweinfurt rolling-gate dams. Hilgard, "Natural Waterways, Rolling Dams," 441.

Rolling gate sections before assembly, Schweinfurt, Germany. Hilgard, "Natural Waterways, Rolling Dams," facing 444.

Roller-gate dam installed in Germany. Hilgard, "Natural Waterways, Rolling Dams," facing 444.

View of larger Schweinfurt roller-gate dam. Hilgard, "Natural Waterways, Rolling Dams," facing 444.

these kinds of loadings, drums spanning up to 125 feet between piers have been employed. A 1913 *Engineering Record* article compares gate types:

The alternative for rollers are Tainter or sliding gates. It is difficult to say exactly where the economic limit lies for the Tainter type, but it may be said with certainty that gates 30 ft. wide and 12 ft. deep are not far from the economic limit. For sliding gates of the Stoney type, those used in the Panama spillways, which are 46 ft. wide and 19 ft. high, are about as large as gates of that type can be built with economy. Furthermore, the Stoney gates, on account of their submerged rollers, with their bushed journals and roller guides, offer too many chances for trouble. Sliding gates without rollers—friction gates—are in many cases prohibited because of slowness in operation and the excessive cost of operating machinery.[16]

In terms of winter operations, the roller gate was clearly superior, as a 1914 article noted:

Difficulties have been encountered in the operation of movable dams and gates during winter. As soon as the cold weather sets in ice forms around the gates, especially in the guides. The leakage adds to this formation, so that soon practically the entire back of the gate is covered with ice. Ice accessible with crowbars can easily be removed, while that at the bottom and in the guides must be thawed out.

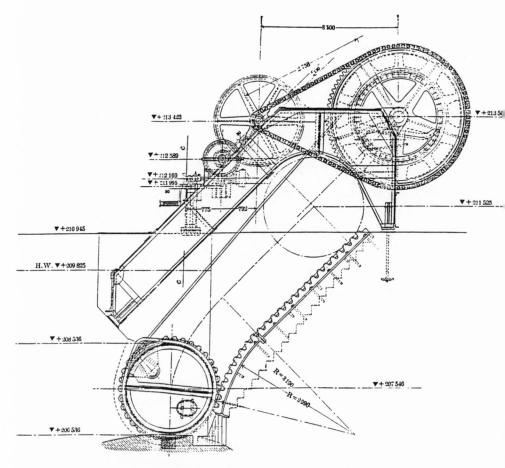

Operating machinery for Schweinfurt Dam with a cross-section of the roller-gate mechanism. Hilgard, "Natural Waterways, Rolling Dams," plate 34.

In one case it was found that as soon as one part had been thawed out and the steam jet directed on another, ice began again to form, so that method had to be abandoned. An attempt was then made to heat the gate itself (which was made of steel), but even this was a failure. Finally after two days' hard work the task was given up and the gate left to be thawed out when the weather got warm. This gate was of the sliding type. Stoney gates are even worse in this respect, as it is impossible to remove the ice formed in the roller nests.[17]

Tainter gates were less prone than Stoney gates to freezing, but they still posed severe problems in this regard.

Cognizant of the many advantages of roller-gate dams, the Corps of Engineers employed this system with alacrity not only on the Great

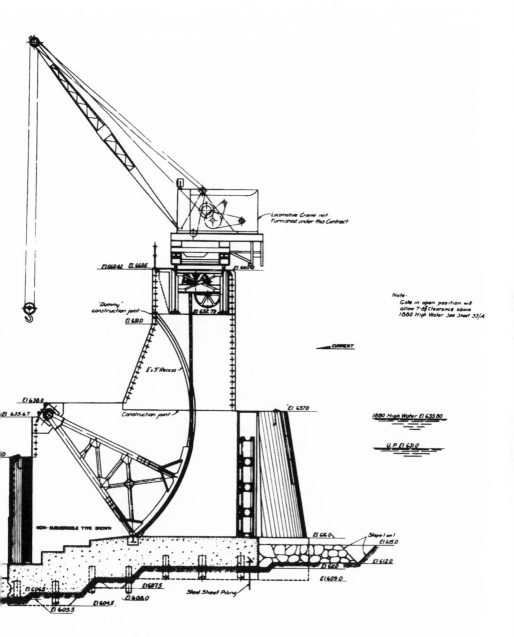

Cross-section of a typical Tainter gate, first used on Dam 8, Upper Mississippi River, by the Corps of Engineers. O'Brien, Rathbun, and O'Bannon, *Gateways to Commerce*, following 73.

Tainter gates in operation at Morgantown lock and dam. John Nicely, Institute for the History of Technology and Industrial Archaeology, West Virginia University, Morgantown, W.V.

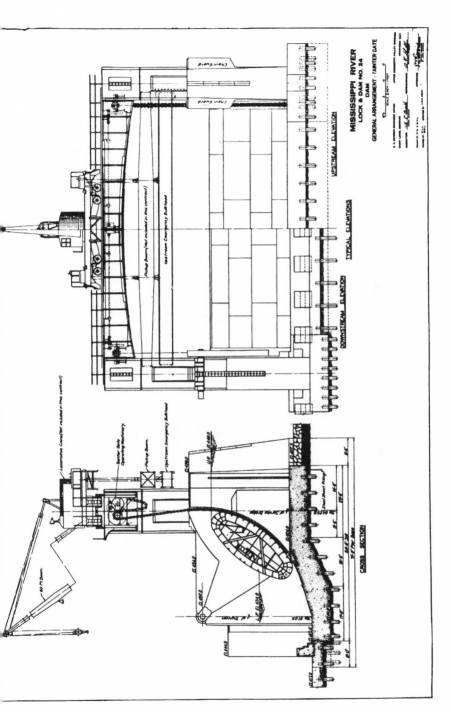

Later development of the elliptical, submersible Tainter gate used on Dam 24, Upper Mississippi River, by the Corps of Engineers. O'Brien, Rathbun, and O'Bannon, *Gateways to Commerce*, following 73.

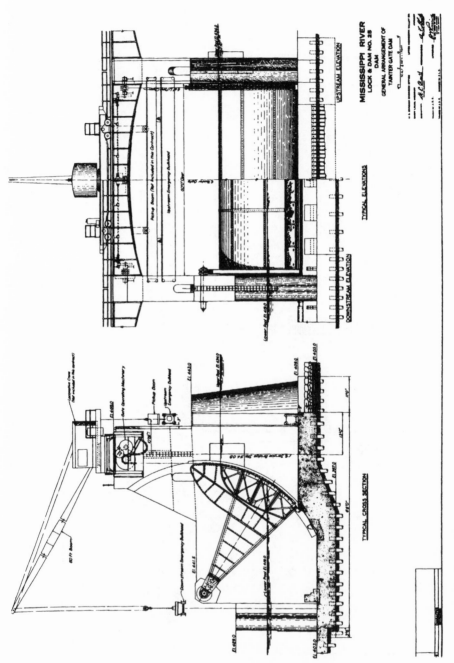

A further development of the submersible, elliptical gate used in Dam 25, Upper Mississippi River, by the U.S. Army Corps of Engineers. O'Brien, Rathbun, and O'Bannon, *Gateways to Commerce*, following 73.

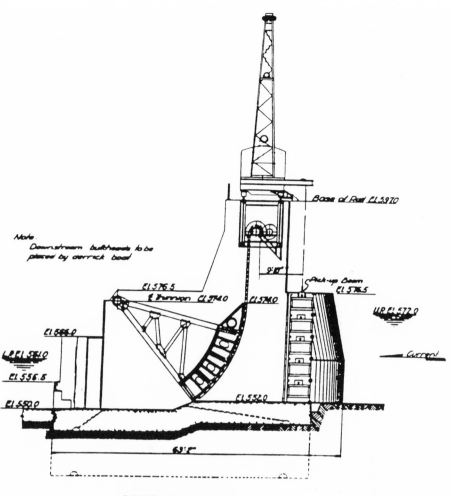

Base of Rail EL.590

Note:
Downstream bulkheads to be
placed by derrick boat

EL.576.5
℄ Trunnion CL.574.0   EL.574.0

9'8"

Pick-up Beam
EL.576.5

U.P. EL.572.0

EL.566.0

Current

L.P.EL.561.0

EL.556.5

EL.552.0

EL.550.0

69'2"

SECTIONAL VIEW

A non-submersible gate used in Dam 14, Upper Mississippi River, by the Corps of
Engineers. O'Brien, Rathbun, and O'Bannon, *Gateways to Commerce,* following 73.

Kanawha Navigation but most notably at twenty-two locations on the
Upper Mississippi Navigation. The use of roller gates was controlled by
basic patents held by the Maschinenfabrik Augsburg-Nurnberg and the
Krupp Company in Germany. Licenses were granted in the rest of Eu-
rope and in North America. The American rights were held by the Dravo
Corporation in Pittsburgh under a license from Krupp, while S. Morgan
Smith Company, of York, Pennsylvania, was licensed by MAN.[18] The Dravo
Corporation subsequently built the roller dams on the Kanawha and the
Gallipolis locks and dam on the Ohio River. In 1939, after the completion

of the Great Kanawha system, *Engineering News Record* reported that 156 individual roller gates had been erected in the United States, the majority employed on the Upper Mississippi slackwater system.

In the design of roller gates, and indeed other movable gated dams, the work begins with a comprehensive analysis of the loads imposed upon the roller drum. Hydraulic loads vary with the position of the gate and the water level in the slackwater pool behind the dam, which is normally controlled at a constant level but can rise significantly during freshets, before the gates can be raised clear of the water. The greatest load occurs in the nearly closed position, just as the gate rises clear of the dam crest and has to be supported at each end. A graphical method of determining the loads on the roller gates was presented by Harry Cole in a paper published in 1935, at the time of the construction of the roller dams on the Kanawha.[19] The basic idea is that the pressure acts radially on the apron and the drum. These forces can be represented as vectors to a convenient scale for each lineal foot of the roller gate and apron. The forces for each are then resolved graphically into a total resultant, which is used to develop shear and bending-torsion moment diagrams on the roller gates and the end reactions. The end reactions were used to design the gearing and determine the loads on the drive chain, as well as bearing conditions on the drum itself.

Once the shear, moment, and torsion diagrams were prepared, the stresses on the roller gate were determined using standard elastic analysis for beams and girders subjected to bending and twisting. The analysis, however, had to take into account the curved surface of the roller gate and its supporting framework. The allowable stresses in the example cited by Cole were: tensile stress, 16,000 psi; compressive stress, 13,500 psi; shear stress, 10,000 psi.

With these governing stresses, it was possible to check the splices and framing, as well as the stresses on the steel plates forming the surface of the gate. The Alton Dam on the Mississippi served as the example for Cole's paper. He acknowledges not only his civilian colleagues, but also Col. E. L. Daley and Lt. Col. P. S. Reinecke of the St. Louis Division Office. Thus it appears that this was the accepted analytical design method used for the Kanawha roller gates, since the St. Louis Division included the Huntington District.

Not all engineers subscribed to the so-called "normal pressure theory."

Professor E. Jacoby of Riga, Latvia, claimed the theory to be wrong and proposed using two forces, one horizontal and the other vertical.[20] One of the forces was equal to the horizontal hydraulic force acting on a vertical plane of the same depth as the roller drum; the other, a vertical force, equaled the water displaced. These forces were then combined with the dead load to yield the total force that must be supported at the piers. It does not appear that the debate on methods was engaged by Corps personnel, nor did it affect the traditional analytical method that they employed. Subsequent modifications in the design of roller gates had to be accounted for in any stress analysis, regardless of the method used.

In the earliest design, the drum rested directly on the sill. The water seal was effected by securing a longitudinal timber to the bottom of the drum. The drum pressed down on the dam because of water pressure, and a seal resulted between the fixed crest and the drum. The first modification was to add an apron at the bottom of the drum to rest on the crest of the dam. It was a curved device attached to the drum and resting on the crest. Being at the bottom, it had to sustain the highest hydraulic pressure, which forced the bottom of the apron hard against the crest of the dam. In a number of cases, a rubber seal was used to ensure that the system was watertight.

In the case of the Great Kanawha Navigation, one gate at each lock-and-dam site had a flap-type drum.[21] The flap was raised by a hydraulic jack, rather like the flaps on an aircraft wing. Raising the flap increased the depth to match the other roller-gate slackwater elevations, while lowering the flap allowed ice and debris to pass over the dam. Since the dams were founded on rock, the movable flap drum was a more economical alternative to a submersible roller gate because in the latter case a pit excavated in the rock would be necessary to receive the submersible gate.

In A. G. Hillberg's 1913 summary paper on roller dams, he used "Jacoby's method" and demonstrated how it could be applied to roller drums with attached sheaths. The addition of a sheath in front of the roller increased the depth of water retained for a given drum diameter.[22]

By 1939, when the Mississippi and Kanawha systems were completed and in operation, C. R. Martin of the Allis-Chalmers Manufacturing Company of Milwaukee presented yet another modification.[23] His new design reduced the usual apron to a small protrusion to act as a sealing device on the bottom of the drum. In concept it was similar to the original timber

A roller gate in its raised position showing the lower apron. U.S. Army Corps of Engineers, Huntington District Archives.

ledger mounted on the first roller dams in Europe. The second change was to put a fixed flap on top of the drum, in essence moving the apron from the bottom to the top of the roller gate. Martin demonstrated, by balancing the forces acting on the drum and flap could result in considerable savings. He argued that the usual location of the apron was objectionable since it needed to resist the highest pressures of the roller gate. In addition, since the gate had to be raised into the river current, heavy loads were placed on the entire lifting mechanism. Martin compared the two systems and claimed for his design a considerable saving in materials. Nevertheless, the modified gate was not used on the first dams, nor in any of the replacement gates on the Corps of Engineers systems. The gates employed on the Great Kanawha Navigation were a standard design in conformance with the Krupp patent.

Interior view of a roller gate. U.S. Army Corps of Engineers, Huntington District Archives.

A flap gate roller gate being fabricated at the Dravo company's Neville Island plant, December 1933. U.S. Engineer Office, Pittsburgh District, Dec. 21, 1933, file 8014.

Assembly of the driven end of a roller gate of the Dravo company's Neville Island plant, December 1933. U.S. Engineer Office, Pittsburgh District, Dec. 21, 1933, file 8013.

Erection of a roller gate with flap at Marmet Dam, 1934. U.S. Engineer Office,
Huntington, W.V., Jan. 19, 1934, file MD 226.

Gear mechanism for opening and closing flap gate at Winfield Dam. U.S. Engineer
Office, Pittsburgh, June 8, 1936, file 9815.

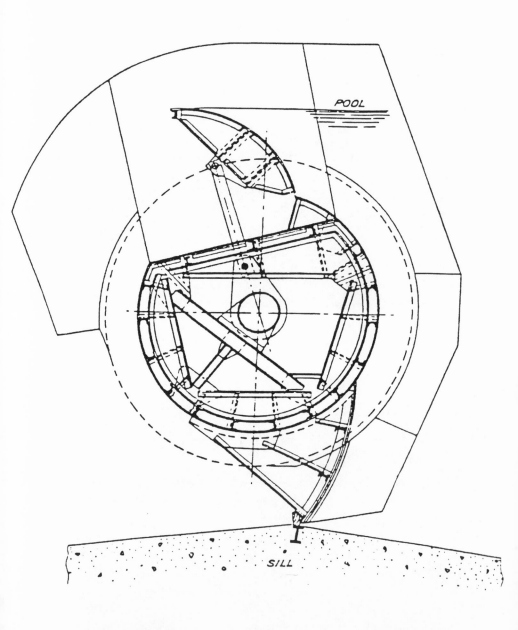

Cross-section showing structure of flap-type roller gate. McAlpine, "Roller Gates in Navigation Dams," 423.

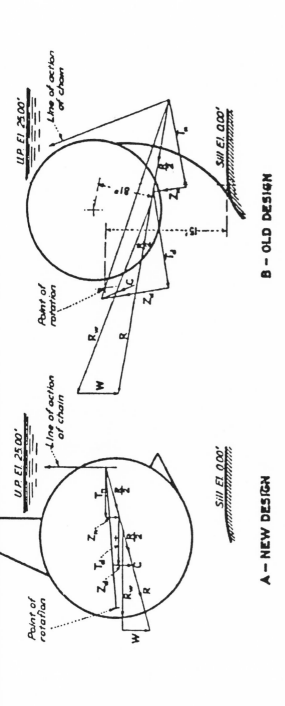

A – NEW DESIGN

B – OLD DESIGN

U.P. El. 25.00'

Line of action of chain

Point of rotation

Sill El. 0.00'

Nomenclature

C, chain pull.....
Z_d, tooth load, driven end.....
Z_n, tooth load, non-driven end.....
T_d, track load, driven end.....
T_n, track load, non-driven end.....
R_w, resultant water load.....
Eccentricity of resultant, inches.....
W equals weight of gate and R is the resultant of R_w and W

	Loads in Lbs.	
	New	Old
	Gate raised 4 ft.	Gate in closed position
	173,000	348,000
	60,000	640,000
	125,000	300,000
	625,000	869,000
	625,000	790,000
	843,000	1,797,000
	1½	81

Comparative weights, loads and forces in new and old designs of roller gates.

Martin modification of a roller-gate design. Martin, "New Design Cuts Costs of Roller Gates," 66.

Concrete

Whereas the late nineteenth- and early twentieth-century construction techniques for locks and dams favored stone masonry, by the 1930s concrete, both plain and reinforced, was the preferred construction material. For the four locks and dams of the Great Kanawha Navigation system, Portland cement was specified and was to be provided by the contractor. It should be noted, however, that natural (that is, hydraulic) cement was specified as an additive to reduce the heat of hydration for concrete cast in large sections, in contrast to the earlier system, where natural cement was still widely applied. In the case of the first locks and dams, the government even provided the cement for the contractor.

The specifications for concrete ingredients for the locks and dams to be constructed at London and Marmet, and later at Winfield and Gallipolis, have a modern appearance. They are quite specific in the requirements for the basic ingredients of cement, fine aggregates, and gravel, which are the basic components of the concrete that was used. Not only were the characteristics of the ingredients specified, but also the gradation of the aggregate to insure that an acceptably proportioned concrete would result. Although the specifications do not formulate concrete mixtures, they do insist that the concrete be proportioned by the water-cement method.[24] This method, developed by Duff Abrams nearly twenty years earlier, is the foundation of modern concrete mixture design. Known values for both the cement and water content are listed in the specifications as guidelines for the contractor. Corps engineers prepared and reviewed sample mixtures to insure that the minimum strength would be obtained throughout the concrete work on both the locks and the dams. They also specified mixing, conveying, and placing of the concrete to insure that the concrete did not separate, and would obtain at least the minimum required strength.

Later, during the construction of the Winfield and Gallipolis locks and dams, specifications called for Class A and Class B concrete. Class A was used for all the piers, the power house and operating houses, and for grouting, machinery, installation of bridge anchors, and other applications requiring high-strength concrete. It was reported that slumps, which are a measure of the wet concrete's stiffness, varied from 2.5 inches to 7 inches, with the average being 5.7 inches. With this water-cement ratio and the approved aggregate gradation, average strengths at twenty-eight days were reported as 4,986 psi. This is greatly in excess of the minimum required of 3,000 psi. Class B concrete, on the other hand, was used for all thick reinforced concrete sections, such as sills, lock walls, aprons, and structures using mass concrete solely for stability. The minimum strength called for was 2,400 psi after twenty-eight days. The average for the Winfield project was 4,832 psi. These values were reported during the construction of the Gallipolis locks and dam. The water-cement ratio and appropriate aggregate gradation are essential for obtaining high-strength concrete. It should also be noted that compaction and the avoidance of segregation are also important factors in obtaining maximum density for a given mix. Controls were maintained over all the concreting operations at all four sites. In addition, for Class A concrete, a total of six ninety-four-pound bags of cement were specified, whereas a minimum of five were required for Class B concrete. Thus, all the conditions were present to obtain concrete strength considerably in excess of the minimums required. Strength is clearly related to durability, so that the high strengths obtained on these projects insured, in part, the long-term durability of these hydraulic structures.

Instead of establishing a large batch plant near the work site, as was done in the case of the Tygart Dam, which was under construction during this same time, the Corps of Engineers built the London and Marmet locks and dams using floating mixing plants. This method featured barges loaded with cement, which could be delivered to the mixers by a pneumatic system, as well as barges supplying fine and coarse aggregates.[25] The Winfield and Gallipolis sites used traditional batch plants erected on shore.

Other items connected with the construction included specifications for metal work; painting, design and erection of both the lock and dam gates; details of the Stoney gate valves for controlling water within the lock chambers; and general conditions for the erection of cofferdams, cribs, and timber piles. The specifications for all four of the lock and dam sites have a decidedly modern look about them and could be easily identified with contemporary large public works.[26]

Structural and Hydraulic Analysis

The locks and dam at each site were founded on rock and designed as gravity structures using conventional design methods previously employed by the Corps of Engineers in similar work. Stress diagrams for the various components clearly indicate the analytical approach used to account for hydraulic pressures under various loading conditions associated with changes in water elevations on the dams, and principally in the lock chambers, during operations. The same elastic design and analysis methods were applied to the stop logs, service bridges, and lock gates, all of which were designed by Corps engineers.[27]

By the late 1920s, the Army Corps of Engineers routinely used models for designing hydraulic structures, including locks and navigation dams as well as large multipurpose dams. Hydraulic model studies for structures and for determining flow patterns in rivers and canals had been carried on at places like St. Anthony's Falls, in Minneapolis, and at various universities during this period. Under the direction of Col. Wildurr Willing, who was serving as district engineer at St. Paul, Minnesota, the Corps of Engineers established a field unit at the Iowa Institute of Hydraulic Research of the University of Iowa in November 1929. Colonel Willing's idea was that this experiment station would serve future projects that were contemplated for the Upper Mississippi Valley division of the Corps of Engineers. A series of locks and dams were subsequently built on the Upper Mississippi that benefited from hydraulic studies at the Iowa Institute of Hydraulic Research. The justification for such work was stated succinctly: "It has been found that hydraulic models when constructed and operated in accordance with the proven laws of similarity serve as an effective aid to the designing engineer in solving doubtful problems. They, furthermore, enable him to develop economical and efficient works that will be safe and adequate when subjected to actual operating conditions."[28]

Because of the large number of variables involved in producing the design of a lock or a dam, or indeed investigating the flow characteristics of a river, hydraulic models provided an attractive alternative to mathematical and analytical solutions for hydraulic designs. This is not to say that hydraulic model studies are devoid of theory. They involve basic principles of similitude in order to correlate the model and prototype behavior. It is essential to simulate the physical behavior of the prototype by considering the similarities that are needed in the design and operation of the model. These are defined as:

1. Geometric similarity. The model is simply a scaled-down version of the prototype in three dimensions.
2. Kinematic similarity. This insures that all the velocities and accelerations are equal in the model and the prototype.
3. Dynamic similarity. This requires that ratios of all the forces be the same in the model and the prototype. If the structure under study is controlled by gravity, then the problems of similitude are greatly reduced.

Dynamic similitude is satisfied by the parameter V^2/GL, commonly known as the Froude number, where V is the velocity, G the acceleration of gravity, and L the depth of flow. This was named after William Froude, a British engineer who first utilized this similitude parameter in a study of ship models. The Froude number can be interpreted as the ratio of two dynamic terms or as the ratio of geometric terms or two energy terms. It was with this background that models were made for a new generation of Great Kanawha structures.[29]

Since the roller gates were a new device in the experience of the Corps of Engineers, questions were raised regarding the flow of water under the rollers at various elevations of the roller, as well as about the operation of one or several of the gates. The first question really concerned the design of the dam crest below the roller gate to insure that cavitation would not occur and that energy could be dissipated at the foot of the dam. There was also concern about erosion characteristics downstream from the dams, which depended not only on the hydraulic flow but also on the characteristics of the rock at the bottom of the river. In addition, for navigation purposes, it was necessary to determine the flow characteristics of water released from the dams, which could create crosscurrents and eddies at the lower end of the lock and the guard wall. There appeared to be no difficulty if all the gates were operated simultaneously. However, if the flow was confined to a limited number of gates, a hydraulic jump might form requiring adequate toe protection. A hydraulic jump can occur when the slope of flow changes from a steep grade to a more gentle slope. A long, smooth apron with an end weir or sill was not found to be adequate. A stilling basin was equipped with baffle piers, or

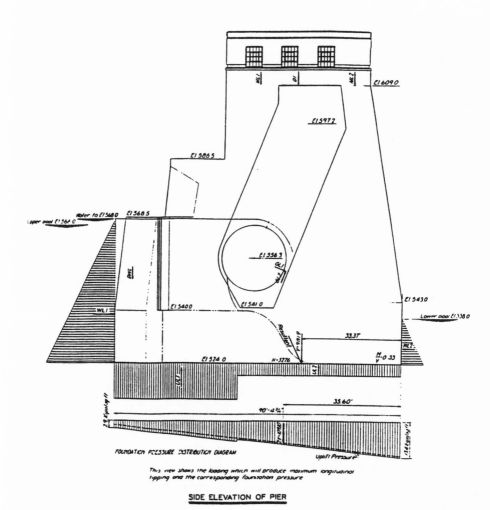

SIDE ELEVATION OF PIER

Cross-section of pier showing stress distribution on side of pier and downstream elevation. U.S. Engineer Office, Huntington, W.V., April 1935, file 023-L1-40/A.

so-called dragon's teeth, providing suitable dissipation of energy. Model studies also indicated that the piers would provide erosion control if properly designed in terms of position and elevation.[30] Models were constructed and tested from December 1930 to July 1931. Direct supervision of the experiments was under Martin E. Nelson, assistant engineer with the Corps of Engineers and associate director of the institute.[31]

There is an interrelationship between the structural design and the results of the hydraulic model studies. In the first place, preliminary structural designs are needed to produce the model. The model, in turn, sug-

Photograph looking down the shaft of a Stoney gate valve at Winfield Locks and Dam. John Nicely, Institute for the History of Technology and Industrial Archaeology, West Virginia University, Morgantown, W.V.

gests certain modifications or additions to the basic structure to insure that it works satisfactorily in hydraulic terms. The test results in the case of Marmet, also applicable to the other sites, indicated that a stepped sill should be designed for the roller gates. This consists of a series of steps whose points follow very nearly the theoretical path of the jet of water issuing under the roller gates. This detail was incorporated into the final design.

It was found that the navigability of the downstream lock entrance was very much affected by the method of operating the dam, but not influenced greatly by the length of the lower guard wall. To determine the backwater influence resulting from the operation of the dam, tests were undertaken on a model with a scale of 1:100. It was found that if a single gate were operated to the left of the center of the dam (that is, with gates toward the power station), a definite crosscurrent was set up at the lock approach. When, however, all roller gates were operated simultaneously at any flow level, no crosscurrents or eddies were set up. This indicated that the operation of the roller gates could have a pro-

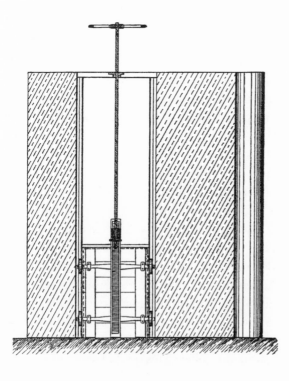

(Above) Photograph of lock-gate mechanism. John Nicely, Institute for the History of Technology and Industrial Archaeology, West Virginia University, Morgantown, W.V.

(Left) Stoney gate valve. Addison Scott Collection, Marshall University, Huntington, W.V., Box 3 FF11.

(Opposite, top) Lock gate operating machinery at Marmet locks and dam. U.S. Engineer Office, Huntington, W. V., Jan. 1934. File 023-L2-22/1.

(Opposite, bottom) Emergency bulkhead being lowered into position at Marmet Dam. U.S. Engineer Office, Huntington District Archives, Jan. 11, 1935.

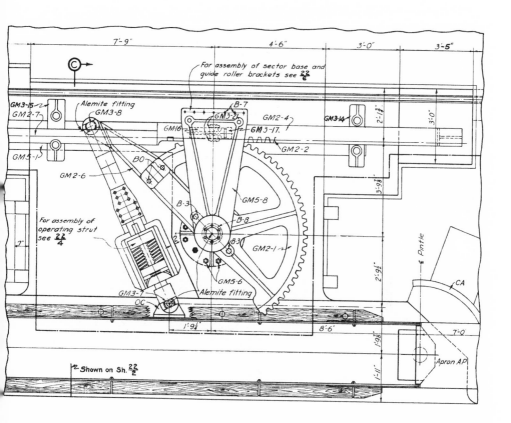

Emergency dam components in place, Marmet locks and dam. U.S. Engineer Office, Huntington District Archives, n.d.

found effect on navigation, and should be carefully controlled by the lock master.

Water, of course, was discharged from the power house located at the far left side of the dam. When the dam was operating under full head, it was found that a crosscurrent occurred at the lower lock approach. This effect could be greatly reduced by constructing a training wall in a line coinciding with the center line of the second bay from the abutment.[32] These model studies were then used to modify the preliminary design of the dam.

During the construction of the Gallipolis locks and dams, rivermen complained that navigation in the upper reaches of the pool, approaching the locks and dam upstream, would be hazardous because of adverse currents. Therefore, in the middle of construction, a series of small-scale test models were undertaken by the Hydraulics Laboratory at the Carnegie Institute of Technology in Pittsburgh. This is the same laboratory that had undertaken tests for the design of the spillway and stilling basin for Tygart Dam.[33] The purpose of tests on this small-scale model was to in-

Lockhouse dwelling at Winfield locks and dam. U.S. Engineer Office, Huntington District Archives, photo no. 11, May 11, 1936.

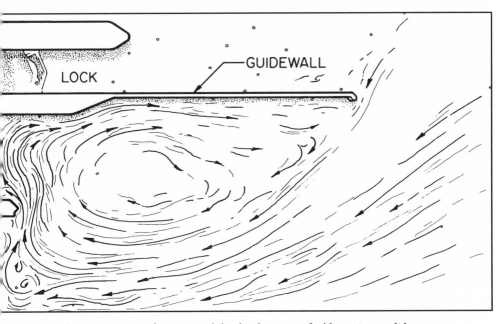

Model testing using confetti to reveal the development of eddies using a solid masonry wall extending from locks. Marmet locks and dam. *Laboratory Tests on Hydraulic Models at Marmet Lock and Dam, Kanawha River* (Iowa City, Iowa: War Department, Engineer Field Office, July 1932), 86.

vestigate the approaches to the upper lock entrances with a view to possible structural modifications that would provide safer navigation. The engineers were also concerned to develop a schedule for opening the gates that would be most favorable to navigation downstream from the locks and dams, as well as to mitigate any erosion of the riverbed and banks below the dam. As in the case of Marmet, there were additional tests to develop the hydraulic designs for the sill and stilling basin.

Several guide-wall designs were considered, but only design number two was appropriate for field checking since it involved a wall extension of 500 feet farther than the originally constructed upper guide wall built following the testing in Pittsburgh. One of the observations of the model test was that for discharges from 171,000 cubic feet per second (cfs) to 343,000 cfs, crosscurrents of rather high velocities were formed from the end of the upper guide-wall extension, and they extended for approximately 800 feet. This observation was made using small confetti particles in the model that were observed to cut in and back up on the left bank in a slow counterclockwise direction for flows up to 125,000 cfs. In higher flows, the confetti particles indicated a sharp crosscurrent that progressed downstream through the upper lock approach as the discharge increased.

It was the formation of eddies in the model that led to field testing. There was a marked line of transition between comparatively high velocities in the channel, well upstream from the dam, and the observed sluggish velocities in the channel immediately upstream from the dam, which were much less than expected. It was concluded that this was obviously a surface condition in the model. The field observations of velocities and directions of flow, both above and below Gallipolis locks and dam, were undertaken by the simple device of using spars consisting of two-inch square timbers, eight feet long and weighted at the bottom so that they would float vertically in the river, not unlike a bobber used in fishing. With this arrangement, six feet of the spars were under water. The floats were placed in the river a short distance upstream from the area to be observed, and most were recovered by boat. Three transits on shore were used to triangulate the location of each of the spars at one-minute intervals. No eddies or other crosscurrents were observed except for a crosscurrent appearing between the upstream ends of the guard and guide walls.

The earlier model test indicated that current paths through the lock approach could be expected to travel in a slow counter-clockwise direc-

View of Winfield Dam showing the crest design and lower apron. U.S. Engineer Office, Huntington District Archives, Aug. 25, 1936.

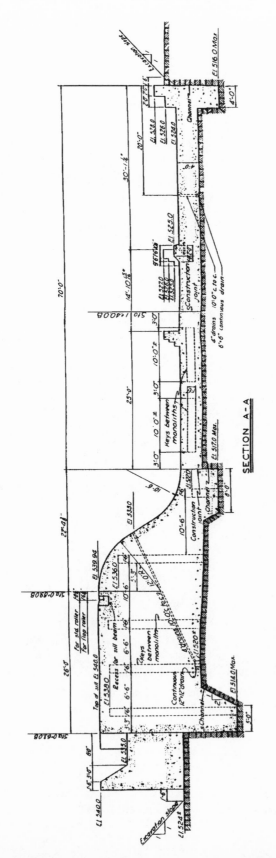

Apron and sill details, Winfield locks and dam. U.S. Engineer Office, Huntington District Archives, April 1935, file 023-L1-40/20.

tion for flow rates of 125,000 cfs, while the field observations of comparable flows indicated a steady uniform flow through the area. Comparison of the model test for flows in excess of 171,000 cfs with field observation show the results to be very similar. For those of 100,000 cfs or less, the field velocities in the main channel, where the hydraulic stream lines are parallel, were found to exceed the model velocities from 200 to 400 percent. In addition, the sharp crosscurrents indicated by the model tests in flows up to almost 150,000 cfs were not shown in any of the field observations. Thus, it was concluded that hydraulic similitude was obtained in the Gallipolis models only for open river conditions with the rollers completely clear of the water. It was further concluded that the divergence of test and field results was largely influenced by the relatively small scale of the test model and the fact that it did not have exact geometrical similitude with the prototype. In addition, in defense of the laboratory models, there was dredging and grading subsequent to the completion of these model studies that would have influenced the test results in the field. Thus, it was recommended that improved instrumentation be used on the models to obtain velocity and direction of the currents instead of relying entirely on floating confetti particles to portray the currents.

The field studies were extended to verify the model studies made at Marmet. The Marmet and London locks and dams were of such similar design that they could be considered sister structures. The model for river flow used in the Marmet studies was ten feet wide by thirty feet long, which allowed a scale of 1:100. This model proved satisfactory for an investigation of river current patterns, but was too small for accurate design of the gate sills and toe protection for the dam. As a result, a model of one-half of a roller gate, gate sill, and pier was built to a scale of 1:22.53. The main conclusions of the model tests were that the length of the upper guard wall was not a factor in influencing flow conditions, but that the patterns could be improved considerably by having a rounded instead of a blunt nose on the guard wall. In addition, it was concluded that the best conditions downstream from the lock and dam would result if all of the rollers were operated together, rather than having individual gates opened. This would preclude any crosscurrents developing at the lower entrance to the locks.

Discharge from the power station gave some concern, and it was concluded that flow conditions could be improved and crosscurrents eliminated by constructing a training wall three hundred feet long. At the time these field observations were undertaken, the work at Winfield was not complete, and the pool level at the foot of Marmet was not at an operating level. Therefore, despite the fact that the early model studies were made on Marmet only, the float tests were conducted at London. Even though these were sister locks and dams, the alignment of the river with the lock and dam varied slightly from London to Marmet. Approaching the lock and dam upstream, the spars traveled with an apparent uniform velocity in a path approximately parallel to the lock approach. They then turned riverward, opposite or just above the upper end of the guide wall, and through one of the fifty-foot openings just above the guard wall.

Several of the floats leaving the power house passed across the channel at the foot of the lower approach to the lock. No vortexes were observed, but these crosscurrents would have to be dealt with by river pilots entering the lock. The results of the field tests were, therefore, inclusive, but in general agreement with the test studies. With the completion of Winfield and observations in the field subsequent to these float tests, it did not appear that the construction of the deflection wall indicated by the model studies was necessary.

Thus, the hydraulic studies provided important information for the design of the sills, deflection baffles, and the stilling basin, but the small-scale models indicating flow patterns above and below the locks and dams appeared to have given results that did not coincide with the limited field tests. The lack of velocity measurements in the model further hampered a comparison between the field and model test results.

During the Second World War, German prisoners from Rommel's Afrika Corps were employed to build a large Mississippi model basin at the Waterways Experiment Station in Vicksburg, Mississippi. The intent was to model all of the lower reaches of the Mississippi, and proceed up the Ohio as far as the falls at Louisville, Kentucky. In a memorandum dated August 20, 1946, the Waterways Experiment Station proposed to make a model of certain mountain streams, and the one selected was the Great Kanawha. It was decided to model the August 1940 flood using the Froudin discharge scale. The purpose of this was to investigate whether floods could be modeled using the Mississippi Basin Model approach.[34] The model had a fixed bed, molded in concrete, with a slightly larger cross section than theoretically required so that surfaces of various roughness could be introduced without reducing the theoretical cross-sectional area. The model was built, as were others of the Mississippi, to a horizontal scale of 1:2000 and a vertical scale of 1:100. The study indicated that such modeling could be done with accuracy, so that in theory the Mississippi model basin could be extended, in the case of the Ohio Basin beyond Louisville, and that the Great Kanawha River could be modeled for flood-control measures. Model studies would be important in the hydraulic design for tributary dams such as Bluestone, Summersville, and Sutton Reservoirs.

CHAPTER SEVEN

The Work at
London and Marmet
Begins

The General Contracting Corporation of Pittsburgh, Pennsylvania, received the contract for the construction of Lock A at Marmet with a low
bid of $968,802.[1] Within three weeks of the opening of bids for the Marmet
locks and dam, bids were invited for the first lock at the London site, with
a stipulation that they would be opened on March 16, 1931. Indicative of
the difficult times during the Great Depression, ten companies bid on the
London lock. Fegle Construction Company of Minneapolis, Minnesota,
was the apparent low bidder with an offer of $914,295. The Dravo Cor-
poration was second with a bid of $914,571.[2] An even lower bid than that
of the Fegle Company was submitted by Northport Sand and Gravel
Company of New York State, in the amount of $844,782.

R. N. Dravo noted in a March 24 letter to the Chief of Engineers,
Maj. Gen. Lytle Brown, that Northport Sand and Gravel would probably
have difficulty furnishing a bond, and that the company had no experience in river locks and dams and further had no equipment to undertake
such work. Thus it seemed clear that they were not a qualified bidder.
With regard to Fegle's bid, Dravo pointed out that the company did not
have equipment in the vicinity, nor manpower to undertake a rapid start
on this project. In addition, Dravo pointed out that his own company's
bid was only $276 higher than the Fegle bid, and that no bond had been
submitted by the low bidder after notice of award. The Dravo Corporation was in a position to make a rapid start on the project and put the

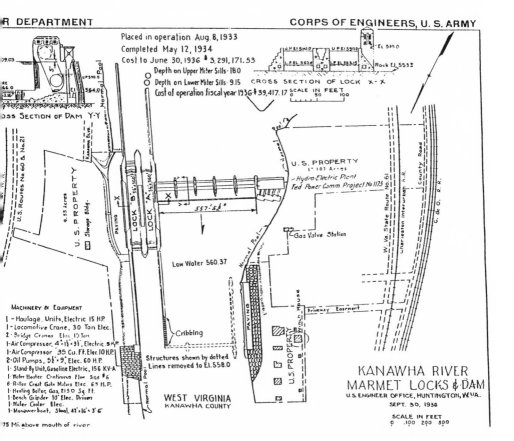

Marmet site map showing locks, dam, and powerhouse. U.S. Engineer Office, Huntington, W.V., Sept. 30, 1936.

system in operation at the earliest possible time, in the process relieving unemployment in the Kanawha Valley.[3] Lt. Col. E. L. Daley, representing the division office, wrote in response that no decision could be made on the Dravo proposal unless the low bidders clearly indicated their incapacity or lack of intent to enter on the contract.

The London lock estimate prepared by the Army Corps of Engineers was just over one million dollars, at $1,200,421, but the Army Engineers was willing to consider close bids that were under their estimate.[4] While there was some delay in awarding the contract for Lock A at the London site, work was progressing rapidly on the Marmet lock. In mid-August, the district engineer, Maj. Fred W. Herman, submitted an addition to the Marmet contract for the installation of vents in the river wall and in the chambers immediately adjacent to the wall, in accordance with drawings that accompanied his memorandum.[5] Additional work under the contract for the Marmet lock included vents for the culverts, changes in pipes and trenching recesses, and keyways joining river and intermediate walls. The work was requested by the Corps of Engineers and represented an increase in the contract in terms of a change order issued January 5, 1932.

On August 22, the district engineer forwarded to the Chief of Engineers in Washington plans and specifications for the construction of the second lock at the Marmet site. Rather than let a single contract for the second lock and dam, the district engineer proposed that a separate contract for the lock be let to avoid any break in construction. It appeared that the contractor would complete the work on the river lock prior to December 31, 1931, seven months in advance of the contract deadline. The Corps of Engineers considered it impossible to complete the plans for the dam in a timely fashion because further study was felt to be necessary to coordinate the plans and specifications for the dam and the proposed power-generating station for the Appalachian Electric Power Company. The district engineer pointed out that Lock B could be started by using the existing cofferdam erected by the General Contracting Company, which meant that Lock A could be put in operation before work was started on the dam and power station.[6]

Col. George Spalding, division engineer, organized a symposium in conjunction with a meeting of the Ohio Valley Improvement Association on October 12–13, 1931. President Herbert Hoover was invited to speak to the conference, but he regretfully declined the invitation. The speaker was the Chief of Engineers. A feature of the conference was a boat trip and banquet held at Montgomery.[7] Later that month, the *Montgomery News* announced that the last phase of work for the first lock at Marmet had begun. The lock was to be completed by July 1932. Once the contractor finished casting 2,500 cubic feet of concrete for the upper guide wall, his work on the lock would be done.

The Chief of Engineers requested that the Secretary of War allocate a modest sum of $20,000 for dredging in the lower reaches of the river to insure that a minimum six-foot draft was available. This allocation would be in addition to funds appropriated for the construction of the Marmet locks and dam. It appeared to be an appropriate response to navigation interests in the river who were continually complaining about the channel depth.[8]

The request was approved, and on September 23, 1931, an invitation for bids was issued for the construction of Lock B at Marmet.[9] When bids were opened on October 23, 1931, A. G. Rothey of Elizabeth, Pennsylvania, was the apparent low bidder. Later, the district engineer, Major Herman, in a letter to the Chief of Engineers dated November 3, 1931, recommended "that the low bid be rejected for the reasons that the bid is unbalanced, fails to comply with the specifications in all respects, and that the bidder lacks the necessary experience to construct the work of the kind required jeopardizing the interest of the United States, particularly in the matter of maintaining existing navigation past the site of the new work." Herman added, "These reasons are discussed in detail in the following paragraphs."[10]

On large public works using government money, it is difficult from a legal standpoint not to accept a low bid unless the bidder can be proven, beyond a reasonable doubt, to be incompetent to carry out the work. Within a week, Congressman Clyde Kelly of the 33d District of Pennsylvania wrote to the Chief of Engineers asking for a delay in awarding the contract in order that Rothey might present additional information in support of his bid. The Congressman concluded, "Permit me to say again that if it is possible to grant this favor it will be deeply appreciated by me."[11]

Rothey was obviously working behind the scenes to put together a consortium that would be acceptable to the government. In a letter dated November 13, 1931, the General Contracting Corporation told Rothey that they would be willing to have him "take over" their organization, which was then on site at Lock A. (This may be an offer to act as a subcontractor to Rothey.) The letter outlined the qualifications of the men currently working on Lock A and expressed the hope that Rothey would be successful in revising his work plan.[12] Joining Congressman Kelly, A. W. Temple of the 25th District of Pennsylvania indicated to the Chief of Engineers that the Rothey bid was some $9,000 below that of the next lowest bidder, which happened to be the Dravo Corporation of Pittsburgh. Temple requested that Rothey have the opportunity of presenting additional facts in connection with his bid. Like Kelly, Temple said that he would greatly appreciate his request being honored.[13] Despite these interventions, Dravo was later awarded the contract.

In preparation for bidding on the Marmet Dam, the Greenbag Cement Company of Pittsburgh wrote to Lt. Hugh J. Casey, serving as assistant chief of the River and Harbor Division, with regard to the specification for supplying bulk cement. If cement met the twenty-eight-day strength-test requirement in seven days, the company inquired, might shipments be approved after only a week and without waiting a full month? They pointed out that it would be a very great hardship on them to carry bulk cement at their plant in storage until the twenty-eight-day test had been approved. The intention of this company was to transport bulk cement by barge from their Kenova Works to the site.[14] Replying to this letter on November 17, 1931, Lieutenant Casey indicated that after due consideration it had been decided that waiving this requirement would establish a dangerous precedent and, in addition, be unfair to other cement manufacturers.

In November 1931 the General Contracting Corporation finished its project for the first lock at Marmet ahead of schedule. By March 1932, Wheeling Steel Company had submitted an affidavit stating that it was still owed a balance of $11,472.88 by the general contractor. The document was submitted so that Wheeling would have the right of action against the bonding company in the event that they failed to receive final payment.[15]

On all large public works, change orders are to be expected. The fifteen submitted by the General Contracting Corporation amounted to only $24,516.02, which is a comparatively small amount considering the total contract price. Nearly two years after the contract started, a notice was submitted in late June 1932, soliciting bids for the construction of a roller-gate dam and the installation of a permanent upper-lock gate at the Marmet site.[16]

A landslide that occurred at Marmet Lock B on April 23, 1932, interrupted routine construction work. The moving earth killed six men and injured eleven others. The disastrous landslide was a culmination of minor earth movement reported as early as January. At the time a crevasse appeared that threatened the U.S. Engineers' temporary field office. The crevasse was discovered at 7:00 A.M. and by 10:00 A.M. the temporary office had been moved to a safe area.

One could hardly claim that the bank failure had occurred without warning. Yet Major Fred W. Herman exonerated Dravo Corporation publicly in a news release given to the Associated Press and in an official Corps of Engineers document. J. Thomas Ward, an attorney for the victims and their families, wrote to Gen. George B. Pillsbury, Associate Chief of Engineers, requesting clarification on the jurisdiction and authority of the district engineer to exonerate the construction company. The essence of the matter rested upon whether Major Herman had acted on his own authority or for the entire Corps of Engineers and hence the federal government.[17] On August 10, 1932, the attorney wrote directly to the district engineer. He clearly wanted to draw out Major Herman in order to strengthen his case against the company. He ended his request for a written response by Major Herman by stating:

> Major Herman, you perhaps do not realize the weight of the opinion of yourself and your subordinates given by a jury of laymen. On behalf of the widows and children and permanently injured men, I ask you to be considerate and let their cases be tried on their merits without the handicap of having the jury feel that the United States Government, as stated by Mr. Fowler, acting as a judge and jury, and through your speaking for the government found Dravo Company blameless. I will mention here that I have before me a sheaf of evidence to the contrary and I am quite confident that this evidence has undoubtedly never been put before you. I await a reply at your earliest convenience.[18]

A letter from the Dravo Company to Major Herman described the measures that the contractor had undertaken so that the accident that occurred on Saturday night, April 23, at Marmet Lock B, would not be repeated. In an attempt to preclude a change order by the company, the district engineer wrote to Dravo Corporation on May 16, 1932, saying that a forty-five-degree slope was assumed for estimating quantities by the Corps regardless of what the natural slope of the material happened to be. The district engineer did not propose to make extra payment for additional excavation necessary to preclude any further landslides. Herman was willing, however, to refer a formal request from the contractor to a higher authority. Responding in late May with a request for fifteen change orders, the contractor stated:

> During the period the work was underway, we accepted verbal orders for all changes, and it was not until the later part of October 1931 that we learned that your field representatives and our engineer were not in agreement regarding their respective understandings of the contract and specifications. Later we compared quantities for the final estimate, there was further differences in evidence which could not be adjusted by our engineer and your field representative. Accordingly, under the terms of Article No. 3 of the contract, we request the contracting officer to make his decisions regarding the value of the 15 items in questions.[19]

The Dravo Corporation sought additional compensation because the landslide had to be cleaned up and a flatter slope put in on the bank, involving additional excavation.[20] The district engineer repeated his claim that the forty-five-degree angle was assumed for estimating quantities of earth, and had nothing to do with the angle of repose at a given site because soil conditions varied from site to site. Sometimes the contractor had to make more extensive excavations and lost money, but in other cases a steeper slope could be safely excavated, saving the contractor money, although the bid was based on a nominal forty-five degrees. The Corps of Engineers denied the Dravo Corporation claim.

The matter of claims by the General Contracting Corporation in Pittsburgh had not been resolved a year after completion of the project. The fifteen claims totaled $24,658.81. Although the sum was later reduced slightly to $24,516.02, the government was only prepared to pay $2,426.40.

While work continued on the two locks and dams on the Upper Kanawha, a public hearing was held in July 1932 to receive public comments on the proposed construction of two locks and dams below Charles-

Marmet operations building, 1995. John Nicely, Institute for the History of Technology and Industrial Archaeology, West Virginia University, Morgantown, W.V.

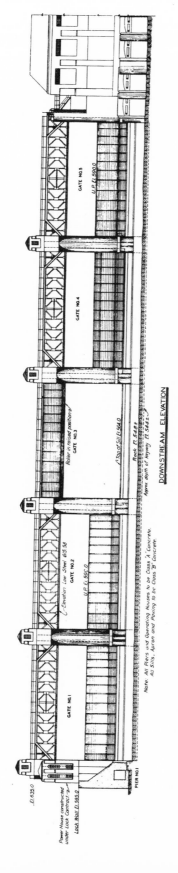

General plan and elevation of Marmet locks and dam. U.S. Engineer Office, Huntington, W.V., Dec. 1931, file 023-L2-10/0.

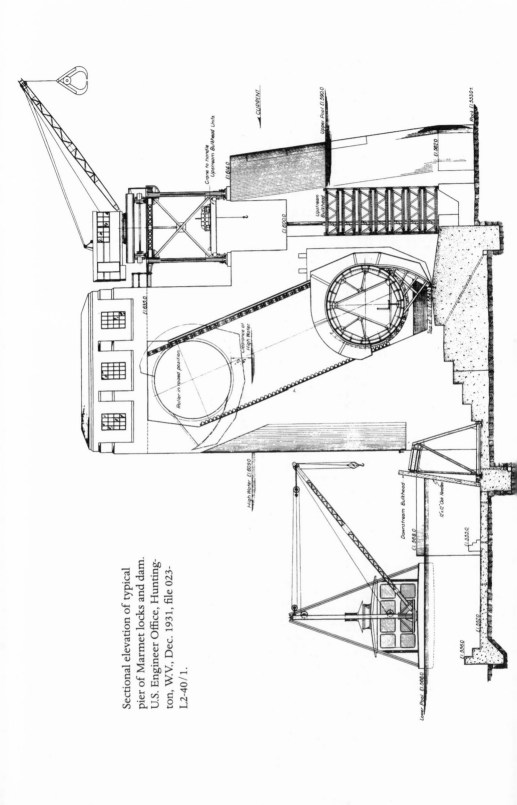

Sectional elevation of typical pier of Marmet locks and dam. U.S. Engineer Office, Huntington, W.V., Dec. 1931, file 023-L2-40/1.

ton, which would replace the existing Locks and Dams 6, 7, 8, 9, 10, and 11. The meeting reviewed proposed locations, elevations of pools, lock sizes, and other issues for those with a vested interest in navigation on the Lower Kanawha. Two proposals were presented. One, which had been revealed to the public earlier, consisted of two dams on the Kanawha River with twin locks at each site measuring 360 feet in length with a clear width of 56 feet. They would parallel the developments at London and Marmet. The second alternative was, in fact, much more creative and, in the end, was the one selected. This was to put one dam and set of locks in the Kanawha River at Winfield, with twin locks measuring 360 feet in length by 56 feet width in the clear, and to move the lowest proposed site on the Great Kanawha to a position near Gallipolis on the Ohio River. There an auxiliary lock of 360 feet by 56 feet would be installed to match those on the Great Kanawha, along with a lock 600 feet long by 110 feet wide on the Ohio River. Both of these locks and dams would have movable floodgates over the entire length of the dam, but the type of floodgate was not specified. If the second or lowest locks and dam were placed in the Ohio River, Dams 24, 25, and 26 on the Ohio River could also be eliminated. This second alternative was ultimately built, but not until several years later under a New Deal program.[21] It is interesting to note that not only was the district engineer, Major Herman, in attendance at this public meeting but also William H. McAlpine, head civilian engineer in the division office at St. Louis; F. B. Duis, the principal engineer at the district office; and senior engineer T. S. Burns and assistant engineer L. E. Fitts, both of the Huntington office. Also attending were representatives of the Marietta Manufacturing Company, Pittsburgh Coal Exchange, and others.[22]

On August 9 the Dravo Corporation of Pittsburgh, as low bidder, received the contact for the Marmet gated dam and the installation of a lock gate. The bid was considered reasonable, and the contractor had been thoroughly investigated and was believed to be reliable. Therefore, the district engineer recommended that in the interest of the United States this low bid be accepted.

The long-awaited survey of the Kanawha River from Lock 5 to the mouth at Point Pleasant was submitted to the division engineer on August 15, 1932. The report recommended replacing the six locks and dams with two high-lift dams to provide a navigable depth of nine feet at an estimated cost of $10.3 million. The district engineer, however, recommended the previously described alternative, whereby high lift locks and a dam would be constructed at Gallipolis on the Ohio River at an estimated cost of $12.2 million. But because it was to be constructed on the Ohio River, a credit of $834,000 would be applied to the elimination of the three locks and dams on that river. He recommended an initial appropriation of $3 million, with the remainder to come in equal installments. The preferred alternative would cost a net amount of $11.36 million.[23]

No sooner had the bids for the Marmet lock and dam been received than the West Virginia Rail Company, a firm producing reinforcing bars by rerolling used rail, wrote to Senator H. D. Hatfield in Charleston. Their complaint was that specifications for the construction of the dam ruled out the use of rail steel because, despite the fact that it had a higher strength, it was more brittle than mild steel bars and not trusted to pass the ductility tests in terms of standard bending of selected specimens. The company noted that rail steel, according to the American Society for Testing and Materials, had been used on the work at London and Marmet. The company had requested Major Herman to submit a personal request to the St. Louis office to allow such steel to be used. The company quoted the building code report of the committee appointed by President Hoover and published by the Bureau of Standards. In a subsequent letter of August 1, 1932, the company supplied additional information to Senator Hatfield with regard to the standard bending tests. Their argument was that, since the Dravo Corporation was from western Pennsylvania, they would probably order reinforcing steel from firms in the Pittsburgh area, precluding the involvement of West Virginia firms.[24]

One of the inherent disadvantages of a Stoney lift gate, a Tainter gate, or a roller gate is that the water issues from the bottom, thus preventing a self-cleansing action. Debris collecting behind the gates has no way of passing over the dam. The solution in the case of the Upper Mississippi was to use a submerged Tainter gate. A submersible-type roller gate was considered, but its pit would have to be excavated into rock and it too was subject to the collection of rubbish. During a discussion with German engineers, who indicated that submerged roller gates had been abandoned in Germany, Col. George R. Spalding telegraphed the Chief of Engineers indicating that they should abandon the idea of one of the gates being of the submersible type, and in its place substitute a flap gate. The advantage here was that the flap could be lowered like the flap on an aircraft wing, allowing debris to pass over the top of the dam. When

Downstream view of Marmet Dam showing flap-gate roller in operation. U.S. Engineer Office, Huntington, W.V., file MD 299.

cleared the flap could be raised to maintain the same level as the other roller gates.

It was at this time that the design for one of the gates at both London and Marmet was modified to incorporate flap gates rather than submerged roller gates.[25] Head engineer William McAlpine joined the discussion with a memorandum to General Pillsbury and Major Herman conveying his doubts and those of Colonel Spalding with regard to submersible roller gates. He concurred with the change recommended by Major Herman for an adjustable top flap on a standard roller gate.[26] The Dravo Corporation responded on October 14, giving details of both the submerging-type roller gate and the alternative of a smaller diameter roller with an adjustable flap. The design had already been worked out on the flap-type roller gate by the Krupp Corporation, a drawing of which was forwarded by Dravo Corporation to the district engineer.[27]

After due consideration, the Chief of Engineers informed the Dravo

Corporation that their request for extra payment would not be honored.[28] Proposals for constructing a roller gate dam, the second lock, alterations for the upper miter gate, and a power house at London locks and dam were reported on October 17, 1932. It was very close bidding. The Dravo Corporation succeeded in offering the low bid of $1,559,425, against a bid by Lowensohn Construction Company of Cleveland, Ohio, who bid $1,599,532. At this stage it was becoming apparent that Dravo Corporation was the company to beat in any competitive bidding on the Great Kanawha Navigation system.[29] The district engineer recommended to the Chief of Engineers that the Dravo Corporation be offered the bid.[30]

An interesting exchange took place between Local 1207 of the Brotherhood of Carpenters and Joiners of America and the War Department, beginning with a letter from the union dated November 15, 1932. The letter advised that as early as 1930 a complaint had been lodged with the district attorney of southern West Virginia concerning contractors involved in government projects on the Great Kanawha River. The complaint stated that numerous laborers and mechanics were working ten to twelve hours and, in some cases, even fourteen hours per day, which the union contended was a violation of federal laws. Under the New Deal, a maximum work week of thirty hours per week had been established as a way to provide more jobs for unemployed workers. Only supervisory staff were allowed to work longer hours. F. H. Payne, the Assistant Secretary of War, replied a fortnight later, stating that the War Department had no legal control over wage rates paid by contractors, but he assured the union that the department would see to it that the requirements of the law were rigidly enforced. In practice, this meant assuring that the thirty-hour law was enforced under the Emergency Relief and Construction Act of 1932.[31] Other New Deal agencies would be responsible for wage rates.[32]

The construction year 1933 saw a number of change orders. A typical example was a letter from the Dravo Corporation, dated February 15, 1933, concerning flooding of the cofferdams on the London B lock and dam, for which they had the contract. The district engineer replied on February 21, after reviewing all of the data with regard to a freshet in the Kanawha River, and concluded that flooding was not due to any negligence by the contractor and he was, therefore, willing to extend the contract by four calendar days. In such a situation, with a sudden rise in the river, the sluice gates were opened on the cofferdam and pumping was discontinued. In this case, the river level was one and one-half feet above the height of the cofferdam. The water level dropped, the sluice gate was closed, and pumps were restarted to drain out the cofferdam so that work could resume.[33]

Many if not most of the change orders were the result of foundation problems, in which subsurface conditions were not completely known until work was underway. In a separate change order, Major J. S. Bragdon, chief of the finance division, Corps of Engineers, agreed in a memorandum to the Chief of Engineers to pay an additional $1,005 to the Dravo Corporation with regard to test piles being driven in the steel sheet-pile guard piers. (Steel sheet piles are interlocking pieces used to form watertight walls for cofferdams and, in this case, guard piers.) There was also a slight change in alignment of the guard pier. In recommending a change order, Bragdon wrote, "it is stated in the order that this change is in the best interest of the United States and it is, therefore, recommended that it be approved."[34]

Although the Dravo Corporation had the contract for Lock B and the dam at the London site, Northport Sand and Gravel Company had responsibility for building Lock A. King and King, attorneys for Northport Sand and Gravel, were called in on a case that began on December 22, 1932, with eight claims for additional payments.[35] In a letter to the division engineer, Major Herman summarized the claims and noted, in reference to the attorneys' letter of March 9, 1933, that only three claims were being pursued.[36] It is interesting to note, in the original claim, that the eight items were for rock excavation, excavation pumping, damages suffered from interference with the concreting work, de-watering the cofferdam twice, additional cofferdam construction, the cost of extra castings, additional cost of cement, and finally a damage claim. Herman responded to the first claim, for the extra cost of rock excavation, on behalf of the Corps of Engineers. As part of detailed comments that involved quotations from the specifications, as well as details of all aspects of rock excavation, Herman stated: "The character of the rock was not different than should have been anticipated from the borings shown on the contract drawings. It is my opinion that the claim is without merit."[37]

The second claim, for the extra cost of pumping during excavation inside the cofferdam, included not only the actual work done but the cost of supervision and clerical services, compensation insurance, and liability and contingent insurance in connection with the change order. Again Herman wrote, "The claim for consequential damages resulting from the grounding of foundation is, in my opinion, without merit."[38] The third item was for damages suffered because of interference with concreting work. In this case the contractor was pressing for an additional payment for de-watering the cofferdam on two separate occasions. It is the only claim that the Corps of Engineers found to have merit because a literal interpretation of the specifications indicated that payment could be made for floods that exceeded an elevation of 601.57 feet above mean sea level, and both of the floods in question exceeded this elevation. The three items claimed out of the original eight amounted to $36,533.31, of which only the third item, for de-watering the cofferdams, in the amount of $6,000, was approved.[39] The examples show the great detail in which the Corps of Engineers reviewed each and every claim for extra compensation. Response to claims began at the district engineer's office, and proceeded to the division offices in St. Louis, and ultimately to the Chief of Engineers in Washington. These examples are typical of what one would expect on such a project.

A subsequent change order by Dravo Corporation resulted from an action by the Corps of Engineers' inspector, Roy T. Taylor, when he reported that "cracks have appeared in the concrete of Pier No. 1 of London Dam to such an extent as to warrant taking immediate definite measures to prevent a condition existing in the remaining concrete to be placed."[40] Cracks were thought to be so serious that all concreting was stopped until an appropriate solution could be recommended. When concrete sets it produces what is known as the "heat of hydration," which may be sufficiently high to cause cracking in large masses of concrete. This problem occurred in some of the large dams, like Hoover Dam in the West. The heat of hydration is produced, in large part, by two components of the cement, namely, tricalcium aluminate and tricalcium silicate. (Low-heat cement has a minimal amount of these two compounds and optimizes dicalcium silicate.) In addition, the fine grinding required for cement used in dams means that more surface area is available for hydration as soon as water is added to the mixture.

The Corps decided to replace one of the bags of the six-and-one-half-bags-per-cubic-yard mix with a ninety-four-pound bag of hydraulic cement because natural cement had a much lower amount of tricalcium silicate and aluminate. A stop order was issued on June 16, 1933.[41] Dravo Corporation was quick to protest that is was not their responsibility since they were following precisely the contract specifications for concrete. They further questioned the design, saying, "in view of the fact that the plans for the piers on your roller gate dams in the Kanawha River do not call for reinforcing to overcome shrinkage and your specifications are very clear as to the amount of cement, water, sand, and coarse aggregate, and method and time of mixing, there is no opportunity for the contractor to do anything either to prevent or cause shrinkage cracks. Consequently, it cannot be a contractor's responsibility."[42] The company was willing to cooperate, but they were not willing to accept responsibility for this situation.[43]

In a concrete mixture, the water-to-cement ratio is important in determining the strength of the concrete paste. Adding cement generally increases the strength of a given mixture. However, a mixture rich in cement also produces greater shrinkage cracks. Shrinkage cracks are also associated with hot-weather concreting, and this seemed to be the problem at the London locks and dam. In ordering a new mix design, the Corps of Engineers specified that hydraulic lime approved by the contracting officer and equal to "Flamingo" brand from Riverton, Virginia, constituted a change of the specification. In a rather miserly fashion, the Corps agreed to pay an extra twenty-five cents per cubic yard for this alteration in the concrete mixtures, estimating that the total would be approximately $350.[44] J. S. Miller, vice president of Dravo Corporation, was quick to respond. He made it clear that he held the U.S. Government directly responsible for the delays and increased expenses that had to be met by his company. After reciting all the technical reasons for possible cracking, he ended his letter to the Chief of Engineers by saying, "We would further call to your attention that a delay of two or three weeks at this season of the year may have far reaching consequences due to extending the work period into the rainy season with resultant delay and additional expense far beyond the actual present delay."[45]

In response to Miller's letter, the district engineer replied with a detailed statement indicating that the contractor was required to place just one additional lift, and that the interval between the various pours was about the same as before the restrictions placed, that is, forty-eight hours between lifts.[46] Therefore, the District Engineer's opinion was that the contractor should not receive additional compensation beyond the twenty-five cents per cubic yard previously offered. As for work on this pier, the district engineer also made an interesting observation. There was no delay because the second roller gate did not arrive until July 27, or seven days after all concrete work on Piers 1 and 3 was completed. Dravo Corporation, claiming a delay, could not have continued their work within the cofferdam until the roller gates had arrived. Thus, the district engineer felt that he had compelling reasons why extra compensation, beyond the minimal amount offered, should not be provided to the contractor. Apparently this decision was not appealed, since there is no evidence in the archives to sustain their claim on this matter.

With work at London and Marmet rapidly reaching completion, a flurry of claims by the contractor was met by reluctance on the part of the Corps of Engineers to honor change orders. Then, in February 1934, General Markham, the Chief of Engineers, wrote in response to a claim by Dravo that he had reviewed the situation and was unable to find any grounds whatsoever to grant extra compensation for the change in the concrete mixture.[47] Unhappy with repeated refusals to honor this request, Dravo wrote a month later they were not content simply to accept twenty-five cents per cubic yard as additional payment, but required an additional $8,903 for expenses caused by a change in specifications by the Corps of Engineers. The request for additional compensation was resubmitted, and on May 10 was again refused by the Chief of Engineers.[48]

Downstream view of roller gates in operation, Marmet locks and dam. U.S. Engineer Office, Huntington, W.V., file MD 304.

By midsummer 1933, both the London and Marmet projects were open for navigation even though the dams were not completed until the following summer, nor had work begun on the hydroelectric generating stations, which would be built later by private enterprise. The remaining work at both sites was being constructed inside a cofferdam extending from the completed bays of the dam to the left bank of the river. With the opening of the locks it was necessary to remove the old structures, which presented a hazard to navigation. The district engineer informed the Chief of Engineers that Lock and Dam 5 had been abandoned as an operating structure on August 1, 1933, and replaced by the new Marmet locks and dam. That did not mean that the project was finished, since only two of the five roller gates were completed and in operation. The remainder were still under construction in the contractor's cofferdam. Nevertheless, this amounted to a milestone in this large public work. In celebrating this opening, Major Herman commented that Lock and Dam 5 had been the first Chanoine wicket dam constructed in America, while

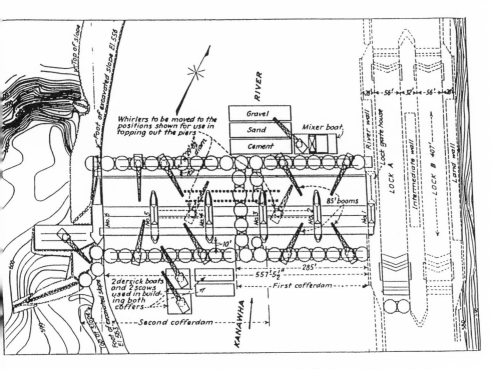

Plan showing construction layout and organization of cofferdams at Marmet locks and dam. "Roller Gate Dams for River Improvements," *Engineering News Record*, Sept. 21, 1933, 339 (redrawn and simplified 1999).

Aerial view showing locks under construction while original wicker dams and single lock are still in operation at Marmet locks and dam. U.S. Engineer Office, Huntington, W.V., ca. 1933.

General view from esplanade showing locks, dam, and hydroelectric power station, 1995. John Nicely, Institute for the History of Technology and Industrial Archaeology, West Virginia University, Morgantown, W.V.

the new Marmet dam was the first roller-gated dam in America to be operated for navigational purposes, based upon a patented German design. He also commented that fifty years appeared to be the economical life of such structures as Chanoine wicket dams. Despite his concern for history, he indicated that the Chanoine design was unsuitable for the current needs of commerce.[49]

The London and Marmet projects were undertaken by the federal government before the institution of the New Deal. However, by September 1933, it was clear that public-works funds associated with the New Deal were available to the Corps of Engineers. With this in mind, the district engineer wrote to the Chief of Engineers requesting $700,000 for these twin projects, to be expended between September 1, 1933, and June 30, 1934, for such items as the construction of esplanades, improvement

General view showing dam and Kanawha Valley Power Company power plant, Marmet locks and dam. U.S. Army Corps of Engineers, Huntington District, Aug. 20, 1953, file MD-53-1.

of grounds, clearing of banks in the London and Marmet pools, removal of old work, purchase of additional flowing easements in both the London and Marmet pools, and the purchase of land at the Marmet abutment site and the London lock and abutment site.[50] In turn, the Chief of Engineers suggested to the Secretary of War that the sum of $600,000, which was to be appropriated for improvements on the Mississippi River between the Illinois River and Minneapolis, should instead be allocated to the Kanawha Project. The Secretary of War approved General Brown's request, and $600,000 was transferred to the Upper Kanawha River project on October 7, 1933.[51] By the end of the year, the Corps of Engineers received a $1.25 million allotment from the National Industrial Recovery Administration Fund.[52] This amount was to insure the completion of the London and Marmet locks.[53]

Additional claims were made by the contractor after the Marmet lock was put into operation, while work was still underway at London. At London there was an unusually deep rock excavation for certain piers and sill foundations, both required by the Corps of Engineers. For these the contractor requested that an additional five calendar days be added to

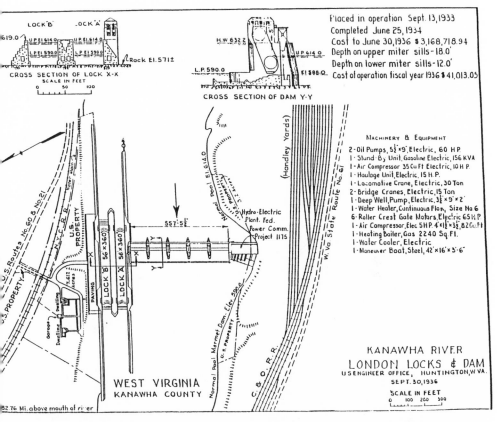

General plan of London locks and dam. U.S. Engineer Office, Huntington, W.V., Sept. 30, 1936.

the contract. Failure to complete work at the locks would result in fines in the amount of $200 a day, and the Dravo Corporation was clearly trying to extend the contract so that the assessments would not have to be paid. Dravo reiterated their claims at the end of July 1934, after all of the contract work was completed at Marmet and London. The first claim reopened the debate on the change of specifications for the concrete mixtures. The second claim was for the additional excavation required, and a third was for damages subtracted from the final estimates that, in the contractor's mind, had been improperly assessed and should be reimbursed. The liquidated-damages claim was that the contract was to be completed by December 28, 1933, but with change orders the date was extended to May 21, while in fact the contractor received final acceptance

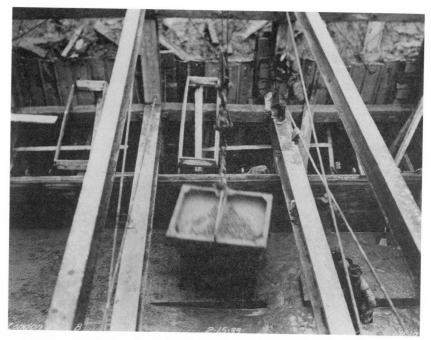

Concreting typical structure. Note the very fluid state of the concrete, which would hardly meet the slump requirements of the specifications despite the fact that an inspector appears to be on site. U.S. Engineer Office, Huntington, W.V., Feb. 15, 1933, file L.B.-19.

for the work on June 25, 1934, leaving a period of thirty-five days subjected to liquidated damages in the amount of $7,000. Dravo claimed that at least forty-six additional days were required to perform the extra work entailed in excavation and in the mixture controversy. That would extend the contract period until July 6, 1934, well beyond the actual completion of their work on June 25. As a result, they claimed that $7,000 should be remitted to them.[54] Not only did the Chief of Engineers reply, but he was supported in his decision by the Secretary of War, who wrote directly to the Dravo Corporation on August 6, 1934, stating that there was no basis for an allowance of any kind in the amount claimed.[55]

Despite the fact that the Marmet project was finished on May 10,

(*Opposite, top*) Construction of locks at London locks and dam. U.S. Engineer Office, Huntington, W.V., June 13, 1933, file L.B.-51.
(*Opposite, bottom*) Construction of cofferdams, January 1933. U.S. Engineer Office, Huntington, W.V., Jan. 22, 1933, file L.B.-11.

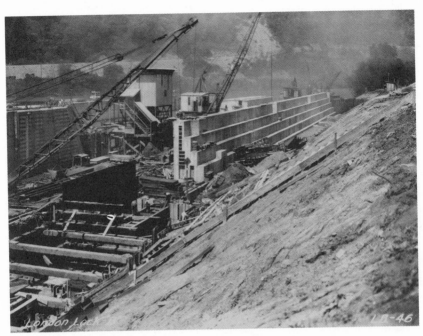

Erection of landside wall at London Lock B, 1933. U.S. Engineer Office, Huntington, W.V., May 18, 1933, file L.B.-46.

1934, and the pool behind the dam and the sister locks at London were filled by June 25, disputes continued until the end of the year. The government did not contest the company's request for liquidated damages from December 28, 1933, until May 21, 1934, and supplied a voucher for $28,800 to the contractor on August 29, 1934.[56] The $7,000 was still disputed and remained active throughout 1934. In late December, Capt. Philip G. Bruton, on behalf of the Chief of Engineers, wrote to the Dravo Corporation indicating that their claims would be viewed by the Comptroller General for settlement as soon as the administrative examination had been completed.[57] The parties involved remained intransigent. The Dravo Corporation pressed its case, but in February 1935, Major J. S. Bragdon, chief of the finance division, rendered a decision favoring the Corps of Engineers, except for $800 for four days that he determined should be remitted to the contractor.[58] Apparently, this ended the Dravo pursuit of extra compensation for the three claims. It did not, however, end their involvement with a series of change orders long after the Marmet and London locks and dams were in operation. Because of delays in completing the London Lock B and dam, the Corps of Engineers decided to modify

A fleet of barge-mounted whirlers used in the construction of London locks and dam, 1932. U.S. Engineer Office, Huntington, W.V., Nov. 29, 1932, file L.B.-4.

View into completed lock walls at London locks and dam. U.S. Engineer Office, Huntington, W.V., Dec. 21, 1933, file L.B.-68.

Erection of lower miter gate at London Lock B, February 1934. U.S. Engineer Office, Huntington, W.V., Feb. 28, 1934, file L.B.-74.

Erection of upper miter gate and the installation of form work for emergency dam sill, London locks and dam, March 1934. U.S. Engineer Office, Huntington, W.V., March 17, 1934, file L.B.-77.

the Dravo contract, although the company had not finished the upper miter sills in the locks. It was possible to put the locks into operation and have the modifications made the next winter by the regular district repair fleet, which would otherwise be idle. Thus, $18,000 was removed from the original contract price.[59]

Considering the magnitude of the projects undertaken at Marmet and London by the Dravo Corporation, there was not an excessive number of change orders to be contested. However, in the spring of 1936, the Dravo Corporation was contesting increased costs associated with the National Recovery Administration Act, which regulated the number of hours that workmen could work and also increased their rates of pay.[60] This was to have repercussions for laborers who were paid less but allowed to work longer hours. The claim submitted to the General Accounting Office by the Dravo Corporation was in the amount of $34,122.74, for work on which increased costs were claimed, under a contract entered into prior to August 10, 1933, before these provisions were put in force. The district engineer, Maj. John F. Conklin, recommended that only $23,347.82 be paid, and that the balance be disallowed for the reason that the claimant did not prove such costs were directly caused by compliance with these new regulations. The district engineer's recommendation was endorsed by the division engineer, Col. Roger G. Powell, who approved $21,750.69 for increased labor costs and $959.86 in additional insurance costs. Final approval was given by Brig. Gen. G. B. Pillsbury, Acting Chief of Engineers.[61] Since no further claims by the construction company were forthcoming, the company officers presumably accepted the decision of General Pillsbury to pay partial compensation.

The Dravo Corporation was not the only claimant regarding the Marmet locks and dams. The General Construction Corporation was responsible for one lock only, designated Lock A on the river side. As early as December 31, 1931, the contractor submitted five claims for payment, with four additional claims being submitted on January 25, 1932, and six more on February 16, 1932. In answer to these claims, Army engineers prepared a report in March of that year with recommendations to the district engineer, who was willing to settle for $2,426.40. The recommendation was forwarded to the division engineer, who, on October 21, 1932, recommended that allowances totaling $6,162.14 be approved. In November the Chief of Engineers directed the district engineer to make a direct settlement with the contractor in the amount of $5,364.71, as authorized by the Comptroller General. With nothing to lose, the contractor protested the settlement and requested a further review. It started the whole chain of events over again, with the Comptroller General requesting the Chief of Engineers to reexamine the case and furnish another report. Seeing the report and review, the Comptroller General sustained his settlement in a letter to the contractor dated December 20, 1933. Again, on March 18, 1935, the contractor petitioned for twelve claims totaling $19,671.15, which included interest based on the date of his original claim. All of the claims were carefully examined by the Corps of Engineers, which precipitated a court case with Claims No. 42796.[62] Information on the court decision has not been located.

CHAPTER EIGHT

Gallipolis and Winfield
Locks and Dams

After years of discussion, debate, and planning, the Huntington, West Virginia, *Advertiser* jubilantly announced that bids would be taken for the Winfield and Gallipolis locks and dams during September 1933.[1] Months before there was a public announcement, Lt. Hugh J. Casey, in a letter to the division engineer dated February 8, 1933, indicated that the Chief of Engineers had the report of the Board of Engineers for rivers and harbors recommending the construction of both of these locks and dams. This letter confirmed there would be twin locks at both locations. The projects would be funded under the National Recovery Act of 1933 for an estimated total of $7 million out of a total of $70 million earmarked for Corps of Engineers public works. The request for the two locks and dams represented an expenditure of $5.3 million.[2] The contract for the Gallipolis locks was awarded to the Dravo Corporation on October 23, 1933.[3]

The bids for Winfield were opened on October 2, 1933. Three days later the acting district engineer, A. M. Neilson, wrote to the Chief of Engineers informing him that the low bidder was the Brader Construction Corporation of New York City. Neilson did not believe, however, that the Brader company was the lowest *responsible* bidder, a requirement stipulated in Section 13 of the Federal Emergency Administration Public Works Bulletin 51. This regulation was intended to eliminate bidders who lacked experience in large public works or sufficient equipment to com-

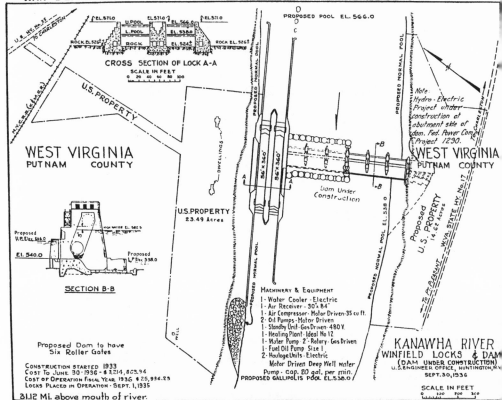

Plan of Winfield locks and dam. U.S. Engineer Office, Huntington, W.V., Sept. 30, 1936, no file no.

plete the work and meet contract schedules. Furthermore, the district engineer noted that the bid for the Stoney gate valves, which controlled the water through the locks, was less than half the cost estimated by the Corps, confirming that this company was not qualified to undertake the project.[4]

Later the same month, the Chief of Engineers, Maj. Gen. Lytle Brown, wrote a memorandum to the Secretary of War indicating that the Dravo Construction Company had submitted a bid of $1,921,130, whereas the Brader Construction Corporation's bid was for $1,874,506. Four additional bids had been recorded, all in excess of $2 million.

There was great concern by the Huntington District engineers that the Brader Construction Corporation did not have sufficient equipment to undertake the work. With this in mind, the district engineer had re-

Excavation for upper guide wall and cofferdam construction at Winfield Locks, 1933. U.S. Engineer Office, Huntington, W.V., Dec. 26, 1933, file W.L. 16.

Construction at Winfield, 1934. U.S. Engineer Office, Huntington, W.V., July 2, 1934, file W.L. 165.

Detailed view of pile foundation for upper guide wall prior to concrete placement. U.S. Engineer Office, Huntington, W.V., Aug. 8, 1934, file W.L. 189.

quested that the Brader Corporation give him the location and description of the plant they intended to acquire. In addition, he visited the company's offices in New York City, where they were unable to give him the information he requested. And while he was shown a quantity of land-based equipment, the company had no means of providing the floating concrete plant that was to be an essential part of the construction. By using barges it was possible to put together a complete concrete batching plant that could be floated and repositioned as work progressed on the locks and the dams. General Brown further indicated that the bidder did not fill out the requisite sheets, and he concluded by saying, "As a result of two hearings granted the Brader Construction Corporation in his office Brown found that it was not the lowest responsible bidder and that it had not fully complied with the requirements of the advertise-

(Opposite, top) Concreting a typical monolith at Winfield locks and dam. U.S. Engineer Office, Huntington, W.V., Aug. 8, 1934, file W.L. 190.

(Opposite, bottom) General view of Dravo's concrete batch plant at Winfield locks and dam. U.S. Engineer Office, Huntington, W.V., Aug. 14, 1934, file W.L. 198.

Placing concrete in Lower Guide Wall Monolith M-12,
looking riverward from Sta. 5+20.B
8-8-34

Lock No.1-
Kanawha River
PWA Cont. W.516 Eng.726

Contractor's Mixing Plant, taken from within coffer
at Sta. 6+50.B, looking downstream
8-14-34

U.S. Engineer Office
Huntington, W.Va.
W.L. 198

Lock No.1   Foundation for Lower Guide Wall Monolith M-10,   U.S.Engineer Office
Kanawha River   looking downstream and riverward from Sta.5+80B,   Huntington, W.Va.
PWA Cont.W516 Eng.726   8-21-34   W.L. 209

Progress view taken from river arm of coffer at   U.S.Engineer Office
Lock No.1, looking downstream and landward.   Huntington, W.Va.
                    9-6-34   W.L. 215

Lock construction, looking upstream, September 1934. U.S. Engineer Office, Huntington, W.V., Sept. 18, 1934, file W.L. 228.

ment. In as much as the second low bidder did so comply, I have authorized award to that company."[5]

A week later the Assistant Secretary of War, Henry H. Woodring, wrote to the Assistant Secretary of the Treasury, Steven B. Gibbons, with regard to the contract, restating the arguments of the Chief of Engineers.[6] A letter from the Comptroller General to the Secretary of War, dated November 17, 1933, revealed that the attorneys Buckley and Buckley of Washington, D.C., had protested the award of this contract to the Dravo Construction Company, a subsidiary of Dravo Corporation, and asked that the award be reviewed by the Secretary of War. In an undated reply to the Comptroller initialed by the Secretary of War, reference was made to the Comptroller's letter of November 17 requesting additional bid document information on acquiring the concrete batching plant and other

---

(*Opposite, top*) Preparing foundation rock for casting the first monolith (M-10) at Winfield locks and dam. U.S. Engineer Office, Huntington, W.V., Aug. 21, 1934, file W.L. 209.

(*Opposite, bottom*) Construction of locks at Winfield locks and dam, September 1934. U.S. Engineer Office, Huntington, W.V., Sept. 6, 1934, file W.L. 215.

View of lock chamber and gates for twin locks at Winfield locks and dam. U.S. Engineer Office, Huntington, W.V., Dec. 21, 1934, file W.L. 285.

equipment.[7] The Secretary of War noted that the Chief of Engineers considered the possession of an adequate floating plant to be of major importance. As a result, hearings were held in the Chief of Engineer's office beginning October 6, 1933, with representatives of the Brader Construction Corporation. The company executives presented a number of telegrams from equipment suppliers indicating they could supply the needed equipment. Stating that the bidder had failed to complete the directions for preparing his bid, the Secretary of War also reiterated that the National Industrial Recovery Act required that men be put to work in the most expeditious manner. He did not feel after his interviews that the Brader Corporation could meet this requirement.

After two hearings were granted to Brader, the Chief of Engineers determined that the company was not the lowest responsible bidder and

(Opposite, top) View of interior lock wall detailing filling ports in lock wall. U.S. Engineer Office, Huntington, W.V., Dec. 21, 1934, file W.L. 284.

(Opposite, bottom) Erection of roller gate at Winfield locks and dam, June 1936. U.S. Engineer Office, Huntington, W.V., June 22, 1934, file W.D. 94.

..king downstream and riverward
Upper Guide Wall at Sta. 6+00A.
12-21-34

U.S. Engineer Office
Huntington, W. Va.
W L 284

U.S. Engineer Office
Huntington, W. Va.
Winfield Dam
E.R. Cont. W 516 Eng-3
June 22 1936 WD-94

(*Above*) View showing piers, roller gates, and details of lock crest and downstream apron. U.S. Engineer Office, Huntington, W.V., July 27, 1936, file W.D. 106.

(*Opposite, top*) Early stages of erection of roller gate at Winfield locks and dam, June 1936. U.S. Engineer Office, Huntington, W.V., June 22, 1934. file W.D. 93.

(*Opposite, bottom*) Roller gate fabrication completed, June 1936. U.S. Engineer Office, Huntington, W.V., June 24, 1934, file W.D. 96.

Construction view of dam and piers at Winfield Dam, May 1936. U.S. Engineer Office, Huntington, W.V., May 25, 1936, file W.D. 88.

had not complied with the requirements of the invitation for bids. The Secretary of War urged the Comptroller General to approve the appointment of the Dravo Corporation for the work at the Winfield locks and dams. On January 17, 1934, the Comptroller General wrote to the Secretary of War conveying his decision on the Brader bid.[8] What had seemed to be a simple decision on the part of the Corps of Engineers was upset by the Comptroller General's reply. He found no objection to the low bidder on the grounds of either experience or financial resources and pointed out that many general contractors relied on subcontractors to supply equipment and personnel. Further, on October 24, 1933, the Corps of Engineers had authorized the Dravo Corporation to undertake the project, and the Comptroller General did not feel that this followed proper procedures for notification of the parties concerned. He ended his letter

(Opposite, top) Erection of piers and service bridge at Winfield locks and dam, July 1936. U.S. Engineer Office, Huntington, W.V., July 29, 1936, file W.D. 109.

(Opposite, bottom) General view inside cofferdam showing foundation conditions at Winfield Dam. U.S. Engineer Office, Huntington, W.V., Oct. 9, 1936, file W.D. 128.

Installation of lock gate at Winfield Locks, June 14, 1937. U.S. Engineer Office, Huntington, W.V., June 14, 1937, file W.D. 224.

by saying, "In such circumstances, the Dravo Contracting Company was not the low bidder and, it necessarily follows and is so decided, that the appropriation involved is not available for payment under a contract entered into with such a bidder."[9]

This must have caused considerable consternation in the channels between the district engineer and the Secretary of War, since Dravo was already at work on the site. Earlier the Comptroller General had requested detailed information on the matter from the Secretary of War. Having received this information, he wrote to the Secretary on February 14, 1934, reviewing all of the pertinent information. He ended by saying, "However, giving full weight to the additional facts now submitted and to all of the circumstances, this office would seem justified in withholding objection to award to the Dravo Contracting Company if, as apparently as sug-

(Opposite, top) View of gear train used to raise and lower roller gates installed in typical pier. U.S. Engineer Office, Huntington, W.V., June 8, 1936, file 3816.

(Opposite, bottom) Roller gates in operation at London locks and dam. John Nicely, Institute for the History of Technology and Industrial Archaeology, West Virginia University, Morgantown, W.V.

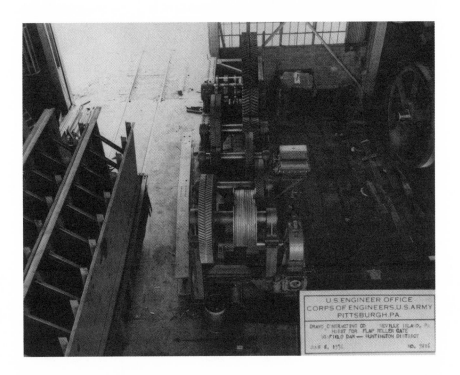

ROLLER GATED DAMS AND LOCKS

gested in the 11th paragraph of your letter of January 30th such company will consent to amending its contract by fixing the amount payable thereunder to that of the low bid. Thus, enabling completion of the work without unlawfully depleting the appropriation."[10]

Clearly the Comptroller General felt that, in the interest of the public and in order to save money, the Dravo Corporation should complete the work under the terms of the low bid submitted by the Brader Corporation. Needless to say, this did not end the controversy. The Secretary of War, George H. Dern, wrote to the Comptroller General two days later indicating that he had forwarded the Comptroller's decision to the Dravo Corporation.[11] Company executives replied by telegram, declining to accept an award based on the Brader bid that was less than their own bid price.

At the end of January, the district engineer had supplied the Chief of Engineers with reasons why he felt the contract should not be awarded to the Brader Corporation. The salient points were that the company was not the lowest responsible bidder in accordance with the rules of the National Industrial Recovery Act. This was thought to be a bureaucratic misdemeanor on the part of the contractor. The district engineer further pointed out that the Brader bid was irregular and did not comply with the bidding specifications, and finally he mentioned that the Brader estimates for the Stoney gate valves, which controlled the flow of water into and out of the locks, were ridiculously low compared to estimates completed by the Army engineers. It appears that this letter was the basis for the Comptroller General's change of mind.[12] The president of the Dravo Corporation, F. R. Dravo, wrote to the Chief of Engineers on February 19, 1934, on the issue of the low bid: "We do not understand where your department got the idea that we were willing to amend our contract because we have consistently declined to do so unless we can have the question between us adjudicated by a Court of Claims without prejudice."[13]

On March 19, 1934, the Comptroller General wrote to the Secretary

---

(Opposite, top) View of operations building at London locks and dam, 1995. John Nicely, Institute for the History of Technology and Industrial Archaeology, West Virginia University, Morgantown, W.V.

(Opposite, bottom) Overall view of London locks, dam, and powerhouse. John Nicely, Institute for the History of Technology and Industrial Archaeology, West Virginia University, Morgantown, W.V.

of War to clarify his position in regard to the low bid submitted by the Brader Corporation. He indicated that the Dravo Corporation's award could be sustained if they agreed to work on the basis of the Brader low bid and thus work could continue without interruption. He believed that the Dravo Corporation could submit a claim against the government for work performed in excess of the low bid. In essence the difference between the two bids would be handled by a change order, and the matter would finally be resolved only after the project was completed and any other change orders had been settled.[14]

Apparently, the Dravo Construction Company was willing to proceed on this basis. However, the issue remained somewhat confused in the mind of the district engineer, who wrote to the Chief of Engineers on November 9, 1934, raising the issue once again and urging him to make a decision. The problem was that if the Corps of Engineers modified the contract through change orders or reductions in the work to be performed, under which unit prices should these changes be made? Specifically at issue were five change orders that resulted in a net deduction in the amount of the contract, making a difference between the Dravo and Brader bids of $31,779.52, as opposed to the original bid difference of $46,624.00. Thus, the amount in dispute could vary quite considerably as the work progressed. It is little wonder that the Corps of Engineers wished to settle this all at one time after the completion of the work.[15] This discussion was followed by a detailed estimated final payment for the Winfield locks prepared by the district engineer on February 20, 1934, suggesting that the difference would be $32,000.[16] Since there is no specific evidence on this matter, one assumes it was resolved by change order.

Late in 1933, S. P. Puffer, managing director of the Chamber of Commerce in Charleston, met with the district engineer, Maj. Fred W. Herman, with regard to the contracts on the new Winfield lock and dams, wondering whether priority would be given to local suppliers and subcontractors.[17] The district engineer wrote in reply on November 3, 1933, listing the quantities of materials estimated to be needed on the Winfield project and saying that preference would be given to local suppliers and subcontractors if the choice did not involve higher costs, inferior quality, or insufficient quantities.[18] This seemingly routine exchange of letters set the stage for yet another controversy between the contractor and the government involving the supply of sand and gravel for the job. These were the main ingredients in the massive amount of concrete needed for both the Winfield and Gallipolis projects. R. M. Dravo wrote to Major Bragdon, assistant to the Chief of Engineers, noting that there were a number of suppliers in the area—including Wilson Sand and Supply and Union Sand and Gravel of Huntington, and Pfaff and Smith and West Virginia Sand and Gravel of Charleston—but that these local suppliers were unable to meet the requirements for both quantity and quality of aggregates to meet Dravo's demanding construction schedule and the Corps of Engineers' specifications. For the aggregates, they preferred to use the Keystone Sand and Gravel Company, a Dravo subsidiary located in Marietta, Ohio, that was the largest producer of sand and gravel in the Upper Ohio, Allegheny, and Monongahela Rivers.[19]

The problem was that relief funds provided through New Deal agencies were apportioned among regions so that all parts of the country could benefit from government projects. Congressman Fred Vinson, well known as a leader of the New Deal, wrote to the Chief of Engineers on February 3, 1934, pointing out that Keystone Sand and Gravel Company was in Region 3, whereas the Winfield project was in Region 4. He strongly opposed using a firm outside the region. In addition, he disagreed with the district engineer that local suppliers could not meet the requirements of the Dravo Company.[20] Four days later, the Chief of Engineers, General E. M. Markham, wrote to Congressman Vinson that he had referred the question to the division engineer in Cincinnati and ordered him to undertake an investigation and report, promising to inform the congressman when the report was "forthcoming."[21]

The report was supplied to the Chief of Engineers on February 9, 1934. In it the four local companies were evaluated together with the production capacity of the Dravo Corporation. The report seemed to indicate that the local suppliers could meet the demand based on the nearby location and size of the sand and gravel bars on the Kanawha and Ohio Rivers.[22] R. E. Plimpton of the National Recovery Administration wrote to the Chief of Engineers regarding General Pillsbury's letter of February 20, asking whether certain deliveries of sand to the Dravo Company were permissible under the code established by the New Deal. He apparently did not know how the code could prevent the proposed delivery of sand and gravel by the Keystone Company to the Dravo Company, provided that the work was done in compliance with the labor and other New Deal code provisions.[23]

If nothing else, the Dravo Corporation was persistent. Its president,

R. M. Dravo, wrote to Major Bragdon, Assistant Chief of Engineers, on February 22, 1934, stating that, notwithstanding the district engineer's position on the matter, the company did not feel that the sand and gravel industry in the Point Pleasant area could make the deliveries required to enable the company to finish the two contracts on time. In addition, their price was thirty cents a ton more than what it would cost the company to dig it themselves. He further indicated the work could be expedited by Keystone because their large number-nine sand digger would be "ready to go as soon as the ice flows out of the rivers in perhaps a week or two." Although it was not an overt threat, the president indicated that he would like to call Pennsylvania Congressman Kelly into the matter. There was no objection to this suggestion on the part of the Army engineers.[24] Apparently, the Dravo Corporation was allowed to supply, at least in part, the sand and gravel necessary for these two projects since there is no further evidence in the archives regarding this matter.

The next administrative difficulty arose when Secretary of the Interior Harold L. Ickes, in a letter of July 20, 1934, to the Secretary of War, informed him that, in accordance with the provisions of the National Industrial Recovery Act of 1933, he was allotting $2.2 million to the Corps of Engineers for construction of the Gallipolis locks and dam. On the same day, Ickes also informed the Secretary of the Treasury of his action.[25] New Deal funding was provided by the Department of the Interior, while all phases of the construction were the responsibility of the Corps of Engineers. General Pillsbury, Acting Chief of Engineers, wrote to Fred E. Schnepfe, who was director of the Federal Projects Division, Federal Emergency Administration of Public Works, on August 8, 1934, informing him that the amount allocated was insufficient to permit the construction of the dam at Gallipolis. However, the structural parts of the Gallipolis dam could be completed at an estimated cost of $2.5 million. Since it was highly desirable to undertake this work in a single con-

---

(Opposite, top) Overall view of completed locks, dam, and hydroelectric power station at Winfield, January 1953. Corps of Engineers, U.S. Army, Huntington District, Jan. 28, 1953, file W.D. 53-1.

(Opposite, bottom) View of operations building at lockside, Winfield locks and dam, 1995. John Nicely, Institute for the History of Technology and Industrial Archaeology, West Virginia University, Morgantown, W.V.

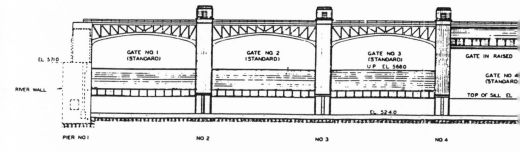

General plan and section of the Winfield locks and dam. U.S. Engineer Office, Huntington, W.V., April 1935, file 023-L1-40/0.

tract, he requested that $375,000 of $500,000 that had been earmarked for channel work in the Ohio be transferred to the Gallipolis project.[26]

Three alternate plans were developed to expend the $2.2 million for what was known as the Lower Kanawha Project. Under Plan 1, $1.4 million would be spent on masonry and steel construction of four bays of the dam, complete with machinery. The remaining funds would be used to finish all work at the Gallipolis and Winfield locks, including the machinery and operations building, which were not included in the earlier contracts. This could be done for $435,000. In addition, bulkheads, a barge, and a whirler derrick boat for use at both dams could be obtained for $290,000. With a contingency of $75,000, this would allocate all of the $2.2 million. This would leave the second half of a dam to be constructed at Gallipolis for $1.2 million and the complete dam at Winfield for $2 million. Flowage rights, clearing, removal of old works, buildings, grounds, and esplanades at both dams would require an additional $2.3 million, making a future allotment of $7.7 million necessary to complete the works. If only the sills and not the roller gates were to be built, a navigable pass of 550 feet would be left between the locks and the half of the completed dam. With suitable water levels, river traffic could bypass the locks.

The second plan called for construction of all the masonry in the dam at Gallipolis for $1.5 million, but there was no provision for roller gates, machinery, or a service bridge. To finish all work at both Gallipolis and Winfield locks, including machinery and operating buildings in excess of the amount already appropriated, would require $435,000, the

 ROLLER GATED DAMS AND LOCKS

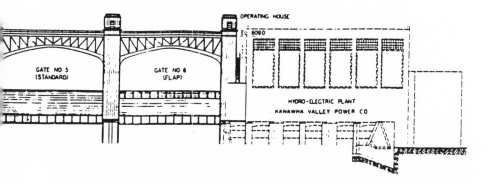

same as Plan 1. However, Plan 2 would provide one barge only and bulk-heads at both dams but not the whirlers. The contingencies would remain the same at $75,000. This would distribute the entire amount appropriated. With this plan, it would have been necessary to complete the roller gates for the entire Gallipolis Dam under a separate contract, at a cost of $950,000. The service bridge and electrical work would need an additional $100,000, the whirler derrick boat would require $150,000, and an estimated $2 million would be needed at Winfield. Flowage rights, clearing, removal of old works, buildings, grounds, and esplanades at both dams would require $2.3 million. It was noted that bids could be opened on either plan on September 15, with the required thirty days' advance notice. Either plan could be undertaken without interference with the existing lock. However, in Plan 2, the river traffic would have to use a 360-foot by 110-foot auxiliary lock at all times and Lock 26 on the Ohio River during low water.

Plan 3 was to build the Winfield Dam. The cost was estimated at $2 million, plus provisions for bulkheads and a barge for both dams at $140,000, and contingencies of $60,000, for a total of $2.2 million. This would leave, for the future, an additional $2.6 million to complete the Gallipolis Dam, and $435,000 to finish all work at the Gallipolis and Winfield locks covered by present contracts. (This was the same amount as in the previous two plans.) Additional costs would be a whirler derrick boat at $150,000 and again $2.3 million for flowage rights, clearance, removal of old works, buildings, grounds, and esplanades. With a contingency of $15,000, the total estimate equaled $7.7 million. The difficulty

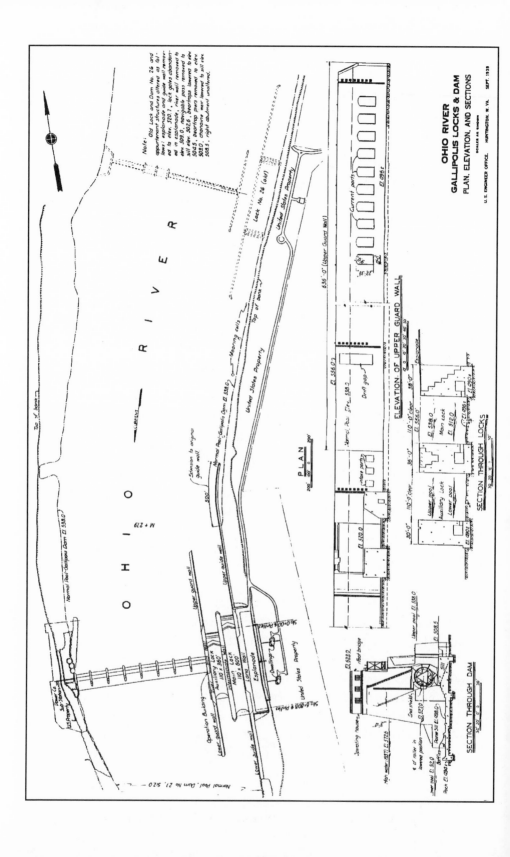

OHIO RIVER
GALLIPOLIS LOCKS & DAM
PLAN, ELEVATION, AND SECTIONS

U. S. ENGINEER OFFICE.   HUNTINGTON, W. VA.   SEPT. 1939

SCALES AS SHOWN

PLAN

ELEVATION OF UPPER GUARD WALL

SECTION THROUGH LOCKS

SECTION THROUGH DAM

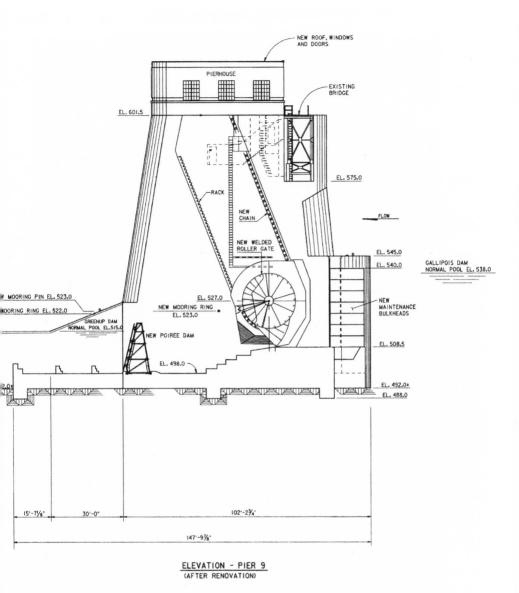

NEW ROOF, WINDOWS
AND DOORS

PIERHOUSE

EXISTING
BRIDGE

EL. 601.5

EL. 575.0

RACK

NEW
CHAIN

FLOW

NEW WELDED
ROLLER GATE

EL. 545.0
EL. 540.0

GALLIPOIS DAM
NORMAL POOL EL. 538.0

MOORING PIN EL. 523.0

EL. 527.0

MOORING RING EL. 522.0

NEW MOORING RING
EL. 523.0

NEW
MAINTENANCE
BULKHEADS

GREENUP DAM
NORMAL POOL EL.515.0

NEW POIREE DAM

EL. 508.5

EL. 498.0

EL. 492.0±
EL. 488.0

15'-7⅛"   30'-0"   102'-2¾"

147'-9⅞"

ELEVATION - PIER 9
(AFTER RENOVATION)

(Above) Plan and elevation of Pier 9 of the Gallipolis locks and dam. U.S. Army Corps of Engineers, Nashville District (Nidi), file KHG Pier 9.

(Opposite) Plan, elevation, and sections of the Gallipolis locks and dam. U.S. Engineer Office, Huntington, W.V., Sept. 1939, no file number.

Ohio River
Gallipolis Dam
PWA Cont. W516 Eng 903

Progress View taken from top of bank at Sta. 3+56B
looking riverward showing general view of progress.
6-28-35

U.S. Engineer Office
Huntington, W. Va.
GD 47

U. S. ENGINEER OFFICE
HUNTINGTON, W. VA.

GALLIPOLIS DAM
OHIO RIVER

P. W. A. CONT. W516 eng - 903
MAR. 23, 1937   GD - 276

Illustration of one bay of Gallipolis Dam. U.S. Engineer Office, Huntington, W.V., Oct. 25, 1935, file GD 98.

here was one of timing since it was stated that the work could not be undertaken until December 15, and that under this plan all river traffic must use the outer of the new locks while the dam was being constructed.[27]

Apparently, there was a delay in having the money transferred, so that Schnepfe advised General Pillsbury, Acting Chief of Engineers, that transfer of additional funds from the open-channel work in the Ohio River would be delayed until the $2.2 million was transferred.[28] These funds were transferred effective August 27, 1934.[29] In order to complete the outstanding contracts at both Winfield and Gallipolis, the district engineer, Major John Conklin, requested of the Chief of Engineers that $350,000 be transferred to the district office.[30]

Distribution of the $70 million appropriated to the Corps of Engineers had been something of a mystery. A letter from the Secretary of

(Opposite, top) Construction details inside cofferdam for Gallipolis Dam. U.S. Engineer Office, Huntington W.V., June 28, 1935, file GD 47.

(Opposite, bottom) Details of pier construction formwork at Gallipolis Dam. U.S. Engineer Office, Huntington, W.V., March 23, 1937, file GD 276.

Overall view of construction showing completed locks and cofferdam for constructing roller-gated dam at Gallipolis. U.S. Engineer Office, Huntington, W.V., Aug. 18, 1936, file GD 218.

War, George Dern, to Harold Ickes, finally revealed how this money was distributed. Apparently, Ickes was not familiar with these developments, which occurred early in the New Deal administration. A general estimate for the Kanawha Project by the Chief of Engineers was for $5.3 million, a figure included in a letter dated September 20, 1934. The Secretary of War asked for $3 million to continue these two projects for the fiscal year 1935 for construction of the dam at Gallipolis, Ohio. The Public Works Administration, however, found it necessary to reduce the funds to be provided.[31] It was decided in a meeting of the Chief of Engineers with H. M. Waite, deputy to Harold Ickes, and F. E. Schnepfe, director of federal projects, to reduce the request to $2.2 million. This allocation was re-

(Opposite, top) Construction detail of Gallipolis Dam showing rail-mounted cranes, cofferdam, and installed service bridge and roller gate. U.S. Engineer Office, Huntington, W.V., April 26, 1937, file GD 291.

(Opposite, bottom) Erection of typical roller gate, Gallipolis Dam, May 1937. U.S. Engineer Office, Huntington, W.V., May 26, 1937, file GD 298.

U.S. Engineer Office
Huntington, W. Va.
Gallipolis Dam
Ohio River
P.W.A.Cont. W516eng-903
April 26, 1937   GD-291

U.S. Engineer Office
Huntington, W. Va.
Gallipolis Dam
Ohio River
P.W.A.Cont. W516eng-903
May 26, 1937   GD-298

Illustration of lock-gate repair at Gallipolis Locks, May 7, 1938. U.S. Engineer Office, Huntington, W.V., May 7, 1938, file GLD-OR2.

Gallipolis Dam in operation, showing water passing under roller gates. John Nicely, Institute for the History of Technology and Industrial Archaeology, West Virginia University, Morgantown, W.V.

Detail of both locks from the downstream gates at Gallipolis, 1993. John Nicely, Institute for the History of Technology and Industrial Archaeology, West Virginia University, Morgantown, W.V.

ceived July 29, 1934, and on October 21 the Accelerated Public Works program (APW) approved the transfer of an additional $375,000 to the project, bringing the total funds available to $2.5 million.

As a result, the Corps of Engineers decided to hold the work undertaken at Gallipolis to a minimum. In seeking additional funds, the Chief of Engineers recommended to the Secretary of War that open-channel work on the Ohio River, as well as projects at Augusta, Georgia; Brunswick Harbor, Georgia; the Wolf River in Tennessee; Milwaukee Harbor in Wisconsin; the St. Mary's River in Michigan; and the Winooski River in Vermont could yield a total of $539,310.87, which could be transferred to the Gallipolis project. This would provide sufficient funds to meet the low bid that had been received in the amount of $3,117,400.[32] Ten days later, Ickes replied to the Secretary of War that his request was receiving careful consideration.[33]

In order to continue the work without a break, the Secretary of War requested of Harold L. Ickes on January 7, 1935, that the work be awarded with a proviso that, since funds were at present insufficient to complete the entire project, the United States would reserve the right, on or before July 31, 1935, or indeed at a later date mutually agreed between the contractor and the government, to limit the work to be done in the first and second cofferdams, which would comprise two-thirds of the entire project. Further, work on or within cofferdam number 3 would be curtailed unless further funds became available.[34] Thus, continuous employment was insured on the Corps projects in West Virginia for the winter of 1934–1935.

It was announced that bids would be received on February 28, 1935, for the operations building and machinery for the locks at Winfield. In preparing for competitive bidding, the Corps estimated a cost of $37,383 if the work were undertaken by the government. The cost by private contractors was projected to be $34,610, a difference of 7 percent; this finding justified going to outside contractors. Of the six companies bidding on the project, Robinson-Branin Company of New York City was the apparent low bidder at $32,000, a figure that was considerably lower than the government estimate.[35]

Following the contracts for machinery in the operations building, Major Conklin, the district engineer, submitted to the Chief of Engineers, for final approval, plans and specifications for constructing the dam at Winfield and certain alterations in the upper gate of Lock A. The design contemplated a roller-gate dam with five standard roller gates and one crest flap-type gate, adjacent to the abutment, whose flap could be lowered to pass debris from the upper pool over the crest of the dam, as an alternative to a submersible-type roller gate. The design also included a footbridge connecting the piers, strong and light aluminum bulkheads for the emergency dam, the traditional Poirée needle dam for the lower emergency gate (in case one of the bays had to be de-watered for repairs), and the installation of permanent upper lock gates in Lock A.

Model tests on the dam were underway at the University of Iowa and had progressed sufficiently to determine the type of sill, apron, and baffles necessary to dissipate energy below the dam in order to control erosion. It was also noted that construction would start at the abutment so that the cofferdam and sheet piles could be left in when work commenced on the hydroelectric power station. The low land at the abutment end was to be reserved for the hydropower station, necessitating that the contractor for the dam provide a staging area on the right bank of the river.[36]

On May 28 the district engineer informed Maj. D. O. Elliott at the division office in Cincinnati that a meeting had been held the day before in Washington in which all questions concerning the Winfield plans and specifications had been resolved. As a result, William H. McAlpine, chief civilian engineer at the division office, informed the district that he would forward the plans and specifications to the district office, with copies, at the end of the month. It appeared that they would be able to advertise bids for the Winfield Dam on or about June 15, providing that sufficient funds had been transferred to the district by that time.[37]

On June 15 advance notice was given that bids would be received on July 18, 1935.[38] In connection with the bidding, the Corps was required to prepare estimates comparing expenses for outside contracts with the cost of hired labor working under the direct supervision of the Corps. In the case of the Winfield Dam, the hired-labor estimate was $2,194,025, whereas the estimate for contract work was $1,973,752, a difference of 10.4 percent, or nearly a quarter of a million dollars. This finding justified going to competitive bids.[39] Therefore, in order to attract the best bids, the Corps of Engineers invited seventy firms nationwide to offer bids on the Winfield Dam.

Much to the relief of the Army engineers, Walter King of the U.S. Treasury Department informed the district engineer that $5.5 million would be transferred to the district for the lock and dam project.[40] This approval came only days before the bids were received.

Turning to the Gallipolis project, the Secretary of War wrote Harold Ickes about his concern over the lack of sufficient funds to complete the project and the possibility that the Corps might be forced to abrogate the contract and finish the work with hired labor. He reminded Ickes that, on January 24, 1934, authorization had been granted to transfer the funds to be added to the allotment of $2.2 million, for a total of $2.5 million. This total was granted on August 27, 1934, for the partial construction of the dam at Gallipolis.[41]

At that stage, work at the Gallipolis locks and dam was well advanced, with the masonry work practically finished. The funds secured from the Emergency Relief Appropriation were applied to the completion of the dam. The remaining work at the lock, the installation of the gate and lock machinery, was the most technical aspect of the whole project, and the Secretary could not recommend that it be performed by hired relief labor. To bolster his argument, he also pointed out that a delay in completion of the lock would slow progress on the dam, since the final cofferdam could not be installed if the locks were not functioning to pass river traffic around the dam. The estimated cost for the completion was $328,000. Evidently a bureaucrat experienced in requesting funds, the Secretary also suggested a source for the money, noting that $129,600 could be made available through the Administration of Public Works and be supplemented by $98,399 provided earlier for the Gallipolis dam. The Secretary of War ended his argument by stating, "The above transfers will permit the efficient and economical completion of the work at the Gallipolis locks and dam and are in the best interest of the government. I strongly recommend their approval in accordance with the attached list."[42]

In June 1935, the district engineer, Major Conklin, submitted a progress report to the *Manufacturers Record* in Baltimore, Maryland. He reported that plans for the construction of the Winfield Dam had been forwarded to the Chief of Engineers for approval, and indicated that a notice for bids would soon be forthcoming. He reported that the Gallipolis locks and dam, where construction had begun in October 1933, were approximately 85 percent complete, with 213,000 cubic yards of concrete already placed and 258,600 cubic yards required to complete the work. A section of the steel miter lock gate and a Tainter valve gate, which controlled the water in and out of the lock, had been started in June. Conklin also noted that the Dravo Contracting Company had secured the contract for the construction of the dam, as well as the locks at Gallipolis. As of June, the work had just started and only the first cofferdam was completed, so that excavation of earth and rock was currently in progress. The dam was to be built with three cofferdams. This would lessen the contraction of the river channel, maintaining open navigation and avoiding excessive river velocities through a constricted passage. The cofferdam of the Ohio bank was being built from the shore so that the abutment and two complete roller gates could be built within its confines. The completed dam would consist of eight roller gates; the estimated completion date was the summer of 1937.[43]

In the fall of 1935, Capt. E. J. Bean, of the Corps of Engineers Finance Department, informed the Chief of Engineers that $7,000 had been transferred from the flood-control accounts to the district for the Winfield project.[44] By early December 1936, General Pillsbury, Acting Chief of Engineers, informed the Secretary of War that the Winfield locks had been placed in full operation on September 9 and the navigation pool raised on October 20. He noted that commercial traffic on the Kanawha

River for the past five years had averaged 1,838,872 tons per year, bringing an annual value of just short of $10 million. He further requested that the Secretary approve the allotment of funds totaling $332,000 for the completion of the two locks and dams. This request was made on December 3 and approved on December 4, 1936.[45]

Earlier in the summer, the district engineer, Major Conklin, submitted to the division engineer for his approval plans and specifications for several dwellings at the Winfield Dam at an estimated cost of $10,000 each. This apparently trivial contract, at least in comparison with the great work on the locks and dams themselves, provides an important architectural insight into the esthetics of the entire site:

> In order to carry out the line and feeling created in the design of the locks and dams and at the suggestion of a consulting architect, the dwellings have been designed in the so-called "modern style." The flat roofs recall the operation building and operating houses and at the same time eliminated complicated roof framing. Stucco had been chosen in order that the general character of the wall surfaces will more closely harmonize with the walls of the locks and dams and, at the same time, give the houses individuality through differences in texture. The steel joist floor construction has been chosen to minimize deflections over the long spans and to eliminate the difficulties often encountered in running electrical and plumbing pipes through wood joists.[46]

Conklin further noted that the plans and specifications for the dwellings had been reviewed by an architect formerly of Charleston.

The Winfield contractor, the Dravo Corporation, of which the Dravo Construction Company was a subsidiary, announced on November 11, 1936, that the company was going through a reorganization,[47] and the district engineer confirmed that contracts would be transferred to the new company. The new firm was simply known as Dravo Corporation.[48]

While construction was going on, river traffic was heavy on both the Kanawha and Ohio Rivers. Although the incident was not reported in the papers, district engineer Maj. John Conklin, with approval from Roger G. Powell, the division engineer, reported to the Chief of Engineers that the motor ship Lelia, owned by a firm in Winchester, Kentucky, had collided with the upper guide crib. The 120-horsepower tow, bound downstream, had approached the lock at 5:30 in the morning, pushing three steel barges, 26 by 170 feet in size and loaded with coal. The pass of the earlier lock was down, so that open navigation was the rule of the day. When the tow was still 200 yards above the upper guide crib, danger signals were sounded by the lock master and his crew, warning the tow not to approach the partially opened pass. It nevertheless continued, so that the head of the tow was drawn into the pass. When the tow-boat captain attempted to reverse engines, the barges struck the outside of the river wall and damaged a gate spar. The damage to the tow boat and barges was not reported, but the payment from the responsible party amounted to only $24.37.[49]

Ironically, after all the struggle to secure sufficient funds for both projects, the district engineer informed the Chief of Engineers that approximately $140,000 would remain in the project budget, and would have to be spent by June 30, 1937. He expected the Winfield project to be finished in July and the Gallipolis Dam in August 1937. He therefore recommended that the surplus funds be obligated for paving the esplanades and for improvement of roads and grounds at both the Winfield and Gallipolis locks and dams. Plans and specifications could be provided by April 15, 1937.[50] In a telegram, Conklin informed the division engineer that apparently only $45,000 would be available to the district for work on the esplanade, roads, and grounds at Winfield.[51] Details of the subproject for Winfield were submitted to the Chief of Engineers on April 19, 1937.[52] The project for the esplanade and other work was modified August 10, 1937, to include some additional work, mainly the provision of a binding material for the gravel base and the erection of a flag pole that was not considered in the original contract. The change order amounted to only $2,008.48.[53]

In May 1937, the Dravo Corporation put in a claim for increased compensation as a result of its compliance with the President's reemployment act. The General Accounting Office in Washington correctly pointed out that the act was passed June 16, 1934, and that the Dravo Corporation had signed a contract later that summer without qualifications, including all subsequent agreements. Therefore their claim was disallowed.[54]

Many of the claims dragged on well after the completion of the locks and dams. One of the most protracted of these was a decision by the Court of Claims of the United States involving the General Contracting Corporation and a contract dated March 27, 1931. A decision was handed down eight years later, on January 9, 1939, and the company was awarded $1,570.62, and an additional $784.64 for a claim involving increased costs for embedded timbers.[55] Considering the magnitude of the job and the many difficulties of administering such a large project, the work at both sites was completed in a remarkably short time.

The West Virginia State Road Commission requested of the district engineer information on both the Gallipolis and Winfield projects. In an August 1937 reply, the district engineer was pleased to announce that the Marmet, London, and Winfield locks and dams had been completed and were in operation.[56]

On June 8, just weeks before the surplus funds would revert at the end of the fiscal year, bids for the operations building were opened, and the apparent low bidder was Boscoe and Ritchie of Ravenswood, West Virginia, with a bid of $22,336 out of a proposed contract of $45,000.[57]

The Winfield project was finished in the summer of 1937, followed closely by the Gallipolis project in October. The planned opening, however, was delayed until fair weather the following summer, on June 12, 1938. It was to be a joint celebration, with the major events occurring at Gallipolis. By the end of 1937, all four locks and dams of the Kanawha Navigation were completed and in operation. The cost for Gallipolis exceeded $10 million, and at Winfield more than $7 million.

The completed projects at Gallipolis and Winfield were succinctly described by the district engineer, Maj. John Conklin, in a letter to the Federal Writers' Project organization in West Virginia:

> The operations building is a two-story structure built on the river wall of the locks and is not to be confused with the operating houses on top of the piers. The building houses the equipment necessary for the operation of the lock gates and valves, the switchboard for the electrical system of both the locks and the dam, as well as the office of the lockmaster, repair shop and storage space.
>
> The principal items of construction for the Gallipolis locks and dam include 719,000 cubic yards of common excavation, 62,000 cubic yards of rock excavation, 351,000 cubic yards of concrete, 12,550,000 pounds of structural steel, 2,723,000 pounds of reinforcing steel, 668,000 pounds of steel and iron castings, and 910,000 pounds of miscellaneous metal work.
>
> The estimated total cost of the Gallipolis lock and dam project, including rights to lands inundated by the higher pool level and damages to roads, bridges and other structures, is $10,600,000. It is expected that the project will be completed in September, 1937.
>
> The Gallipolis locks and dam project is primarily a navigation project and is of little value in the control of flood waters. By raising a roller gate, a varying opening can be made between the bottom of the gate and the sill, permitting water to pass beneath the gate. As the river flow increases, the upper pool level can be main-

tained by increasing the opening. In times of flood flow, the roller gates are raised clear of the water, thus causing a minimum obstruction to the free flow with the consequent lack of build-up of the water level above the dam. It is possible to raise the roller gates a maximum distance of 67 feet, at which height the bottoms of the gates are still three feet above the water level of the maximum flood of record—that of January, 1937.

Principal items of construction in the Winfield locks and dam include 373,000 cubic yards of common excavation, 69,300 cubic yards of rock excavation, 182,000 cubic yards of concrete and 4,750 tons of steel and iron. The project will be completed in August, 1937, at a total cost of approximately $7,000,000, including rights to lands which will be inundated by the higher pool and other flowage damage.

The Kanawha Valley Power Company has been granted a license for constructing a hydro-power plant at the abutment end of Winfield Dam and this plant is now under construction. The plant will have a total capacity of more than 26,000 horsepower, using three turbines. It is estimated that the power plant will be completed in 1937 at a cost of approximately $2,500,000.[58]

In the 1945 report of the Chief of Engineers, the Kanawha River project was summarized with information on the locks at London, Marmet, Winfield, and Gallipolis. In addition to location and dimensions, the estimated cost of the dams is given as a summary.[59]

CHAPTER NINE

Labor and Land

Labor

The unheralded heroes at London, Marmet, Winfield, and Gallipolis were the workers engaged in building the four locks and dams, both those hired from the relief rolls and those skilled in various trades. We know little of the crews or the individual workers unless they were involved in a noteworthy event, such as an accident or a strike. We do, however, know the job skills required in certain aspects of the work. Perhaps the most visible equipment on site was the large barge-mounted whirlers (boom derricks) on derrick boats as well as rail-mounted whirlers. Job descriptions, established in connection with the New Deal public works projects, indicate the skills required of operators:

WHIRLER OPERATORS:
Men operating the Dravo Whirler need to be mentally alert, physically capable and experienced in the operation of this particular type of derrick. Men experienced on other types of articulated boom derricks need at least six months experience, and usually more, to become capable, safe operators of the Dravo Whirler. A training period of not less than two years is required to develop a capable operator, sure and safe at all times, of a man who has become familiar with the machinery of the derrick thru the duties of a fireman or oiler.

OPERATOR OF DERRICKBOATS:
Dravo Contracting Company Derrickboats are of the whirler boat type, being steam powered whirlers mounted on approximately square hulls. In addition to the skill

required to operate the whirler when the boat is in position for work, the Derrickboat Operator must also have the ability to move the boat by its own power. Movement is accomplished by means of a cast steel deadman, called a moving weight, which is attached to the fall line of the derrick and moved about by the derrick for placing in position. Movement is accomplished by placing the moving weight out away from the boat and drawing the boat to the weight by raising the boom high and straining on the fall line. Experience in movement of boat under its own power in swift water is positively essential.[1]

Before the establishment of the New Deal programs that completely changed the working relationships between labor, contractors, and the government, workers traditionally were hired directly by the contractor. The district engineer had no direct involvement in labor-management affairs, other than to assure that reasonable wage rates were part of the contractor's bid. Thus, in the absence of company records, little information remains on the day-by-day working conditions on site, except when an accident occurred.

In the vast administrative paperwork required both for the contractor and the Corps of Engineers in order to manage a project of this magnitude, the records indicate just three deaths associated with the work at London and Marmet, in addition to the six previously mentioned that occurred in connection with a landslide. This is not to say there were not other accidents and possibly other fatalities, but the records simply do not reveal such information, in contrast with today's rigorous reporting requirements. The first mentioned is the recovery of the body of R. M. Cope, who was lost on January 21, 1933, when he fell from a derrick boat on the London project. His body, however, was not recovered until March 30.[2] Later in the year, on October 5, Tony DeMarco, an Italian immigrant worker, fell into the cofferdam and drowned before rescue efforts could be organized.[3] The third reported case was also caused by falling, this time on January 14, 1934, when Clivy C. Wilson lost his balance, fell off a pier, and died of injuries sustained in the fall.[4]

Injuries were not the only unwanted events that were kept to a minimum. Strikes and other "industrial actions" were remarkably few considering the magnitude of the job and the period over which it extended. With the government controlling the hiring, wage rates, and working conditions through the National Industrial Recovery Administration Act, strikes were averted, and the only "industrial action" was a dispute over wage rates for skilled whirler operators, which was quickly resolved.[5] This is not to say that the attempt to implement a comprehensive new way of doing business did not encounter problems.

In the early days of the New Deal, President Roosevelt visited Grafton, West Virginia, to inspect the construction then underway on the massive Tygart Dam. At the time, he was getting criticism from certain quarters for his New Deal legislation. He appeared at the back of the presidential train and addressed the crowd, saying that he was not there to defend the New Deal but rather to proclaim it.[6] One vehicle of the New Deal was the National Industrial Recovery Administration Act. In typical Roosevelt fashion, the President declared it a frontal attack on unemployment itself. He described these great public works as "a bridge over which men may pass from a relief status to normal employment."[7] The NIRA Act contained specific provisions regarding the employment of labor on public works financed under the act.

To avoid certain obvious shortcomings in the NIRA Act, which would result from an unorganized and disorderly labor market, a special board was empaneled for public works and chaired by Harold Ickes, Secretary

Payday at Winfield locks and dam. U.S. Engineer Office, Huntington, W.V., June 24, 1934, file W.L. 159.

of the Interior. The provisions of the act included recommendations for distributing jobs among qualified workers on a geographical basis, in order to avoid excessive migration of labor in quest of work. Unemployed persons would be asked to verify that they were residents of counties included in the work area. A national reorganization of labor required a considerable bureaucracy to carry out the intentions of the act. It was on large public works such as the Great Kanawha Navigation that the details of the NIRA Act were worked out.

The district engineer, Maj. Fred W. Herman, used newspaper announcements to inform the public that work on the locks and dams at Winfield and Gallipolis would be subject to the rules of the Public Works Administration (PWA), which was charged with implementing the NIRA Act. Accordingly, the laborers required by the contractors would be secured through the U.S. Employment Service. The government would employ the men, who would work under contract for the contractor, who in turn would not be authorized to seek labor on the open market. This requirement applied to all projects that were supported by New Deal funding.[8] Col. George Spalding telegraphed the district engineer on September 9, 1933, informing him of designations for skilled, semi-skilled, and unskilled classes of labor, so that there would be no confusion over minimum wage rates.[9] J. S. Miller, the vice president of Dravo Contracting Company, wrote to the district engineer informing him that the company's executives had accepted the president's blanket agreement, and would attempt to conform to the terms of the National Industrial Recovery Act, with the understanding that they would be reimbursed for the increased hourly rates it required. In the case of the Marmet Dam project, all of the workers were put on a thirty-hour week while their hourly wages were increased to approximate what they had formerly earned in a forty-eight-hour week. The company informed the Chief of Engineers that their agreement had been accepted and they would work under the rules established by New Deal agencies.[10]

There was some public confusion regarding the status of the Marmet and London projects, which had gotten underway before the passage of the National Industrial Recovery Act. In order to clarify the situation, the district engineer wrote to the Charleston Building Trades Council informing them that the Dravo company, in its work at London and Marmet, was not subject to the terms of the National Industrial Recovery Act. Nevertheless, the company had agreed to the eight-hour law at Marmet;

at London, it accepted both the eight-hour law and the thirty-hour work-week. Any information that the Corps of Engineers had regarding wages at these two sites had been supplied by the contractor, and they could not insist that Dravo furnish such information. However, the work at both Winfield and Gallipolis would come under the terms of the NIRA Act, and the contractor had to furnish a list of wages to be paid as part of its bid for the job. It was not expected that bids would be opened until October 17.[11] The Huntington District had secured separate funding for clearing the banks of the pool above Marmet. In this case, men working on this contract came under the regulation of the U.S. Department of Labor, who required information on wage rates, hours worked, and other information to insure that the district was abiding by the regulations of the Public Works Administration.[12]

The Dravo Contracting Company attempted, in good faith, to work under the new regulations established by the Public Works Administration.[13] They noted, however, that it was impossible to secure dependable operators or engine men for the cranes and derrick boats at both Gallipolis and Winfield. Thus, the company requested that these skilled men be allowed to work more than thirty hours per week. If approved, the operators or engine men could work two five-hour shifts, or ten hours per day. It was the company's understanding that the eight-hour law did not apply in the cases of skilled men, but that they would work according to the established wage rates.[14]

The eight-hour law was strictly enforced. In May 1934, in anticipation of a major flood, the Dravo company extended the working hours of a number of their employees in order to secure the work site and minimize any damage caused by flooding. In fact, although the floods did not overtop the cofferdams, water rose to less than a foot below the cofferdam elevation. The district engineer defended the company's action as a case of good judgment and recommended that penalties prescribed by the law not be imposed in this case. The division engineer, Lt. Col. R. G. Powell, and the Justice Department concurred in his finding.[15]

A major labor problem arose with regard to the wage rates and the eight-hour law. In an urgent telegram to the Chief of Engineers, Major Herman argued that the thirty-hour-week rule was impractical, and he asked for permission to authorize the contractor to proceed under the construction code.[16] The telegram makes it clear that the steel erectors had walked out because they were paid the local rate of only $.80 per hour, and were restricted to working just thirty hours a week, whereas the PWA contracts called for $1.10 per hour. Major Herman noted that if the contractor were to pay the scale, he would make a claim against the government for the difference, because in his judgment, waiving the thirty-hour-a-week regulation was in the best interest of the government. The request was denied by General Pillsbury, Assistant Chief Engineer, but after reviewing the facts, General Markham, Chief of Engineers, agreed with Major Herman and gave him authority to institute the forty-hour week on this contract.[17]

Acting on behalf of the Attorney General, Joseph B. Keenan approved the recommendation of the District Engineer that no action was needed on the violation of the eight-hour law in connection with the flooding on the Kanawha River. In a similar emergency on August 22, 1934, a foreman with his crew of five men was ordered to work until 9:30 P.M. to complete the installation of a Stoney gate valve. Finding that the job could not be completed in the time estimated, the foreman authorized the men to work an additional two hours. He was advised that he would be discharged for breaking the eight-hour law, despite the fact that he had held the men over for reasons of safety. The foreman requested that he pay a fine and not be discharged. His request was honored and he was fined twenty-five dollars, which represented a good portion of his weekly wage.[18]

In an effort to discourage men from working overtime, the Dravo company discharged W. H. Muck, who worked two and a half hours overtime while assisting a welder making some repairs on the towboat *Sewickly*. In the subsequent investigation, the contractor was exonerated and no charges of criminal negligence were pursued.[19]

At the end of the London and Marmet projects, the Dravo Corporation submitted a summary of the total hours of labor involved in completing Marmet Lock B, the Marmet Roller Gate Dam, and the London Lock B and Roller Gate Dam. It should be noted that Lock A at both sites, undertaken by the General Contracting Corporation, is not represented in these numbers:

MARMET LOCK B

Man hours at site of work	317,192
Man hours at Neville Island Shops	
[on the Ohio River downstream from Pittsburgh]	27,006
Total	344,198

MARMET ROLLER GATE DAM

Man hours at site of work	472,183
Man hours at Neville Island Shops	141,333
Total	613,516

LONDON LOCK "B" AND ROLLER GATE DAM

Man hours at site of work	771,483
Man hours at Neville Island Shops	161,662
Total	933,145[20]

With the completion of the projects at London and Marmet, activity shifted to the Winfield and Gallipolis locks and dams. An article in the Huntington, West Virginia, *Herald Dispatch* of August 3, 1935, reported that bids on the construction of the operations building at Gallipolis would be opened on the following Monday. A total of 601 men were employed on the locks and 352 on the dams. Relief laborers, 250 men, were employed as direct-hired labor by the Huntington District for clearing the banks of the river above the dam. This was a total of nearly 550 relief laborers employed directly by the district during 1935. A total of 160 workers from the relief rolls started in mid-August at Point Pleasant, the confluence of the Great Kanawha River with the Ohio River, and worked their way upstream to the Winfield lock and dam. An additional 175 men were also involved in clearing operations at the Winfield site. According to the National Relief Agency, workers from adjoining counties in West Virginia and Ohio could be employed to work on the Gallipolis locks and dam. This distribution of workers caused some concern, and complaints were filed about the percentage of workers employed from each of the states.[21]

The hiring of labor directly by the Corps was an alternative to having certain projects undertaken by contract. The Huntington District office on December 21, 1934, outlined the work to be done by hired labor: clearing banks at both Gallipolis and Winfield pool, installing a permanent lock gate at London Locks, and undertaking a flowage survey for the Winfield and Gallipolis pools. A number of additional projects in the district were not associated with the locks and dams. These included surveys and borings of the Bluestone Reservoir and site clearing at the Bluestone, Big Bend, and Clendenin Reservoirs.[22]

NIRA policy required newly hired relief workers to undergo a physi-

Preparing lock foundation at Winfield locks and dam. U.S. Engineer Office, Huntington, W.V., June 23, 1934, file W.L. 158.

cal examination. In the clearing operations on the Gallipolis pool, 163 men were examined, 45 of whom were rejected for medical reasons; 9 were discharged with no reason given, and 29 quit. For clearing work on the Kanawha River, a total of 229 men reported for work, and of these 52 were rejected as unfit, 5 were discharged, and several quit. It appeared that many of the relief workers were unable to take the discipline required by NIRA regulations and the supervision of the Corps of Engineers. In a letter written October 1, 1935, G. A. Sisson, the assistant engineer, made a plea to the district office for additional men to complete the projects undertaken by direct labor.[23]

In the summer of 1935, with both the Winfield and Gallipolis projects underway, authorities in Washington called upon the Corps to expedite the work so that it could be completed in sixteen months, as the New Deal regulations required. The district engineer assured the Chief of Engineers on August 20, 1935, that all of the relief funds at the Gallipolis Dam would likely be expended within the sixteen-month limit. Furthermore, nearly all aspects of the project then underway, including work undertaken by direct labor, would be completed within the sixteen-month period. The only exceptions at Gallipolis were the removal of the old wicket locks and dams above the town, the purchase of flowage easements, and construction of the auxiliary lock sill. At Winfield, however, the work could not be completed in the sixteen-month period without additional funding. The Dravo Contracting Company estimated that it would require a $193,000 supplement. The district engineer stated, "The estimate submitted and breakdown thereof are manifestly inequitable, will probably not accomplish the expedition desired, and are therefore totally unacceptable to the United States."[24] This issue was resolved by the district engineer, to the effect that the Winfield Dam should continue under the contract as written, without modification. It was also recommended that additional funds be secured before October 6, 1936, so that the Winfield Dam could be completed even if the War Department were to lose the unexpended work-relief funds, and also so that flowage easements could be acquired.

It was not only the eight-hour limit that was to cause the contractor considerable difficulties in scheduling work, but also the requirement that 90 percent of the workers be secured through the Federal Employment Office from the relief rolls. On July 2, 1936, J. S. Miller, president of Dravo Corporation, wrote to the district engineer seeking information on the "90% rule" since he intended to bid on the remaining contract at Winfield.[25] Capt. C. T. Hunt, Executive Officer to the district, replied to Dravo's letter on July 8, 1935, stating that the rule would be enforced with some modification in the beginning, when the 90 percent requirement could probably not be met. This appears reasonable since Dravo staff would have to organize the project and build up their workforce at the start of the project. However, it was expected that the total number of employees would meet the 90 percent requirement over the period of the contract. The issue here was the contractor's need to hire highly skilled workers without exceeding the 10 percent limit.[26] Not content with the reply from Captain Hunt on behalf of Major Conklin, Miller wrote to General E. M. Markham, Chief of Engineers, on July 15, 1935. Miller pointed out that there were few or no skilled men, such as carpenters, ironworkers, electricians, derrickboat whirlers, and crane operators on the relief roll, and that it would be impossible to carry out the contract requirements without such skilled men. He indicated that the company would have considerable hesitancy about signing a contract that they did not think they could fulfill.[27]

In an interesting aside, Thomas E. Jeffers, of the U.S. Department of Labor, wrote to Major Conklin with regard to hiring relief workers, stating that workers from Eleanor Roosevelt's homestead at Eleanor, West Virginia, near the Winfield site, would not be eligible for work on the dam because they were already registered with the National Reemployment Office (NRO) at Point Pleasant, West Virginia, outside the jurisdiction of the office responsible for recruiting workers from the Kanawha Valley.[28]

Despite the reservations of the Dravo company executives, they did accept the contract for the Winfield Dam, and they agreed to an exception to the 10 percent rule with regard to the diesel towboat that was used for moving the floating equipment at the site and for towing dumpscows of excavated material. The company hired these crews directly, and they were not considered part of the 90 percent relief workers. They won an exception to the rule, claiming these were not part of the full-time supervisory staff.[29] The Executive Officer, Captain Hunt, wrote in regard to the 90 percent rule to the Chief of Engineers on November 4, 1935, commenting on the exception requested by the Dravo Contracting Company with regard to towboat pilots and crews. His letter states, "There appears to be considerable merit in their objections, and for that reason the letter is being forwarded to the Chief of Engineers for consideration by the Department or for reference to the Works Progress Administration."[30] The WPA granted an exception for the survey work, which included the projects undertaken by direct-hire labor. There was no indication of approval for the Dravo towboat crew exceptions. Apparently, the contractor had to proceed under a strict interpretation of the law.

It was on large public works, such as the Great Kanawha Navigation project, that minute details of the New Deal programs were first worked out. It is therefore not surprising that several of the decisions to be made raised a series of issues and prompted an extensive correspondence. Nevertheless, work proceeded according to schedule and with few accidents and no strikes. Occasional flooding caused the only delays, and thanks to close supervision the work was of high quality and has proven to be durable over more than a half-century of operation.

Land Acquisition

The acquisition of land for a reservoir project, such as the Tygart Dam under construction in West Virginia during this time, involved far more property than was required for construction of the locks and dams on a navigable river. Land was acquired at the location of Locks and Dam 2, whereas flowage easements were obtained elsewhere along the main banks. The division engineer in St. Louis sent an endorsement to the Chief of Engineers in Washington on September 16, 1933:

Flowage easements have not been acquired over any of the properties fronting on the Mainstream of the Kanawha River because the new pool elevation does not exceed what is considered the ordinary high water mark of the Kanawha River. The United States has the right, in the interest of navigation to occupy and use that portion of the bed of the stream lying and being below the line of ordinary high water mark without charge or obligation for the injuries sustained thereby. The injuries resulting from such use and occupancy are consequential, for which the United States is not liable.[31]

A case in point was the claim of R. W. Harvey of Belle, West Virginia, who requested in advance of the London pool being flooded compensation for possible damage to his property as a result of the new dam. It was pointed out that his house was below the level of the normal pool for the new dam and the sewer connected to his house was even lower. The Corps of Engineers did not perceive an obligation to provide for damages despite the fact that he appealed to Senator M. M. Neely, who referred the matter to the Chief of Engineers.[32] Harvey's property was in a small, unorganized village, which contained forty-three dwellings, all of which would be affected by the flooding of the sewers that would result from the increase in pool elevation. The Chief of Engineers estimated that the provision of suitable bank protection in front of this village would cost $20,000 and, in addition, $40,000 would be needed to install sewers and raise basements to prevent damage. In December General Markham wrote to Senator Neely with this information. The information was supplied by Lt. Col. E. L. Daley, who informed the Chief of Engineers that a thorough investigation was underway, and the cost of remediation might be included under part of the Public Works Administration construction program, or possibly under the Federal Navigation project.[33]

It was not only R. W. Harvey but apparently most of the property owners on tributaries affected by the ten-foot increase in pool level who were regarded by the Corps of Engineers as unreasonable. Therefore, on August 11, 1933, condemnation proceedings were undertaken for thirty-seven parcels of land. The list of affected properties mentions not only the names of the property owners but also each owner's offer and the U.S. appraisal. In many cases, it appears excessive amounts were offered. Elizabeth Davis and H. G. Skaggs offered $2,050, for example, but the appraised value was $315. Not only were individuals involved but also owners of commercial and religious property. The Montgomery Baptist Church offered $1,550 against an appraised value of $50. It was recommended, therefore, by the district engineer, Maj. Fred W. Herman, that all thirty-seven of these properties be acquired by condemnation.[34]

In an important public notice, the district engineer stated that the flowage rights were simply the right to flood lands, but the title would remain with the present owners. With the completion of the projects expected early in the spring of 1934, pool levels would be raised. This operation would be carried out "even though the purchase or condemnation of easements is not completed" since court orders authorizing such a procedure were expected to be completed before the pools were raised.[35] Despite this statement, the Sharples Solvent Corporation refused to agree to a set price and expected the government to go to condemnation proceedings. Until they received compensation, they would not allow the government to flood their property or damage any of their equipment. One of the issues at stake was tanks located in the expected flood zone, which would probably float out of the ground since they were buoyant unless they were completely filled. The company had called in their lawyers and expected the court to deal directly with them. The Attorney General directed the Secretary of War, George H. Dern, in a letter dated November 9, 1933, to proceed with condemnation of 127 tracts of land located in Kanawha County.[36] The largest acreage, 117 parcels of land, was held by the Quincy Coal Company. In settlement of the dispute, commissioners were appointed by the District Court to review the condemnation cases. In the case of Quincy Coal and numerous other private landowners, the amounts were established and the condemnation proceedings completed.[37]

The Corps of Engineers had need of approximately 4.4 acres of land at the abutment end of the London Dam for storage of the emergency bulkheads, riprap protection of the landward end of this storage area, construction of a head wall and drain, and a steel sheet pile cutoff wall.

Negotiations continued. The government reduced the amount of land it was seeking to 3.2 acres and offered the Chesapeake and Ohio Railway the sum of $3,000.[38] This price was confirmed by the Attorney General in July 1933.[39]

Since the lock, dam, and ultimately the power station were built within the banks of the river, it might initially appear that there would be no difficulties with regard to land acquisition. But the whole point of the government's action was to obtain flowage rights on the tributaries rather than land, as it was obliged to do in the case of reservoir construction.

On March 30, 1933, the Chesapeake and Ohio Railway submitted a formal offer to the Corps of Engineers to sell 3.2 acres at the abutment end of the dam. The acquisition of this property would permit the construction of the hydroelectric power generation station. The offered price was $3,000.[40]

Condemnation proceedings dragged on well into 1935. On May 2, 1935, the *Montgomery News* reported that hearings would be held in Charleston involving thirty-six pieces of land lying between London and Boomer, with a total area of seventy-nine acres. These parcels were owned by individuals, a significant number of coal companies, and the Montgomery Baptist Church. Because it was not expected that the dam would be put into operation before 1936, there did not seem to be any urgency in settling these claims.[41]

Long after the completion of the project, Congress passed a bill allowing the Secretary of War to transfer to the town of Marmet approximately 4.38 acres on the west side of the Kanawha River at Marmet Lock and Dam 2. This bill was vetoed by President Roosevelt.[42]

By 1940 the Corps of Engineers had apparently softened its view in the matter of easements. Its new position was stated in a memorandum dated November 30, 1940.[43] The Corps was now willing to enter into flowage easements on land adjoining the river if such land were capable of being used for agriculture and if flood waters would damage crops. The Corps was apparently willing, according to letters dated March 2, 1934, and March 2, 1935, and addressed to the office of the Chief of Engineers, to offer compensation for the new pool levels that would permanently flood areas between the new dams above Charleston, thus injuring and destroying values assessed for this property. However, the compensation did not include the cost of erosion protection of land at the higher pool level. The issue here was the claim by a number of landowners that raising the pool levels caused excessive erosion of the river bank, thus damaging their properties. The district engineer stated, "Erosion is occurring along the main banks. It is impossible, however, to separate the damage caused by the high stages of flow from that caused by saturation and wind and boat wave action at the new pool level. Evidence not conclusive, but fact that most of the erosion occurred during abnormally high water of 1939 and very little during normal high water period in 1940, supports the contention that the change in pool levels was not the proximate cause of the damage. *No change in present policy seems warranted.*"[44]

The division engineer, however, in endorsing the district engineer's position, suggested that some modification in the present settlement policy was required, since he concluded that the damage at Winfield pool was due to the raising of the pool level. He cautioned, however, that such an action should not provide an opportunity to reopen cases that were already settled, as that might give rise to further complaints. It should be noted that the district engineer reported that the settlement proposed by the division engineer would increase the cost from $22,000 to $176,000, if applied along the main banks of the Kanawha River. The locks and dam site at Winfield would increase this amount to $322,000. He also reported that if this procedure were applied to London, Marmet, and Gallipolis, the total would be $1.3 million. He concluded that the settlement should be restricted to the Winfield pool only, although this would not preclude other claims being made at a later date.

As in the case of many citizen claims against the government, political pressure was brought to bear on the subject when Congressman Joe L. Smith wrote to Louis A. Johnson, the Assistant Secretary of War, calling his attention to the problem of his constituents who resided or owned property along the river west of Charleston.[45] Although it is not clear that this letter had any part in modifying the Corps of Engineers' position with regard to flowage easements on the banks of the Kanawha River, it may well have influenced their decision in this matter. The accession of land associated with the Marmet site dates back as early as September 5, 1933, when the district engineer recommended that a tract of land in the amount of 23.49 acres be acquired through condemnation, land that would be necessary for the construction of the hydroelectric power station, the dam, and locks.[46]

The city of Dunbar made a formal offer to release the Corps of Engineers from damage and to convey to the United States easements at the river ends of ten streets and alleys along the Kanawha River. The city's offer for $30,000 was close to the U.S. appraisal of $29,000. The offer was approved, and payments were made under the River and Harbor Act of July 1937.[47] In the case of both Winfield and Gallipolis, there were a limited number of tributaries flowing into either the Great Kanawha or the Ohio River, and for this reason virtually all of the easement claims were on the banks of the Kanawha and Ohio. A situation developed when the Corps modified its position with regard to flowage rights on these two rivers, originally claiming that the pool level did not exceed the height of the banks of the river and therefore the government was exonerated from any claims. It was apparent that the easiest way to solve this problem was to negotiate easements for flowage without purchasing the land. Such easements would protect the government from any future claims. This procedure was then followed in the case of all four locks and dams.

On June 1, 1939, the town of South Charleston wrote to Senator M. M. Neely, expressing general dissatisfaction with the attitude of the district office in Huntington with regard to claims for property damage, both public and private, associated with the increased pool levels resulting from construction of the Winfield Dam. Responding to the claims, the Corps acknowledged that it was obligated to provide compensation, even though the damage was within the river banks.[48] In connection with these claims, W. M. Dickinson wrote the President of the United States July 9, 1940, stating that he had been unjustly treated and ignored in regard to damage to his properties along the banks of the Kanawha River in South Charleston. He wrote, "Before you refer this letter to the Army Engineers 'for further consideration' I would like to mention that I am a Democrat and firmly believe in and support the present leaders of the Democratic Party. I would very happy to have the privilege of voting for you again if it is your intention to be the Democratic candidate for the coming election. I would like to mention that I am a World War veteran."[49]

As far as the historical record has shown, the public and private pleas for compensation went unrewarded. The district engineer, Major Conklin, wrote to the Chief of Engineers on December 22, 1936, noting that as a result of the new position on flowage acquisitions, additional money would be needed for the new Winfield and Gallipolis pools.[50] A staggering total of $3.8 million was itemized as follows:

Highways	800,000
Railroads	1,282,000
Industrial plants, sewers, utilities, & misc	580,000
Lands	728,000
Negotiations, including titles	487,000
Total	3,877,000

As stated earlier, land acquisition for reservoirs is a much larger and more complicated situation. Nevertheless, the acquisition of flowage easements and property necessary for the construction of the four locks and dams consumed a considerable amount of administrative time and significantly increased the total cost of the overall project.

CHAPTER TEN

Hydroelectric Power Generation

A Drive for Power

In a demonstration of great expectations, the *Montgomery News* on April 27, 1933, proclaimed "Fayette County has one of world's greatest hydroelectric projects. Foundation for a vast steel industry run wholly by electric power, now being laid, will make the Montgomery Community a miniature Niagara Falls."[1] This announcement concerned the completion of work begun in 1929 by the Electro-Metallurgical Company at Hawks Nest on the New River, above the falls of the Kanawha. There had been much interest for more than two decades in the possibility of hydroelectric power generation on several of the tributaries of the Kanawha River. This interest followed a national trend for hydroelectric power generation, in which the federal government played a role in connection with navigation improvements wherever feasible.[2]

The Hawks Nest hydroelectric power dam was not the first on a tributary of the Great Kanawha. The same company had earlier thrown a dam across the Kanawha River at the falls, so that the local inhabitants were fully aware of the possibilities of power generation. From the beginning, it was clear the federal government was interested in power development, but only in a way that would not interfere with navigation on various waterways.[3] A series of congressional acts brought the federal government into the realm of electric-power generation on multipurpose dams and on navigable waterways. It was the report of 1926, commonly referred to as the 308-309 Documents, that required the Corps of Engineers to undertake a comprehensive program of surveys and explorations of navigable waterways nationwide. In Document 309 of the same 1926 report, the raison d'être for these investigations was clearly stated:

There are evidently two principal purposes for which investigations of this nature would be useful, either for the preparation of plans for improvement to be undertaken by the federal government alone or in connection with private enterprise or to secure adequate data to insure that waterway developments by private enterprise would fit into the general plan for the full utilization of the water resources of a stream. This department is now charged with examinations and surveys for navigation and flood control improvements, and with the construction of such projects as are authorized by Congress. In both cases of investigations, departments must by law give consideration to the development of potential water power.[4]

This was the authorization that required the Corps of Engineers to undertake a comprehensive study of the Great Kanawha River. In anticipation of the construction of the London and Marmet locks and dams, the 1927 report of the Secretary of War provided information on the Kanawha Falls power plant, indicating that it had a maximum head (a measure of water pressure) of 27.5 feet and an average of 23.5 feet, which meant out of a total potential energy of 6,000 kilowatts, they installed generators with a total capacity of 5,000. The success of this plant demonstrated that water power could be developed on the upper portion of the river with a maximum total effective head of 55 feet. Previous discharge rates suggested that for 99 percent of the time, a 5,000 kilowatt power output could be expected.

At that time much of the concern for hydroelectric power was focused on large dams, built not only for power generation but also for flood control. Where flood control was the primary concern, pool levels would change dramatically between winter and early summer, and there was a noticeable change in power generation depending upon the season. In the winter, the pool would be lowered to provide capacity for the expected spring floods. During the spring and summer, the pool would gradually be filled to provide for low-water augmentation. Since the Corps of Engineers considered these dams an essential part of navigation, power generation at flood-control dams took lower priority not only to flood control but also to low-water augmentation in late summer and early autumn.

The situation was quite different with regard to locks and dams built for navigational purposes. Here it was highly desirable that pool levels be maintained at a constant elevation as much as possible, so that, in the case of the Great Kanawha River, a nine-foot channel could be maintained for navigation throughout the year. Although power generation also had secondary priority in this case, the private power companies found the prospect of a continuous source of water at a virtually constant head to be highly desirable. Even though the head was low, a significant amount of power could be generated at each of the proposed locks and dams. The report also indicated that there was a market in the Kanawha Valley for the electricity generated.[5]

The Chief of Engineers' 1933 annual report to Congress was not nearly as sanguine about power generation at the proposed Winfield and Gallipolis locks, in part because of the frequent backwater from the Ohio and high water on the Kanawha, or a combination of these two, which would have reduced the effective head for power development at Point Pleasant, where the lowest dam on the Kanawha was proposed. In the case of the dams at Winfield and at Gallipolis on the Ohio, sufficient head would be available for power development for a large portion of the year, but the district engineer did not feel they could be considered to be primary power-development sites. He, therefore, did not feel that the benefits obtained from power generation at Gallipolis or Winfield should be considered in the benefit-cost studies for each of these dams. Nevertheless, a power plant was installed at Winfield, as well as at London and Marmet, but no power-generation facilities were provided in the Gallipolis locks and dam.

From 1927 to 1935, the Corps of Engineers was in an unusual position in being allowed, for the first time, to consider flood control and electric-power-generation dams, but only in terms of their benefits to navigation. For example, Tygart Dam, completed in 1938, was justified for flood control and low-water augmentation for navigation on the Monongahela River. It was also required to provide power-generation capacity, which was never utilized. By 1935, however, the Corps of Engineers was released from this restrictive interpretation, and in that year the district engineer, Maj. Fred Herman, reported that there were attractive possibilities for hydroelectric power generation on the four locks and dams constituting the Great Kanawha Navigation system. So attractive was this possibility that a power license was pending for both London and Marmet. Considering the electrical-generating potential for the entire Kanawha watershed, the district engineer indicated that by considering the New, the Gauley, and the Kanawha Rivers, it would be possible to generate six billion kilowatt hours of electrical energy.[6]

In anticipation of power development at the new locks and dams, a new company was formed on February 24, 1932, the Kanawha Valley Power Company, a subsidiary of Appalachian Electric Power, which in turn was a subsidiary of the American Gas and Electric Company. The new company applied for a license to construct and operate power stations at both the London and Marmet navigation dams.[7] The application proposed 6,400-horsepower turbines for both locations. On February 24, 1932, the division engineer, Col. George Spalding, wrote to the Chief of Engineers concerning the proposed power stations, including the power houses and associated equipment. The colonel pointed out that the project was not essential for improving or developing the waterway, but it was highly desirable as a by-product of navigation in terms of HR Document 190.[8] A section on power development states the charges the federal government would pay.

In March 1932, Lt. Col. John J. Kingman wrote to Spalding in St. Louis to request information on the average static head of water to be used in calculating the power capacity for the London and Marmet dams. This was not only essential engineering information but would be used to establish the annual rent charge to the power company for use of the site. Spalding replied on April 9, 1932, stating that 80 million kilowatt hours would be available per year at Marmet, and since the London facilities had the same head and same equipment, their annual charges would be levied against the power company on the basis of the estimated power generated.[9] The Chief of Engineers wrote to the chairman of the Federal Power Commission (FPC) on April 14, 1932, indicating that their detailed study had determined that the annual charges should be $38,000.[10]

With their license still pending, the power company hired F. W. Scheidenhelm, a consulting engineer from the well-known firm of Mead and Scheidenhelm of New York City. Scheidenhelm, in conference with Major Herman and General Pillsbury, the Assistant Chief of Engineers, established essential understandings regarding the Corps' construction work at the London and Marmet dams and the building of the power stations. For example, the construction operations of the power company would be conducted under the supervision of the district engineer in Huntington. Further, the Corps of Engineers would see to it that an upper wing wall, consisting of a combination of steel piling cells and diaphragms, would be left in place to act as a cofferdam for the power-station construction. When the project was completed, the steel sheet piling would be retrieved at the expense of the licensee and delivered to the Corps of Engineers. If the licensee did not perform in a satisfactory manner, the district engineer could terminate the work.

In addition, the power company was responsible for preventing damage from erosion of the banks, either downstream from the dams or within the limits of the power station fore-bays; further, it would defend all suits brought on account of any damages caused during their construction. The power company was to be exonerated, however, in the case of fire, floods, epidemics, quarantine restrictions, strikes, freight embargoes, unusually severe weather, or other delays that would prevent a timely completion of the contract.[11] At the time negotiations were going on, it was estimated that construction costs for the two power stations would be $3.1 million. Frank R. McNinch, acting chair of the Federal Power Commission, wrote to General Brown on August 19, 1932, requesting information on the relationship between the expenditures to be made by the United States and the Kanawha Valley Power Company. He indicated that until this information was available, he would be unable to issue a license.

A year later, on October 31, 1933, Scheidenhelm again wrote a report estimating the cost of a modern steam electric station, compared with hydroelectric power generation. He estimated that $298,900 would be the annual value compared to a cost of $270,000 for generating the electricity, leaving a net income of $28,900. His estimate was based on the agreement that the power company would provide gratis all of the power needed for navigation purposes at both London and Marmet.[12]

Finally, on January 16, 1934, the Federal Power Commission issued a license through the authority of a congressional act of June 10, 1920, to the Kanawha Valley Power Company to undertake the construction and operation of hydroelectric power stations at London and Marmet. This license was to be in effect for fifty years.[13] Thereafter, Frank McNinch, chair of the Federal Power Commission, wrote to the Chief of Engineers, General Markham, setting out the requirements of the FPC, including cost accounting, official reports, information on the use of equipment, and other details since the Corps of Engineers would supervise the construction.[14] Later McNinch wrote again to General Markham indicating that the license required the construction of the plants to be completed by December 1, 1935.[15]

The Corps of Engineers was concerned about the storage of light-weight bulkheads, which were used to close off one or more bays in the dam and allow repairs to be made in the dry. The lineal descendants of the stop logs used on earlier canals, these bulkheads needed to be readily accessible in case of emergency. It was clear they could not be stored on the other end of the dam because of the two locks between the end of the dam and the bank. A separate contract was signed on July 16, 1934, for bulkhead storage; some were to be kept under the service bridge. It was the responsibility of the licensee to provide appropriate hangers and other devices necessary to store these bulkheads so that they would not interfere with the power station at the end of the dam.[16]

Work commenced on June 10, 1934. In mid-September the chair of the Federal Power Commission wrote to the company indicating that the progress as of that point was not what might reasonably have been expected. He modified his criticism by saying that both plants should be completed by December 1, 1935, if the work was prosecuted with reasonable diligence.[17] The contract allowed additional time in the event of flooding or natural disasters. There was a rise in the river on November 28, which made it necessary to flood the cofferdams at the Marmet and London power-house sites on the morning of November 30; normal work did not resume until December 15. Therefore, the division engineer granted the construction company eleven days' extra time at London and fifteen days at Marmet.[18]

The first of the new series of locks and dams at Marmet was finished on March 10, 1934, and the pool began to rise to its design level.[19] The London locks and dam were completed months later. During 1934 work was underway on the construction of power stations at both of these locations.[20] The contract was awarded to Boscoe and Ritchie of Ravenswood, West Virginia, and nearly a hundred men began work on Tuesday, June 5, 1934. It was estimated, at the time, that 150,000 yards of earth had to be excavated, together with 10,000 yards of rock at Marmet and just 200 yards of rock at London. At the same time the power equipment had been ordered from various manufacturers in the country, and the concrete design was proceeding.[21]

During the New Deal, employment was a paramount concern. It is not surprising, then, that the Commissioner of Labor for the state of West Virginia, C. L. Jarrett, wrote to the district engineer, Major Conklin, inquiring about labor provisions for the construction of power stations at

An early view of power station excavation at London locks and dam. U.S. Engineer Office, Huntington, W.V., Nov. 15, 1934, file L-10.

Construction of power house and draft tube outlets. U.S. Engineer Office, Huntington, W.V., May 25, 1935, file L-33.

Progress view of London powerhouse during formwork on the landward end of the construction. U.S. Engineer Office, Huntington, W.V., March 8, 1935, file L-29.

General view of construction featuring intake draft tubes. U.S. Engineer Office, Huntington, W.V., Dec. 28, 1934, file L-22.

Detailed view of downstream wall of powerhouse with draft tube outlets at Marmet. U.S. Engineer Office, Huntington, W.V., July 8, 1935, file 45.

Marmet and London.[22] Conklin replied two days later that the license issued by the Federal Power Commission did not contain any provision regarding labor under the National Industrial Recovery Administration Act (NIRA). Since it was not a Corps project but only supervised by officers of the Corps of Engineers, Conklin suggested that Jarrett write to the NIRA compliance director in Charleston for clarification. None of the subsequent documents reveal that any special requirement was placed on the Kanawha Valley Power Company with regard to employment of workmen, and especially their wages under the Davis Bacon Act. This act, still in force, establishes prevailing wage rates for all federal construction projects. Since this part of the navigation project was being constructed with private funding, government regulations on labor rates and hours apparently did not apply.

At the beginning of 1935, Frank McNinch, chair of the Federal Power Commission, wrote to General Markham, the Chief of Engineers, requesting a progress report on both of the power stations. Apparently, the commission was concerned as to whether the contractor could finish both

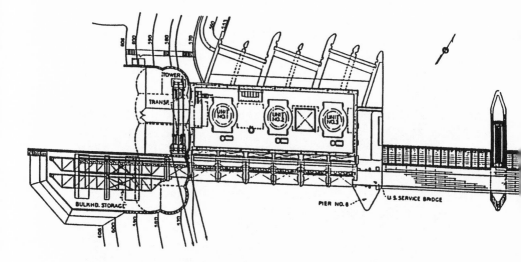

General layout of the Marmet powerhouse. Sporn and Peterson, "London and Marmet," 82.

stations by the end of the year, as stipulated in the contract. Although progress at London had been delayed because of high water, the division engineer felt that both contracts could be completed on time.[23]

With work beginning at Winfield in 1935, the Kanawha Valley Power Company applied for a license to construct a third power station there. The division engineer wrote to the Chief of Engineers on February 12, 1935, giving details of the existing river conditions, including the locks and dams, as well as a list of proposed storage reservoirs to control flooding on the Kanawha and its tributaries. The report also established an annual rental at Winfield of $48,000, a figure that was 1.5 percent of the original cost of the project. In a more mundane vein, the report indicated that the U.S. government would be responsible for disposing of trash by the operation of the flap roller gate located in one of the bays. In addition, permission was granted for the power company to establish a boom in front of its intakes to collect trash and prevent foreign materials from damaging the turbines.[24]

F. W. Scheidenhelm, the consulting engineer for the power company, pointed out that there was, as he termed it, "an economic inferiority" associated with the Winfield project, compared to the London and Marmet power stations. He noted that, in spite of the 25 percent additional capacity at Winfield, the amount of water available was controlled by the roller gates and power station at London; very little additional water entered the Kanawha River between the London and Winfield locks from tributary streams. The consultant's concern was that the higher cost of construction at Winfield could not be matched by increased power capacity during periods of low flow. The company wished to assure that it could generate electrical power more cheaply than the coal-fired stations could.[25]

In an interim construction report to the Federal Power Commission, the division engineer indicated that both the London and Marmet power plants would be ready for operation on December 1, 1935, as specified in the license. In addition, both sites would complete final cleanup by January 1, 1936.[26]

The Kanawha Valley Power Company submitted a claim in the amount of $55,320.93, in connection with the construction of a power-generating building. The claim entailed a hearing before the Federal Power Commission in Washington on September 10, 1935. A year after the claim was submitted, on February 4, 1936, the Federal Power Commission upheld the company. This represents the only claim by the power company against the federal government. All other dealings were between the company and the contractor and suppliers of equipment for the power station.[27]

The power company completed the work at London and Marmet by the end of 1935. On April 28, 1936, a license was issued to this company for the construction of a similar power station at the Winfield site.[28] In all of the work on the Great Kanawha Navigation, the government was always concerned about completion of contract work on time and with a minimum of claims. F. W. Scheidenhelm, the consulting engineer, turned the tables on the government when he wrote on September 9, 1937, that the work at the Winfield project would be completed and ready for operation by October 1. He pointed out that the company had a considerable investment in this project and needed to generate power at the earliest opportunity. For this reason, he appealed to the Corps of Engineers to raise the pool to its final elevation as soon as possible since they could not generate power economically at lower water levels.[29]

It was clear that the Corps of Engineers was caught in an unusual situation. The district engineer responded on October 7, 1937, that the contract specified that the work would be completed and ready for operation on January 1, 1938. (But this date was in error, he noted, since the statement in the license indicated completion of the project by March 1, 1938. The letter then quotes article 6 of the contract as a point of reference.) Although the Winfield locks and dam had been completed on Au-

U.S. Engineer Office
Huntington, W. Va.
Lock No. 3 (London)
Sept. 20, 1935
L - 35

U.S. Engineer Office
Huntington, W. Va.
Lock No. 3 (London)
Sept. 20, 1935
L - 37

General view of Marmet hydropower plant under construction. U.S. Engineering Office, Huntington, W.V., April 15, 1935, file M-36.

gust 20, 1937, the pool had not been raised to its operating level because of negotiations with the state, the railroad, and other private interests whose property would be affected by the new Winfield pool. These parties expected that the water level would not be raised until January 1, 1938. It was estimated that an additional $55,000 would be necessary to compensate owners if the pool was raised before the agreed date.[30]

Leon Fuquay, Secretary of the Federal Power Commission, wrote to the Kanawha Valley Power Company on November 6, 1937, insisting that they keep adequate records of their operation so that annual charges could be determined based upon water usage.[31] In a subsequent letter to the Corps of Engineers, F. W. Scheidenhelm, writing on behalf of the power company, acknowledged that his earlier statement about completion by January 1, 1938, was, in fact, in error, and the date was established in the

(Opposite, top) Nearly completed power station at London locks and dam. U.S. Engineering Office, Huntington, W.V., Sept. 20, 1935, file L-35.
(Opposite, bottom) Interior view of power station during installation of No. 2 turbine, London locks and dam. U.S. Engineering Office, Huntington, W.V., Sept. 20, 1935, file L-37.

Close-up of concrete work adjacent to an intake tube. U.S. Engineering Office, Huntington, W.V., Feb. 24, 1937, file W-43.

license as March 1, 1938. He complained that the company had been urged to complete its work as early as possible, and had no prior knowledge that the pool would not be raised until the locks and dams were completed. He was pleased to note that the pool level had been raised from 556 to 558 feet. The company would attempt to operate at that elevation, unfavorable as it was.[32] At the completion of the Winfield project, the final cost was $1,903,307.39, as reported on April 30, 1938.[33] Based on this agreed sum, the Corps of Engineers was prepared to accept a claim by the Kanawha Power Company in the amount of $83,286.73, for interest during periods of suspension caused by inclement weather.[34] This appears to be the final settlement on this project.

Construction of the power stations at all three locks and dams was carried out by Boscoe and Ritchie of Ravenswood, West Virginia. The London and Marmet installations could be considered to be twin structures and the Winfield a near relative. Construction at all three sites was undertaken in a similar manner. Riprap that had been placed by the government on the downstream slopes to protect the banks was removed. A cofferdam of interlocking steel sheet piling was constructed; it extended

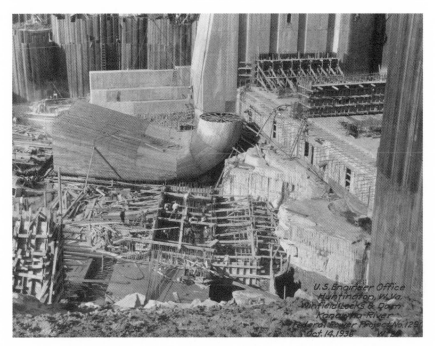

Construction of draft tubes at Winfield locks and dam, October 1936. U.S. Engineering Office, Huntington, W.V., Oct. 14, 1936, file W-20.

Completed Marmet power station. U.S. Army Corps of Engineers, Huntington District, Aug. 20, 1953, file MD-53-2.

Downstream view of completed power station at Winfield locks and dam. U.S. Army Corps of Engineers, Huntington District, Aug. 20, 1953, file WD-53-2.

from the abutment pier of the dam over to the bank so as to enclose the downstream side. The cofferdams on the upstream side had already been constructed by the contractor building the dam. Power equipment was used for the excavation, both drag-line and clam-shell buckets. At all three sites, the excavated material was deposited nearby for grading and filling gullies and depressions in the land.

A small, one-yard mixing plant was erected in the fore-bay area, and concrete was transported to the form work by derricks and concrete buggies. At London, a one-yard plant was augmented with "pump-crete" equipment. At all three sites, particular care was taken to obtain a very dense and durable concrete, since this area in the Middle Atlantic region is subjected to frequent cycles of freezing and thawing that have a deleterious effect on concrete. Care was taken to place the concrete by approved methods to avoid segregation of the aggregate from the cement paste.

The specifications for Class A and Class B concrete were the same for all three projects. Class A concrete had 550 pounds of cement per cubic yard, whereas Class B had only 440 pounds. Class B concrete was used for interior work and in areas not subject to frequent freeze-thaw cycles. In an attempt to secure a strong paste, water was limited to six gallons per bag of cement, which limited the slump of the plastic concrete to one and a half to three inches. (As mentioned earlier, the slump measures the stiffness of the plastic concrete. The slump is a measure of the water in the mixture and hence indirectly of the strength of the hardened concrete.) The fresh concrete was placed in layers not exceeding one and a half feet and carried out in what was known as a continuous process. Normally, the lift did not exceed eighteen feet in one continuous casting, except that height was restricted to eight feet during hot weather. The concrete was placed using vibrators as well as hand spading adjacent to the forms to secure a dense concrete free of honeycombing. Special precautions were taken to assure satisfactory construction joints between lifts. A thin layer of concrete was to be removed at the top of every lift in preparation for receiving the next continuous placing of concrete. All concrete was cured for fourteen days under continuous water spray. This was to improve not only the strength but the durability of the concrete and prevent as much as possible shrinkage cracks from developing. The result was a structure utilizing the latest techniques in concrete design and construction.

From an architectural point of view, these buildings could be described as functional or utilitarian. They had an absolute minimum of decorative features, and their purpose was "to utilize the most practical engineering idea or development regardless of whether it was old or modern, tested or new, so long as it was sound and to produce the power in the most economical and safest manner."[35]

The architecture was to reflect the engineering design of the locks and dams. A significant feature of the interior of these power stations is that the floor is located at or near the top of the generators, leaving a remarkably open bay served by an overhead crane. The bays are almost devoid of equipment except for cabinet governors and other measuring devices.

State-of-the-Art Power Stations

Since these were state-of-the-art facilities, the hydroelectric equipment deserves consideration. To the extent possible, the equipment is automatic and controlled from a remote station. Currently, the power-generation control is at Roanoke, Virginia, with only a maintenance crew assigned to each of the three stations.

Water wheels have an ancient lineage. It was not, however, until the development of the high-speed turbine by Sir Charles Parsons at the end of the nineteenth century that the era of modern turbines began. In the case of water turbines, since about 1925 efficiencies had reached 93 percent.[36] High-speed water turbines can be grouped into two general types. One is the impulse wheel, which converts the kinetic energy of a high-velocity jet into mechanical energy when the jet impinges upon the buckets of the wheel.

The Pelton wheel is a classic example of the impulse turbine. It found wide application in cases where there was a high hydraulic head of water, in a number of cases in excess of 800 feet. Since the head of water available at the navigation dams was in the neighborhood of 20 to 30 feet, the impulse turbine is not suitable for low-head applications. In the earlier wicket-dam system of twin locks and dams, the lifts were in the neighborhood of 8 to 10 feet and really not suitable even for low-head water turbines. Thus, the development of the three high-lift roller-gated locks and dams on the Kanawha River offered the possibility of economical power generation with low-head equipment.

The other family of hydraulic turbines is the reaction type, which converts the action of pressure and velocity into mechanical energy. Within

Cross-section through the Marmet plant showing the Kaplan turbine. Sporn and Peterson, "Design Features of the London and Marmet Hydro Developments," 84.

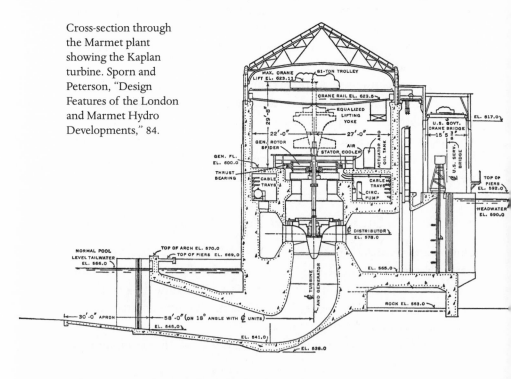

this group is the Francis or reaction type and several versions of propeller turbines. Propeller turbines, with their high speed resulting in lower-cost generators, seemed ideally suited for the low-head operations on the Great Kanawha River. Thus, propeller runners were adopted for all three locks and dams.

The fixed-blade propeller turbine is highly efficient at nearly full operating load, but the efficiency (approximately 88 percent) drops off sharply at lower loads. Thus, fixed-blade turbines should only be operated at ranges near full load or not at all.

To overcome the inherent weakness of the fixed-blade type, the adjustable-blade runners were developed. This type of runner produced nearly uniform efficiencies in excess of 90 percent for all stages of loads. The variable-pitch runner is a near relative of the variable-pitch airplane propeller. One of the leaders in the field was the Kaplan turbine, in which the pitch of the blades is controlled by a servomotor.

In a multiple-unit generating station, an efficient arrangement would be to have just one adjustable turbine and other fixed-turbine runners operating under full-load conditions only.

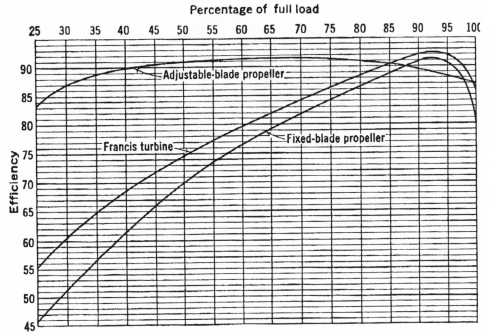

Efficiency curves for fixed- and adjustable-blade turbines. Creager and Justin, *Hydroelectric Handbook*, 833.

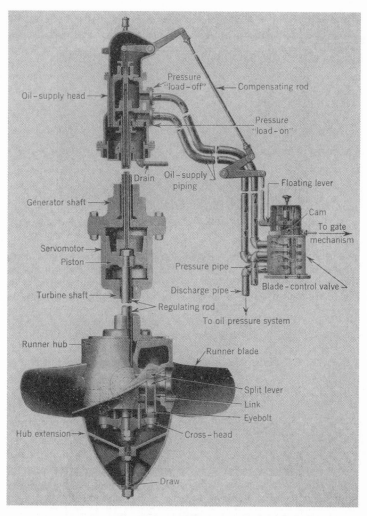

Diagrammetric view of a Smith-Kaplan turbine runner. Creager and Justin, *Hydroelectric Handbook*, 821.

At both Marmet and London, the arrangement was to install three turbine generator units at each station, with two fixed propellers and the third a Kaplan-type turbine. In fact, the adjustable-blade turbine at Marmet is one of the earliest installations of this type of equipment. The fixed-blade runner turbines have a capacity of 6,600 horsepower (hp) under a net effective head of twenty-three feet and a speed of 90 revolutions per minute (rpm). The Kaplan turbines have the same overall dimensions but a rated capacity of 7,200 hp under the same operating speed and head of water.[37]

Detail of control devices for turbines at Marmet power station. U.S. Engineering Office, Huntington, W.V., Jan. 6, 1936, file M-88.

Shortly after the Winfield station came on line, a new automatically adjusted blade-runner unit, developed by the Newport News Shipbuilding Company, replaced one of the two fixed-blade units.

While the Winfield hydroelectric station is a younger sibling of Marmet and London, it differs in important equipment details with a higher but more variable fluctuating head. At least two of the three units were to be of the adjustable-blade type. The reason for the fluctuation in head was, in part, that there are few tributaries between Marmet and Winfield on the upstream side, and on the lower side of the dam, the pool level is controlled by levels on the Ohio. Thus, Winfield, in a sense, is at the mercy of pool levels at Gallipolis and London. After a very satisfactory performance of the variable-blade turbines at London and Marmet, it was decided that all three units at Winfield would be of the adjustable-runner type. Not all of the units, however, are the same. Two feature the Kaplan type, while the third is an automatically adjustable blade system developed by Newport News Shipbuilding Company. It was this type that replaced one of the fixed-blade units at Marmet. Under a twenty-six-foot

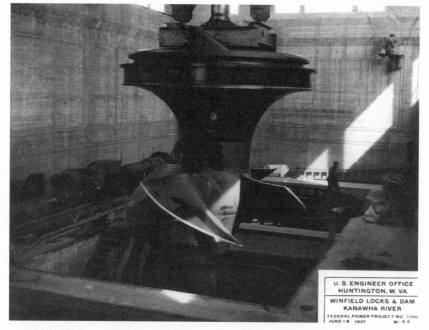

Detail of a variable-blade runner being lowered into position. U.S. Engineering Office, Huntington, W.V., June 16, 1937, file W-65.

head and a speed of 90 rpm, each of the Kaplan units developed 9,200 hp, while the Newport News Shipbuilding unit developed 9,150 hp under the same operating conditions.

The alternating-current synchronous generator, also called an alternator, delivers electricity to the transmission system by stepping up the current to a high voltage to reduce transmission losses. All of the units at all three stations deliver three-phase current. All six of the generators at Marmet and London are identical, rated at 6,000 kva, while running at 90 rpm. (The kva rating is the kilowatt output divided by the power factor.) They feature an 80-pole, 3-phase, 60-cycle unit delivering a 4,150-volt current.[38]

Unlike the turbines, the generators at various load ranges and power factors between 1 and 0.8 remain at more than 90 percent efficiency. As a result, regardless of the turbine type, all of the generators are the same at Marmet and London. The three identical generators at Winfield, although similar to the other units, developed 6,150 kva, or 150 kva more than the Marmet and London generators. These units also run at 90 rpm and feature 80-pole, 3-phase, 60-cycle generators delivering 4,150 volts.[39]

The Marmet and London power stations contain one of the first installations of the Woodward governor in a single cabinet unit. There were also actuator cabinets on the main floor, which controlled the adjustable-blade turbines.

Synchronizing is a necessary operation each time a generator comes on line, as an effort to avoid voltage drops and interruption of service. Creager and Justin identify three conditions necessary to synchronize a generator with its associated electrical system: (1) the voltage of the generator must be the same as that of the bus; (2) the frequency of the generator must be the same as the bus; (3) the phase position of the generator must be the same as the bus.[40]

Before automatic synchronization was installed, the operators at Marmet and London took between one and five minutes to synchronize the generators as they came on line. At Winfield, however, the generators were synchronized in less than one minute through special windings permitting automatic pull-in synchronization. First used at Winfield and later at Marmet and London, automatic flood-control devices were installed that were sensitive to water level changes of only four inches. These devices control the starting and stopping of selected units sequentially. As a result of its performance at Winfield, a similar device was later installed at Marmet.

The following design, construction, and equipment data are provided for Winfield and the Marmet and London hydroelectric power stations:

DESIGN, CONSTRUCTION, AND EQUIPMENT DATA
FOR MARMET AND LONDON HYDROELECTRIC POWER STATIONS[41]

Engineers and Supervisors—American Gas and Electric
    Service Corporation
Consulting Engineer—F. W. Scheidenhelm
Consulting Architect—Eddy Fairchild
General Contractors—Boscoe and Ritchie
Hydraulic Turbines—Baldwin-Southwark Corp. (I. P. Morris Div.) (2);
    Newport News Shipbuilding & Dry Dock Co. (1).
Governors—Woodward Governor Company
Alternators—General Electric Company
Exciters—Westinghouse Electric & Manufacturing Co.
Transformers and Circuit Breakers—General Electric Company;
    Westinghouse Electric & Manufacturing Co.

Auxiliary Dist. Equipment—I.T.E. Circuit Breaker Company

Automatic Switching Equip., Supervisory and Telemetering Equipment—Westinghouse Electric & Manufacturing Co.

Fire Protection—C. O. Two Fire Equipment Company

Structural Steel—Virginia Bridge and Iron Company

Head Gates, Stop Logs, and Trash Racks—Virginia Bridge and Iron Company

Cranes—Phillips & Davies, Inc.

Roof Slabs—Federal-American Cement Tile Company

Roofing—General Roofing & Air Conditioning Corp.

Cement—Diamond Portland Cement Company; Green Bag Cement Company of West Virginia; Penn-Dixie Cement Corporation

Hydraulic Lime—Riverton Lime Company

Winter-Kennedy Piezometers—Simplex Valve and Meter Company

Design, Construction and Equipment Data for Winfield[42]

Engineers and Supervisors—American Gas & Elec. Co.

Consulting Engineer—F. W. Scheidenhelm

Consulting Architect—Eddy Fairchild

General Contractors—Boscoe & Ritchie

Hydraulic Turbines—Baldwin-Southwark Corp. (I. P. Morris Div.) (2); Newport News Shipbuilding & Dry Dock Co. (4)

Governors—Woodward Governor Co.

Alternators—General Electric Co.

Exciters—Westinghouse Elec. & Mfg. Co.

Transformers—Westinghouse Elec. & Mfg. Co.

Auxiliary Switches—Delta Star Electric Co.; Westinghouse Elec. & Mfg. Co.

Automatic Equipment and Supervisory Control—Westinghouse Elec. & Mfg. Co.

Batteries—Electric Storage Battery Co.

Fire Protection—C. O. Two Fire Equipment Co.; Walter Kidde & Co.

Cranes—Phillips & Davies, Inc.

Gates—Virginia Bridge & Iron Co.

Gate Hoists—Phillips & Davies, Inc.

Stop Logs—M. H. Treadwell Co., Inc.

Trash Racks—Phillips & Davies, Inc.

Rack Rakes and Hoists—Newport News Shipbuilding & Dry Dock Co.
Structural Steel—Virginia Bridge & Iron Co.
Reinforcing Steel for Concrete—West Virginia Rail Co.; Concrete
    Steel Co.
Ventilating Equipment—Buffalo Forge Co.; Minneapolis-Honeywell Co.
Concrete Roof, Ceiling and Floor Slabs—Federal American
    Cement Tile Co.
Roof Tile—W. F. Shawver Sons Co., Inc.
Asphalt Tile Floor—David E. Kennedy, Inc.
Cement—Alpha Portland Cement Co.; Green Bag
    Cement Co. of W. Va.; Pennsylvania-Dixie Cement Corp.
Hydraulic Lime—Riverton Lime Co.
Winter-Kennedy Piezometers—Simplex Valve & Meter Co.

With the completion and operation of the Winfield Power Station, all of these installations were state of the art, incorporating many improvements and innovations. Some focused on the most economical generation of power, but other innovations were for convenience of operation or the pleasing arrangement of the components within the power station. They have served with efficiency and reliability for more than half a century. It is interesting to note that replacement lock-and-dam structures built by the Corps of Engineers on the Monongahela River did not incorporate low-head power generation, nor is there any example of such installations on any of the improved locks and dams on the Ohio River from Pittsburgh to its confluence with the Mississippi at Cairo, Illinois, although these facilities were under construction at the same time. The reason may be, in part, that these other locks and dams did not have sufficient head to be considered for power generation, although certainly the Gallipolis locks and dam could have had installations similar to those on the Great Kanawha River. Even such large flood-control dams as the Tygart, while provided with a penstock, never had generating equipment installed, although the possibility was recently considered as a joint operation between the private-power industry and the Army Corps of Engineers. Thus, hydroelectric power installations at London, Marmet, and Winfield represent an exception to the general practice of lock-and-dam building and operation by the Corps of Engineers during the New Deal period. There is currently renewed interest in power generation at a number of Corps of Engineers facilities.

Epilogue

The vision of a central waterway connecting tidewater Virginia with the Ohio River persisted for decades during the nineteenth century, first with the James River and Kanawha Canal fostered by the Commonwealth of Virginia, and subsequently with the Central Water Line endorsed by the federal government. The Central Water Line, cutting through the Appalachian Mountains, would rival the Erie Canal since it would connect with the lower reaches of the Ohio River and, indeed, the entire middle of the country drained by the Mississippi and its tributaries. It was a grand vision, never implemented, but nevertheless became a highly successful regional waterway developing the rich resources of the Kanawha Valley.

The same fate overtook the Chesapeake and Ohio Canal, which was intended to connect the Chesapeake Bay with the Ohio River at Pittsburgh. After years of struggle it finally reached Cumberland, Maryland, but went no farther. The C&O Canal became a regional carrier serving the upper reaches of the Potomac Valley and the ports of Georgetown and Alexandria. There is, however, a significant difference between a controlled river for navigation and a towpath canal. On the latter, the speed and capacity of the canal boats could not be increased, and they could not compete with the increasingly large tows plying the nation's river navigations.

With the rivermen championing open navigation during favorable stages of the river and, at the same time, clamoring for controls to ensure navigation during periods of low flow, the Corps of Engineers responded with the concept of the movable dam. The French Chanoine wicket dam was selected from many other designs as the most suitable, not only for the Great Kanawha but also for the Ohio River. The design featured an open pass over the dam when the wickets were dropped, whereas the adjacent lock was used when the wickets were erected. It was an ingenious solution and deserves to be ranked with other notable achievements of the U.S. Army Corps of Engineers in waterway engineering. With a series of ten low-lift movable dams stretching from its confluence with the Ohio River nearly a hundred miles to the falls, the Great Kanawha became the first controlled-waterway navigation in America. Now, with only the wall of Dam 5 just below the Marmet locks and dam remaining, the entire system is little remembered as historically significant. Even the leaders in building the system of dams in the years 1880–1891 are little known. Who remembers the name of Addison Scott or William P. Craighill?

In the 1920s it became apparent that the oldest dams, Nos. 4 and 5, were in an advanced state of decay and would have to be rebuilt. This justified the replacement of Locks and Dams 2–5 with two new high-lift dams and twin locks at Marmet and London. Because of the greatly increased lifts, engineering studies indicated that open navigation, made possible by movable dams, was not feasible.

Whereas the Chanoine wicket dams were a French import, the replacement dams utilized the German roller gate, which could regulate the pool levels, pass flood waters, and ensure water quality and quantity during low flows. This type of gate, however, could not provide open navigation.

One of the leading themes for historians of technology is the idea of technology transfer. The Chanoine wicket and the roller-gate dams on the Great Kanawha River provide a well-documented case study. The dams on the Great Kanawha River and the Gallipolis locks and dams utilized the roller gates exclusively. Similar structures built on the Ohio and Upper Mississippi Rivers combined bear-trap gates and Tainter gates, as well as roller gates. In addition, the Marmet Dam was the first in the nation to use roller gates for navigational purposes.

It would be difficult to characterize the architecture of the Chanoine wicket system except to say that the dams had a decidedly French accent about them. The most notable feature of the system was the wickets and associated equipment. Masonry portions of the structure were hardly visible during normal operation. The locks were of masonry design and represented a long tradition of the Corps of Engineers, who were responsible for the design and supervision of both systems.

With its towering piers and operations buildings, the second system, featuring roller gates, was in marked contrast to the wicket dams and associated locks. The piers supporting the rollers and the operations building expressed the utilitarian function of this large engineering work but with a hint of the current Art Deco style. Each of the four sites fits the surrounding landscape well. The work was executed by well-known contracting firms, notably the Dravo Corporation of Pittsburgh, under close supervision by the Huntington District of the Corps of Engineers. This system is an outstanding example of a large New Deal public works project.

The immediate result was unemployment relief, but the locks and dams have given significant long-term benefits to the Kanawha Valley. They have proved to be durable structures and have served in essentially their original condition for more than half a century. The system was built to provide a cost-effective means of moving bulk cargo, especially coal, and to a lesser extent, chemicals, along nearly one hundred miles of the Great Kanawha River. Each of the systems provided a means of exploiting the mineral resources of the valley. There was a steady increase in the tonnage passing through the locks and dams, even before the first system was finished.

The importance of the waterway is revealed by the fact that the Winfield Lock is the busiest one in the entire Corps of Engineers' system. Its heavy use has justified the construction of a new 800-foot-long by 110-foot-wide lock to handle the current and anticipated tonnage on the river. Cost-benefit studies are now underway for a similar lock at Marmet. One cannot claim the new 1,200-foot-long by 110-foot-wide lock at Gallipolis is solely the result of the commercial traffic on the Kanawha proceeding down the river, but the Kanawha tonnage has certainly been a significant factor in the decision to build the new lock, which is compatible with the upgrading of other locks on the Ohio River.

The function of the navigation dam is not to provide flood control downstream, but rather to allow excess water to pass over the crest of the dam and, thus, prevent unacceptable rises in the pool behind a particular dam.

The essence of Charles Ellet's mid-nineteenth-century scheme for flood control and low-water augmentation was to build flood-control dams on the tributaries of natural navigable rivers. By the 1920s, and until 1935, the Corps did not consider flood control part of its mandate, which was focused entirely upon navigable waterways. Their only justification for building flood-control dams was to improve navigation. Their shackles were released, however, in 1935 with an expanded mandate that included flood control.

Following the construction of the Hawk's Nest Dam on the New River by private enterprise, three Corps of Engineers flood-control dams were built—the Bluestone, Summersville, and Sutton Dams. They have successfully controlled floods in the heavily industrialized Kanawha Valley and, at the same time, augmented low flows in the late summer to maintain the nine-foot navigation channel and improve water quality in the river by dilution.

By any measure, the Great Kanawha Navigation has been one of the most successful ventures of the Corps of Engineers. Each of the two systems featured innovative designs that proved to be cost effective and environmentally sound.

Appendix A

A DESCRIPTION OF THE LOCKS AND DAMS ON THE GREAT KANAWHA NAVIGATION

The plan of both projects included twin locks and a roller-gated dam, with a powerhouse (operations building), hydroelectric generating station, and associated machinery. The architectural style is typical 1930s public-works concrete construction with a hint of Art Deco.

The London and Marmet locks include the land wall, upper and lower guide walls, river wall, upper and lower guard walls, middle wall, miter gate and emergency dam sills, and mitering gates (upper and lower). The London and Marmet dams each include sills, aprons, piers, gates, hoisting units, a service bridge, a powerhouse with necessary operating machinery, piping, and electrical work. The project also includes two guard piers above the upper guard wall.

Dams

The dams are of the non-navigable, gated-crest type, 557'-5½" in length. The dams consist of five roller gates, each 100'-3½" in length between piers, and 26' in diameter. There are four standard roller gates and one roller gate with a flap to allow for ice and debris discharge. The dams provide a 24-foot lift in the pool elevation. The roller gates are placed between five piers 14' thick and a sixth pier, 10'-6" thick, with concrete sills and aprons, and a five-span service bridge, with electric traveling bridge cranes. At the top of each pier (except pier No. 6) there is a hoisting unit, enclosed by a pier house, for operating a roller gate. The upstream nose of the piers supports five spans of K-type deck-truss bridges. A thirty-ton locomotive crane travels the top deck, and a thirty-ton bridge crane traverses the lower chord.

The standard roller gates installed at London and Marmet are gates 104'-3½" between adjusting edges (recessed), 19'-4" inside diameter, with two end sections and a series of plates connected together to form an intermediate tube section. The gates are circular and have an apron attached that rests on a sill on the upstream side of the gate. The gates are driven from one end and rise above the sill on an angle from the vertical in the downstream direction. When the gates are in a suspended position they clear the sill by 50 feet. The driven sections weigh approximately 35 tons, and the nondriven sections weigh approximately 25 tons. The approximate weight of each gate is 89 tons. The additional steel in the flap gate makes its weight 109 tons.

The roller end-sections travel in the pier recesses. In the downstream sides of the recesses are racks with teeth that engage the end-sections of the rollers, the principle being that of a rack and pinion. In the upstream side of the recess there is a contour guide which is cleared by the roller rim by an average distance of half an inch. The roller teeth on the driven end ride on the rack teeth as the roller ascends, until the apron assumes a position where it is on the downstream side of the roller, at which point the center of gravity of the roller is changed and the teeth in its end-sections ride on top of the rack teeth in the pier recesses.

The roller is raised and lowered by a hoist unit in the pier house at the top of the pier. This unit is electrically driven and consists of a series of gears that operate the lifting chain. The lifting chain or connection between the hoist and roller is made up of sections. The chain is a "triple link," which lifts or lowers the roller as a "drive chain" operating in cogs in the driven end section. The approximate weight of the chain is twenty-nine tons.

The roller gates are raised or lowered to regulate the pool. When all gates are closed and the pool is at its normal elevation, the water level will be at the tops of the rollers.

The hoisting units for the roller gates are anchored into the tops of the piers. The rollers are in all cases driven from the right end, or lock end, of the roller. They were assembled at the Dravo plant in Pittsburgh and barged down the Ohio River to the construction site. The hoisting units, after being placed, were assembled, and the movable parts such as the motors and limit switches were added. The pier houses or operating houses were then built around the units. One door in each pier house opens onto the top of the service bridge. A switch box is located in each operating house. There is one hand-control switch for operating each gate. Limit switches are used to stop automatically the motion of the gates a few inches from the top and bottom of their range of movement. There are two limit switches at each point. These were designed by Westinghouse, and consist of a horizontal, rotating worm rod that travels with the movement of the roller and trips the control switches at the limit points. A by-pass switch near the roller-control switch is used to start the roller moving again beyond the limit points. A dial near the control switch registers the feet of clearance on the roller above the sill. A pit in the upstream side of the pier below the hoist is used to provide a storage place for the lifting chain when the roller is in the suspended position.

Locks

There are two locks on the right bank at the London and Marmet sites. They parallel each other and are of gravity-type construction with concrete walls founded on rock. The upper guard walls are located on rock-filled timber cribs, and the upper guide walls rest on bearing piles. The mitering lock gates are horizontally framed, flat-type steel of single steel plates.

Lock A is the first, or riverward of the two locks, and Lock B is the second and landward lock. Both lock chambers measure 56 by 360 feet. The portion of the land wall upstream from the lock chamber is designed to act as the upper guide wall, and the wall downstream from the lock chamber serves as the lower guide wall. The length of the land wall proper is 544 feet. The upper guide wall is 510 feet long and 11 feet wide at the base, while the lower guide wall is 501 feet long and 20 feet wide at the base. An intermediate or middle wall is 624'-6" long and separates Lock A from Lock B. All of the lock walls are constructed of mass concrete founded on firm rock. The outer wall, or river wall, of Lock A supports the powerhouse (that is, the operations building) and adjoins Pier No. 1 of the dam.

The side-filling locks are provided with 8' × 10' main culverts, three 5' × 8' intake ports, 4' × 5' and 5' × 8' discharge ports and ten lateral ports. Three surge vent wells are provided in each wall to release air that might be trapped in the ports. When there is a surge, water that is vented into the well through the pipes is discharged into the lock chamber through a two-foot-square opening in the wall.

The intake valves were originally opened and closed by four patented Stoney gate valves. These valves included gate-jack cylinders with pistons and packing, as well as four-way double valves for the operation of the intake gates.

The gate jack consisted of a hydraulic cylinder with the piston rod connected to a rack, which in turn was meshed to a toothed sector wheel. An arm attached to the sector wheel connected to the valve. The valves were opened and closed by a single stroke of the piston. The operation machinery was set in a recess in the lock walls, shimmed to grade, aligned and adjusted to the gates, and concreted into place. Each gate is opened by a sector gear and rack that is hydraulically operated. The lock gates consist of two leaves each; when open, they rest in recesses provided in the walls. When closed, they miter in the center of the chamber. Both gates miter at a point upstream from their pintle points. The upper gate is approximately twenty-three feet high and the lower gate forty-one feet high. When in a mitering position, the gates rest against a sill beam in the concrete miter sill. The gates are made up with steel sections and steel castings and are provided with seals and fenders.

Powerhouse

The operations buildings, or powerhouses, were constructed on the river wall of the locks, entirely of concrete. The walls were erected over keyways that had been provided on the top of the wall. Asphaltic expansion-joint filler was used on the keyways prior to placing the concrete, to prevent bonding. The interior partitions were of hollow tile.

The operations buildings are the only buildings on the lock-and-dam structures. They provide space for the equipment and controls necessary to operate the locks. The buildings also provide office space for the lock masters and their staffs.

Hydroelectric Plant

The hydroelectric buildings constructed at the western end of each dam are concrete structures 150 feet long and 55 feet wide containing three turbines spaced 50 feet on centers. The buildings are plain structures that were designed to serve a simple, functional purpose, that of providing power in the most economical way. They are sparse without ornamentation or decoration. Conventional windows have been eliminated, and daylight illumination is provided by glass bricks.

The three turbines at London are of the vertical shaft propeller type, of which two have fixed-blade runners and one has adjustable-blade runners. Marmet was to be constructed the same way, but a new type of Newport News automatically adjustable propeller was substituted for one of the fixed-blade runners. Fixed-blade runners have a rated capacity of 6,600 hp under a net effective head of twenty-three feet at a speed of 90 rpm. The diameter of the runner is 177 inches. The automatically adjustable blade unit for Marmet has the same dimensions and the same capacity. The adjustable blade, Kaplan-type units have a diameter of 169 inches. Maximum output under normal operating conditions is eighteen megawatts. The layout of the turbines is the same at both plants. Though there is different hydraulic output from the three machines in each plant, all can use identical electric units for all generators in each plant.

Engineering and supervisory work was provided by the American Gas and Electric Company. The general contractors were Boscoe and Ritchie, and the turbines were provided by Baldwin-Southwark Corporation and the Newport News Shipbuilding and Drydock Company.

THE WINFIELD LOCKS AND DAM

While not an exact copy of the London and Marmet Locks and Dams, the Winfield site is very similar in all of its details. Instead of five roller gates, the Winfield Dam features six, each 100'-3½" in length, 26' in diameter, and set between piers 15' thick. In addition to the five standard roller gates, there is one with a retractable flap, which can be lowered to pass ice and debris. In the lowered position the gates produce a lift of 28 feet, 4 feet more than the London and Marmet dams. When raised the gates clear the sill by 47 feet for the passage of floodwaters.

The original twin locks, 56 × 360 feet, are identical to those at London and Marmet. Currently the Winfield locks are the busiest on the entire Corps of Engineers system. To alleviate traffic delays, a new 800 × 110 foot lock has been constructed alongside the twin locks. A similarly large lock has been proposed for Marmet.

THE GALLIPOLIS LOCKS AND DAM

Located on the Ohio River below Point Pleasant, West Virginia, the Gallipolis Locks and Dam are part of both the Great Kanawha Navigation and the Ohio River Navigation. For this reason the complex is larger, and it differs from the other three locks and dams on the Kanawha in both dimensions and details.

Like the facilities on the Kanawha River, the dam is of the non-navigable gate-crest type, extending from the Ohio bank in a series of eight bays separated by piers 16 feet thick. The eight bays provide 1,132 feet of opening, controlled by roller gates 29 feet in diameter and 120½ feet in length. The gates at Gallipolis are the largest in the country and are the most distinctive feature of all the locks and dams on the Ohio River.

In order to accommodate barge traffic on both the Ohio and Kanawha Rivers, a standard 600 × 110 foot-wide lock was constructed alongside a 360

× 110 foot auxiliary lock of the same length as the Kanawha locks. A huge 1,200 × 110 foot lock, named for Senator Robert C. Byrd, has replaced the auxiliary lock. This new size is the standard for the Ohio River.

Unlike the other dams, the Gallipolis site does not include a hydroelectric power-generation station.

Appendix B

District Engineers:
Huntington District, 1922–1977[1]

Major Malcolm Elliott	July 1, 1922–August 14, 1922
Major Milo P. Fox	August 14, 1922–April 19, 1923
Major William P. Stokey	April 19, 1923–June 30, 1923
Major Harry M. Trippe	June 30, 1923–May 24, 1927
Major E. D. Ardery	May 24, 1927–October 13, 1930
Major Fred W. Herman	October 13, 1930–July 31, 1934
Major John F. Conklin	July 31, 1934–June 14, 1937
Lt. Col. J. D. Arthur, Jr.	June 14, 1937–September 29, 1940
Lt. Col. F. H. Falkner	September 29, 1940–July 21, 1942
Col. Wilson B. Higgins	July 21, 1942–May 24, 1943
Lt. Col. Harry Pockras	May 24, 1943–January 26, 1946
Col. B. B. Talley	January 26, 1946–March 18, 1946
Lt. Col. John R. Sharp	March 18, 1946–April 18, 1946
Col. F. W. Gano	April 18, 1946–December 3, 1946
Col. A. M. Neilson	December 3, 1946–October 1, 1949
Col. D. T. Johnson	October 1, 1949–July 20, 1950
Col. Walter Krueger, Jr.	July 20, 1950–March 16, 1952

Col. E. R. O'Brien   March 16, 1952–June 2, 1952

Col. J. O. Colonna   June 2, 1952–June 22, 1953

Col. George T. Derby   June 22, 1953–April 30, 1956

Col. Herrol J. Skidmore   April 30, 1956–August 29, 1959

Col. Steven Malevich   August 29, 1959–August 5, 1962

Col. Harrington W. Cochran   August 5, 1962–July 17, 1965

Col. William D. Falck   July 17, 1965–July 14, 1968

Col. Maurice D. Roush   July 14, 1968–June 29, 1971

Col. Kenneth E. McIntyre   August 31, 1971–July 19, 1974

Col. Scott B. Smith   July 29, 1974–January 31, 1977

Col. George A. Bicher   April 26, 1977–

Notes

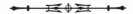

Part 1: Chanoine Wicket Dams and Locks

INTRODUCTION: AN OLD AND CONTRARY RIVER

1. Wilton N. Melhorn and John P. Kempton, eds., *Geology and Hydrogeology of the Teays-Mahomet Bedrock Valley System,* Special Paper 258 (Boulder, Colo.: Geological Society of America, 1991), 30.

2. W. Armstrong Price, *Kanawha County: Part IV—Paleontology* (Wheeling: West Virginia Geological Survey, 1914), 31, 50.

1. THE INTERNAL IMPROVEMENTS MOVEMENT IN VIRGINIA

1. Department of the Treasury, *Report of the Secretary of the Treasury [Albert Gallatin] on the Subject of Public Roads and Canals [1808]* (New York: Augustus M. Kelley, 1968), 1–123.

2. Wayland Fuller Dunaway, "History of the James River and Kanawha Co." (Ph.D. diss., Columbia University, 1922), 9.

3. Ibid., 17.

4. Ibid., 19.

5. Ibid., 66.

6. James L. Kirkwood, *Waterways to the West,* Interpretive Series no. 1 (n.p.: Eastern National Park and Monument Association, 1963).

7. Dunaway, "History of the James River and Kanawha Co.," 89.

8. Ibid., 90.

9. Ibid., 123; Gene D. Lewis, *Charles Ellet, Jr.: The Engineer as Individualist, 1810–1862* (Urbana: University of Illinois Press, 1968), 57–59.

10. Dunaway, "History of the James River and Kanawha Co.," 126.

11. Kirkwood, *Waterways to the West,* 15–17.

12. Lewis, *Charles Ellet, Jr.,* 136 (fn).

13. Charles Ellet, Jr., *The Mississippi and Ohio Rivers: Containing Plans for the Protection of the Delta from Inundation; and the Investigations of the Practicability and Cost*

of *Improving the Navigation of the Ohio and Other Rivers by Means of Reservoirs* (Philadelphia: Lippincott, 1853).

14. Dunaway, "History of the James River and Kanawha Co.," 218–19.

15. U.S. House, *James River and Kanawha Canal,* 41st Cong., 3d sess., 1871, Exec. Doc. 110, 96.

16. Ibid., 1–2.

17. Dunaway, "History of the James River and Kanawha Co.," 223; U.S. House, *James River and Kanawha Canal,* Exec. Doc. 110, 2–12.

18. U.S. House, *James River and Kanawha Canal,* 43d Cong., 1st sess., 1874, Exec. Doc. 219, 29.

19. Ibid., 1–47.

20. Ibid., 4.

21. U.S. House, *James River and Kanawha Canal,* Exec. Doc. 110, 63–73.

22. U.S. House, *James River and Kanawha Canal,* Exec. Doc. 219, 8.

23. Ibid., 36–37.

24. Dunaway, "History of the James River and Kanawha Co.," 237.

25. Ibid.

2. A VIEW FROM THE WESTERN WATERS

1. Dale Van Every, *Ark of the Empire: The American Frontier, 1784–1803* (New York: Morrow, 1963); Leland D. Baldwin, *The Keelboat Age on Western Waters* (Pittsburgh: University of Pittsburgh Press, 1941); Louis C. Hunter, *Steamboats on the Western Rivers: An Economic and Technological History* (Cambridge, Mass.: Harvard University Press, 1949); U.S. Army Corps of Engineers, *The History of the U.S. Army Corps of Engineers* (Washington, Government Printing Office, 1978), 37–46.

2. Otis K. Rice, *Charleston and the Kanawha Valley: An Illustrated History* (Woodland Hills, Calif.: Windsor Publications, 1981), 20; Gerald W. Sutphin and Richard A. Andre, *Sternwheelers on the Great Kanawha River* (Charleston, W.V.: Pictorial Histories Publishing Co., 1991), 4; J. Mack Gamble, "Steamboats in West Virginia," *West Virginia History* 15, no. 1 (Oct. 1953): 124–38.

3. Rice, *Charleston and the Kanawha Valley,* 20–25, 64–65; Sutphin and Andre, *Sternwheelers on the Great Kanawha River,* 4–5; James T. Laing, "The Early Development of the Coal Industry in the Western Counties of Virginia, 1800–1965," *West Virginia History* 27, no. 2 (Jan. 1966): 144–55.

4. Virginia, "An Act to Amend the Act, Entitled 'An Act for Clearing and Improving the Navigation of James River,' and for Uniting the Eastern and Western Waters, by the James and Kanawha Rivers," chap. 56, *Acts of the General Assembly,* Feb. 1820 (Richmond, Va.: Thomas Ritchie, 1820), 39–47.

5. Virginia, "An Act to Amend the Act, Entitled 'An Act to Amend the Act for Clearing and Improving the Navigation of James River, and for Uniting the Eastern and Western Waters, by the James and Kanawha Rivers,'" chap. 46, *Acts of the General Assembly,* Feb. 1821 (Richmond, Va.: Thomas Ritchie, 1821), 48–52.

6. Sutphin and Andre, *Sternwheelers on the Great Kanawha River,* 2–194.

7. Leland R. Johnson, *An Illustrated History of the Huntington District, U.S. Army Corps of Engineers, 1754–1974* (Washington: Government Printing Office, 1977), 57; Dunaway, "History of the James River and Kanawha Co.," 89.

8. Virginia, "An Act Authorizing the James River and Kanawha Company to Borrow Money to Improve the Kanawha River, and to Pledge the Tolls on Said River for That Purpose," chap. 103, *Acts of the General Assembly, 1855–56* (Richmond, Va.: Thomas Ritchie, 1855), 85; Dunaway, "History of the James River and Kanawha Co.," 197; Johnson, *An Illustrated History of the Huntington District*, 61.

9. Charles Ellet, Jr., *Report on the Improvement of the Kanawha and Incidentally of the Ohio River by Means of Artificial Lakes* (Philadelphia: Collins, 1858), 1–125.

10. Rice, *Charleston and the Kanawha Valley*, 63; Johnson, *An Illustrated History of the Huntington District*, 57–62; Stan Cohen and Richard Andre, *Kanawha County Images* (Charleston, W.V.: Pictorial Histories Publishing Co., 1992), 69.

11. (West) Virginia, "An Act to Amend and Re-enact the Act Passed May 15, 1862, Entitled 'An Act to Reorganize the Kanawha Board,'" chap. 40, *Ordinances and Acts of the Restored Government of Virginia, Prior to the Formation of the State of West Virginia, with the Constitution and Laws of the State of West Virginia, to March 2d, 1866*, 1862–63 (Wheeling, W.V.: John Frew, 1866), 27.

12. Addison M. Scott, Charleston, W.V., to Lt. Col. William P. Craighill, Baltimore, Md., Aug. 17, 1874, Addison Scott Collection, Box 2, FF 8, Morrow Library, Marshall University, Huntington, W.V.

13. West Virginia Legislature, "An Act in Relation to the Collection of Tolls on the Great Kanawha River, and to Terminate the Existence of the Kanawha Board," chap. 54, *Acts of the Legislature, 1881* (Wheeling, W.V.: W. J. Johnston, 1881), 321–22.

14. U.S. Army Corps of Engineers, "Great Kanawha River, West Virginia," *Annual Report of the Chief of Engineers* (Washington: Government Printing Office, 1882), 142–43.

15. Secretary of War, "Examination and Survey of the Great Kanawha River, from the Great Falls to the Mouth," *Report of the Chief of Engineers* (Appendix T 28), H.R. Exec. Doc. 1, Part 2, 43d Cong., 1st sess., 1873, 836–42.

16. Ibid., 841.

17. Ibid., 840.

18. Ibid., 509.

3. MOVABLE DAMS

1. Secretary of War, *Hydraulic Gates and Dams in the Ohio River*, H.R. Exec. Doc. 78, 43d Cong., 2d sess., 1875, 1–83.

2. Ibid., 84–131 and plates.

3. L.T.C. Rolt, *Navigable Waterways* (London: Arrow, 1973), 7; "Ohio River Movable Dams," *Military Engineer* 27, no. 151 (Jan.–Feb. 1935), 53–54.

4. Norris Hansell, *Josiah White: Quaker Entrepreneur* (Easton, Pa.: Canal History and Technology Press, 1992), 50–53, 140; Benjamin F. Thomas, "Movable Dams," *Transactions American Society of Civil Engineers* 39 (June 1898): 437; Edward

Wegmann, *The Design and Construction of Dams* (New York: John Wiley and Sons, 1900), 191; Benjamin F. Thomas and D. A. Watt, *The Improvement of Rivers,* part 2 (New York: John Wiley and Sons, 1913), 537–58, 651–65, 697.

5. Leland R. Johnson, *The Davis Island Lock and Dam: 1870–1922* (Pittsburgh: Pittsburgh District, U.S. Army Corps of Engineers, 1985), 24–27; Thomas and Watt, *The Improvement of Rivers,* 595.

6. Thomas and Watt, *The Improvement of Rivers,* 196–97.

7. Ibid., 653.

8. Leveson F. Vernon-Harcourt, "Fixed and Movable Weirs," in *Minutes of Proceedings of the Institution of Civil Engineers,* Paper no. 1655 (London: I.C.E., Jan. 20, 1880), 28.

9. William Watson, "River Improvements in France, Including A Description of Poirée's System of Movable Dams," *Van Nostrand's Engineering Magazine* (New York: D. Van Nostrand, 1878), 393–44; Thomas and Watt, *The Improvement of Rivers,* 559–84; Vernon-Harcourt, "Fixed and Movable Weirs," 151–61, 229–30.

10. Thomas and Watt, *The Improvement of Rivers,* 576–77.

11. Thomas, "Movable Dams," 431–615.

12. Emory L. Kemp, "Stemming the Tide: Design and Operation of the Bonnet Carré Spillway," *Essays in Public Works History* 17 (Dec. 1970): 1–25.

13. Wegmann, *Design and Construction of Dams,* 162–64; Thomas and Watt, *The Improvement of Rivers,* 539, 608–16; Thomas, "Movable Dams," 213–515; Auguste Boulé, "Nouvelle passe navigable," Mémoires et Documents no. 42, *Annales des Ponts et Chaussées* (1873): 98–158; Auguste Boulé, "Un nouveau système de barrage mobile," Mémoires et Documents no. 15, *Annales des Ponts et Chaussées* (1876): 320–74.

14. Wegmann, *Design and Construction of Dams,* 164–71.

15. Thomas and Watt, *The Improvement of Rivers,* 585, 640–45; Wegmann, *Design and Construction of Dams,* 172–74; Jacques Chanoine, "Sur le barrage d'Epineau," *Annales des Ponts et Chaussées* 16 (1839): 238–80; Cambuzat, "Sur les barrages mobiles du système Poirée et du système Chanoine qui fonctionnent simultanément pour les ecluses de l'Yonne," Mémoires et Documents no. 146, *Annales des Ponts et Chaussées* (1866): 135–38.

16. Vernon-Harcourt, "Fixed and Movable Weirs," 35.

17. Wegmann, *Design and Construction of Dams,* 177–81; Watson, "River Improvement in France," 339–44, 458–62; Maurice Levy, "Manoeuvre des barrages Chanoine," Mémoires et Documents no. 23, *Annales des Ponts et Chaussées* (1881): 419–27.

18. Vernon-Harcourt, "Fixed and Movable Weirs," 36.

19. Wegmann, *Design and Construction of Dams,* 185–87; Thomas and Watt, *The Improvement of Rivers,* 641–46; Vernon-Harcourt, "Fixed and Movable Weirs," 36–38.

20. Wegmann, *Design and Construction of Dams,* 181–83; Vernon-Harcourt, "Fixed and Movable Weirs," 38–39.

4. The First Kanawha Locks and Dams

1. Register of the Addison Moffat Scott Papers, "Biography of Addison Moffat Scott," Addison Moffat Scott Collection, Morrow Library, Marshall University, Huntington, W.V.; "Portraits and Profiles," *History of the U.S. Army Corps of Engineers* (Washington: Government Printing Office, 1986), 115–27.

2. "Transcript of Addison Scott's Testimony in the Zimmerman, Traux, and Sheridan Construction Case," Scott Collection, Box 3, FF 9, 1891.

3. Ibid., 4.

4. *History of the U.S. Army Corps of Engineers,* 120; Association of Graduates, U.S. Military Academy, *Register of Graduates and Former Cadets of the United States Military Academy,* entry 1580 (West Point, N.Y.: Association of Graduates, 1990), 277.

5. American Society of Civil Engineers (ASCE), *A Biographical Dictionary of American Civil Engineers,* Historical Publication no. 2 (New York: ASCE, 1991), 2:75–76; Johnson, *The Davis Island Lock and Dam,* 568–69.

6. Secretary of War, *Hydraulic Gates and Dams in the Ohio River,* 1–83.

7. Association of Graduates, *Register of Graduates and Former Cadets,* entry 1825, 282; Johnson, *History of the Huntington District,* 79–101; *Dictionary of American Biography* (New York: Charles Scribner's Sons, 1933), 568–69; ASCE, *A Biographical Dictionary of American Civil Engineers,* 123.

8. *The National Cyclopedia of American Biography* (New York: James T. Waite and Co., 1962), 616–17.

9. *The National Cyclopedia of American Biography,* 51–52; Association of Graduates, *Register of Graduates and Former Cadets,* entry 2641, 298.

10. Association of Graduates, *Register of Graduates and Former Cadets,* entry 2156, 289.

11. Ibid., entry 2159, 289.

12. Eduard Lorraine, *The Central Water-Line from the Ohio River to the Virginia Capes* (Richmond, Va.: Gary, Clemmitt and Jones, 1869), n.p.

13. Johnson, *History of the Huntington District,* 89–91.

14. Scott to Craighill, Aug. 1874, Box 2, FF 8, Scott Collection, Marshall University.

15. Secretary of War, "Examination and Survey of the Great Kanawha River, from the Great Falls to the Mouth," *Report of the Chief of Engineers* (Appendix T 28), H.R. Exec. Doc. 1, Part 2, 43d Cong., 1st sess., 1873, 836. This survey was based on earlier reports by Lorraine, and Lorraine's *An Appeal for the Speedy Completion of the Water Line of Virginia, and Through That of the Great Central Water Line of the Union* (Norfolk, Va.: C. H. Wynne, 1857).

16. Secretary of War, "Examination and Survey of the Great Kanawha River," 836–42.

17. Secretary of War, "Examination and Survey of the Great Kanawha River," (Appendix T 29), 842–43.

18. Secretary of War, "Hydraulic Gates and Dams in the Ohio River."

19. Thomas, "Movable Dams."

20. Secretary of War, *Improvement of the Great Kanawha River, West Virginia* (Appendix M 3), H.R. Exec. Doc. 1, Part 2, 43d Cong., 1st sess., 1873, 505–06.

21. Secretary of War, *Annual Report of Major William P. Craighill, Corps of Engineers, For the Fiscal Year Ending 30 June 1876* (Appendix S), H.R. Exec. Doc. 1, Part 2, 44th Cong., 2d sess., 1876, 153–63.

22. Ibid., 157.

23. Ibid., 158.

24. Ibid., 159.

25. Ibid., 163–65.

26. Thomas, "Movable Dams," 498–99.

27. Secretary of War, *Annual Report of Major William P. Craighill*, 163–64.

28. Secretary of War, *Improvement of the Great Kanawha River, West Virginia* (Appendix G 20), H.R. Exec. Doc. 1, Part 2, 46th Cong., 3d sess., 1880, 681–82.

29. Ibid., 682.

30. Ibid., 683.

31. Ibid., 684.

32. Ibid., 685–89.

33. Lt. Col. William P. Craighill, Baltimore, Md., to Capt. Ernest H. Ruffner, Charleston, W.V., Jan. 25, 1882; Record Group (RG) 77, Entry 1331, Letter 23 (Misc. Officers' Letters, Kanawha River), National Archives and Records Administration, Philadelphia (NARA—Philadelphia).

34. Craighill to Ruffner, Feb. 8, 1882; RG 77, Entry 1331, Letter 35 (Misc. Officers' Letters, Kanawha River), NARA—Philadelphia.

35. Craighill to Ruffner, Aug. 29, 1882; RG 77, Entry 1331, Letter 146 (Misc. Officers' Letters, Kanawha River), NARA—Philadelphia.

36. Craighill to Ruffner, Aug. 29, 1882, RG 77, Entry 1331, Letter 146; and Craighill to Ruffner, April 14, 1883, RG 77, Entry 1331, Letter 75, NARA—Philadelphia. Craighill credits Scott with the preparation of the specifications and not Ruffner, who probably ordered Scott to undertake this work.

37. Lt. Col. John G. Parke, Washington, D.C., to Theodore Wright, Philadelphia, Aug. 24, 1882; RG 77, Entry 1331, Letter 150 (Misc. Officers' Letters, Kanawha River), NARA—Philadelphia.

38. Parke to Ruffner, Charleston, W.V., Jan. 16, 1883; RG 77, Entry 1331, Letter 20 (Misc. Officers' Letters, Kanawha River), NARA—Philadelphia.

39. Thomas F. Hahn and Emory L. Kemp, *Cement Mills along the Potomac River* (Morgantown, W.V.: Institute for the History of Technology and Industrial Archaeology, 1994), 7–23.

40. Ibid.

41. Capt. Thomas Turtle, Charleston, W.V., to Scott, Charleston, W.V., Feb. 21, 1883; RG 77, Entry 1331, Letter 66 (Misc. Officers' Letters, Kanawha River), NARA—Philadelphia.

42. Parke to Craighill, Feb. 8, 1883; RG 77, Entry 1331, Letter 35 (Misc. Officers' Letters, Kanawha River), NARA—Philadelphia.

43. J. L. Merchant and Co., New York City, to Craighill, Baltimore, Md., Feb. 13,

1883, Letter 136; and Turtle to Scott, Feb. 21, 1883, Letter 66. Both RG 77, Entry 1331 (Misc. Officers' Letters, Kanawha River), NARA—Philadelphia.

44. Ruffner to Chief Clerk, War Department, Washington, D.C., Proposal for Building Dam No. 6, Jan. 3, 1883; RG 77, Entry 1331, (Misc. Officers' Letters, Kanawha River), NARA—Philadelphia.

45. Col. Quincy Adams Gilmore, New York, to Craighill, Oct. 14, 1884; RG 77, Entry 1331, Letter 111 (Misc. Officers' Letters, Kanawha River), NARA—Philadelphia.

46. Ibid.

47. Interrogatory of Addison M. Scott, 1891, RG 77, Entry 1347a (General Administrative Files), 18–19, NARA—Philadelphia.

48. William P. Craighill, *Kanawha River Improvement: Proposals for the Iron Work of a Movable Dam on the Great Kanawha River* (Baltimore, Md.: U.S. Engineer Office, 1877), 4.

49. Ibid.

50. Report of the Members of the Board of Engineers, June 21, 1882; RG 77, Letter 123 (Misc. Officers' Letters, Kanawha River), NARA—Philadelphia.

51. Craighill to Scott, March 7, 1883; RG 77, Entry 1331, Letter 219 (Misc. Officers' Letters, Kanawha River), NARA—Philadelphia.

52. Craighill to Scott, March 29, 1884; RG 77, Entry 1331, Letter 26 (Misc. Officers' Letters, Kanawha River), NARA—Philadelphia.

53. Craighill to Scott, April 4, 1884; RG 77, Entry 1331, Letter 28 (Misc. Officers' Letters, Kanawha River), NARA—Philadelphia; Craighill to Scott, April 24, 1884; RG 77, Entry 1331, Letter 38 (Misc. Officers' Letters, Kanawha River), NARA—Philadelphia.

54. Craighill to Scott, Aug. 4, 1884; RG 77, Entry 1331, Letter 77 (Misc. Officers' Letters, Kanawha River), NARA—Philadelphia; Craighill to Scott, Nov. 4, 1884; RG 77, Entry 1331, Letter 123 (Misc. Officers' Letters, Kanawha River), NARA—Philadelphia.

55. Scott to Craighill, Addison M. Scott Collection (MS 14), Box 2, FF 9, 1–18, Morrow Library, Marshall University, Huntington, W.V.

56. Craighill to Scott, Feb. 13, 1885; RG 77, Entry 1331, Letter 20 (Misc. Officers' Letters, Kanawha River), NARA—Philadelphia.

57. Secretary of War, *Improvement of Great Kanawha River, West Virginia* (Appendix I 17), 48th Cong., 2d sess., H.R. Exec. Doc. 1, Part 2, 1884, 930–31.

58. Ibid.

59. Ibid., 933–34.

60. Ibid., 932.

61. Secretary of War, *Harbor of Refuge at Mouth of Great Kanawha River, West Virginia* (Appendix CC 10), 49th Cong., 1st sess., H.R. Exec. Doc. 1, Part 2, 1885, 1826–27.

62. Ibid., 1850–51.

63. Craighill to Chas. H. Strong and Son, Coal Valley, W.V., Oct. 9, 1886; RG 77, Letter 105 (Misc. Officers' Letters, Kanawha River), NARA—Philadelphia.

64. Secretary of War, *Harbor of Refuge at Mouth of Great Kanawha River,* 1848.

65. Ibid., 1855.

66. Craighill to Carkin, Stickney, and Cram, East Saginaw, Mich., March 27, 1889; RG 77, Entry 1331, Letter 33 (Misc. Officers' Letters, Kanawha River), NARA—Philadelphia; Corps of Engineers, *History of the U.S. Army Corps of Engineers,* 120.

67. Albert Mott, Baltimore, Md., for Turtle to Scott, April 16, 1889; RG 77, Entry 1331, Letter 40 (Misc. Officers' Letters, Kanawha River), NARA—Philadelphia.

68. Craighill to Scott, Aug. 29, 1889; RG 77, Entry 1331, Letter 77 (Misc. Officers' Letters, Kanawha River), NARA—Philadelphia.

69. Craighill to Carkin, Stickney, and Cram, May 13, 1890; RG 77, Entry 1331, Letter 49 (Misc. Officers' Letters, Kanawha River), NARA—Philadelphia; Craighill to Carkin, Stickney, and Cram, Sept. 15, 1890; RG 77, Entry 1331, Letter 84 (Misc. Officers' Letters, Kanawha River), NARA—Philadelphia.

70. Craighill to Scott, Oct. 9, 1890; RG 77, Entry 1331, Letter 100 (Misc. Officers' Letters, Kanawha River), NARA—Philadelphia; Craighill to Scott, Nov. 26, 1890; RG 77, Entry 1331, Letter 109 (Misc. Officers' Letters, Kanawha River), NARA—Philadelphia.

71. Craighill to Scott, Jan. 15, 1891; RG 77, Entry 1331, Letter 4 (Misc. Officers' Letters, Kanawha River), NARA—Philadelphia; Craighill to Scott, May 19, 1891; RG 77, Entry 1331, Letter 36 (Misc. Officers' Letters, Kanawha River), NARA—Philadelphia.

72. Craighill to Scott, Jan. 19, 1891; RG 77, Entry 1331, Letter 11 (Misc. Officers' Letters, Kanawha River), NARA—Philadelphia; Craighill to Scott, Feb. 19, 1891; RG 77, Entry 1331, Letter 11a (Misc. Officers' Letters, Kanawha River), NARA—Philadelphia.

73. Craighill to Scott, Aug. 27, 1891; RG 77, Entry 1331, Letter 68 (Misc. Officers' Letters, Kanawha River), NARA—Philadelphia; Craighill to Scott, Oct. 30, 1891; RG 77, Entry 1331, Letter 92 (Misc. Officers' Letters, Kanawha River), NARA—Philadelphia; Craighill to Scott, Dec. 7, 1891; RG 77, Entry 1331, Letter 102 (Misc. Officers' Letters, Kanawha River), NARA—Philadelphia.

74. Capt. W.O. Marshall, Chicago, Ill., to Craighill, Dec. 14, 1891; RG 77, Entry 1331, Letter 104 (Misc. Officers' Letters, Kanawha River), NARA—Philadelphia; Craighill to Scott, Jan. 9, 1892; RG 77, Entry 1331, Letter 7/2 (Misc. Officers' Letters, Kanawha River), NARA—Philadelphia.

75. Craighill to Carkin, Stickney, and Cram, Aug. 10, 1891; RG 77, Entry 1331, Letter 64 (Misc. Officers' Letters, Kanawha River), NARA—Philadelphia; Craighill to Scott, Aug. 10, 1891; RG 77, Entry 1331, Letter 64 (Misc. Officers' Letters, Kanawha River), NARA—Philadelphia; Craighill to Larkin, Stickney, and Cram, July 28, 1891; RG 77, Entry 1331, Letter 64 (Misc. Officers' Letters, Kanawha River), NARA—Philadelphia.

76. Craighill to C. I. McDonald, near Charleston, W.V., Dec. 7, 1891; RG 77, Entry 1331, Letter 101 (Misc. Officers' Letters, Kanawha River), NARA—Philadelphia.

77. McDonald to Craighill, Dec. 4, 1891; RG 77, Entry 1331, Letter 101 (Misc. Officers' Letters, Kanawha River), NARA—Philadelphia.

78. Craighill to Scott, Jan. 2, 1892; RG 77, Entry 1331, Letter 3 (Misc. Officers' Letters, Kanawha River), NARA—Philadelphia.

79. Craighill to Scott, July 22, 1892; RG 77, Entry 1331, Letter 76 (Misc. Officers' Letters, Kanawha River), NARA—Philadelphia.

80. Craighill to Scott, Aug. 12, 1892; RG 77, Entry 1331, Letter 94 (Misc. Officers' Letters, Kanawha River), NARA—Philadelphia.

81. Craighill to Scott, Dec. 8, 1892; RG 77, Entry 1331, Letter 138 (Misc. Officers' Letters, Kanawha River), NARA—Philadelphia.

82. Craighill to Scott, Dec. 31, 1892; RG 77, Entry 1331, Letter 144 (Misc. Officers' Letters, Kanawha River), NARA—Philadelphia.

83. Secretary of War, *Improvement of Great Kanawha River, West Virginia* (Appendix GG 1) 53d Cong., 3d sess., H.R. Exec. Doc. 1, Part 2, 1894, 1953–54.

84. Ibid.

85. Craighill to Scott, Jan. 7, 1895; RG 77, Entry 1331, Letter 213 (Misc. Officers' Letters, Kanawha River), NARA—Philadelphia.

86. Secretary of War, *Improvement of Great Kanawha River, West Virginia* (Appendix FF 1) 54th Cong., 1st sess., H.R. Exec. Doc. No. 2, 1895, 2456.

87. Col. Peter C. Hains, Baltimore, Md., to Scott, Dec. 16, 1895; RG 77, Entry 1331, Letter 322 (Misc. Officers' Letters, Kanawha River), NARA—Philadelphia.

88. Youngstown Bridge Co., Youngstown, Ohio, to Hains, Feb. 14, 1896; RG 77, Entry 1331, Letter 358 (Misc. Officers' Letters, Kanawha River), NARA—Philadelphia.

89. Hains to Youngstown Bridge Co., March 19, 1896; RG 77, Entry 1331, Letter 371 (Misc. Officers' Letters, Kanawha River), NARA—Philadelphia.

90. Hains to Scott, Sept. 16, 1896; RG 77, Entry 1331, Letter 436 (Misc. Officers' Letters, Kanawha River), NARA—Philadelphia.

91. Youngstown Bridge Co. to Hains, Feb. 14, 1896; RG 77, Entry 1331, Letter 358 (Misc. Officers' Letters, Kanawha River), NARA—Philadelphia.

92. Secretary of War, *Improvement of Great Kanawha River, West Virginia* (Appendix FF 10), 55th Cong., 2d sess., H.R. Exec. Doc. No. 2, 1897, 2567–68, 2573.

93. Ibid., 2567.

94. Secretary of War, *Improvement of Great Kanawha River, West Virginia* (1894), 2252–55.

95. Thomas Munford, Point Pleasant, W.V., to Hains, Baltimore, Md., Oct. 24, 1896; RG 77, Entry 1331, Letter 447 (Misc. Officers' Letters, Kanawha River), NARA—Philadelphia.

96. Zimmerman, Truax, and Sheridan, Charleston, W.V., to Hains, Nov. 4, 1896; RG 77, Entry 1331, Letter 456 (Misc. Officers' Letters, Kanawha River), NARA—Philadelphia.

97. Zimmerman et al., Dec. 24, 1895; RG 77, Entry 1331, Letter 350 (Misc. Officers' Letters, Kanawha River), NARA—Philadelphia.

98. Munford to Hains, Oct. 12, 1896; RG 77, Entry 1331, Letter 468 (Misc. Officers' Letters, Kanawha River), NARA—Philadelphia.

99. Maj. William H. Bixby, Cincinnati, Ohio, to Munford, Dec. 24, 1897; RG 77, Entry 1331, Letter 749 (Misc. Officers' Letters, Kanawha River), NARA—Philadelphia.

100. Munford to Bixby, Sept. 14, 1898; RG 77, Entry 1331, Letter 908 (Misc. Officers' Letters, Kanawha River), NARA—Philadelphia.

101. U.S. Army Corps of Engineers, "Improvement of Kanawha River, West Virginia," in *Annual Report of the Chief of Engineers* (Appendix II 5), (Washington: Government Printing Office, 1900), 3322.

102. Ibid., 3323.

103. "River Improvement," *The Charleston Daily Gazette,* Oct. 22, 1898, p. 4, col. 1.

104. Addison M. Scott, "Coal: Commerce and Development on the Great Kanawha Valley, The Cheapest Transportation Known" (pamphlet) (Charleston, W.V.: *Daily Gazette,* 1891), 1–9.

5. OPERATIONS FOR MORE THAN TWO DECADES

1. Memorandum from Office of the Division Engineer, Central Div., Cincinnati, Ohio, to the Chief of Engineers, Washington, D.C., May 13, 1926; RG 77, Entry 1347 A, Economic Study of Kanawha River, File K1549 (General Administrative Files, Kanawha River), NARA—Philadelphia.

2. E. A. Burnside, Campbell's Creek Coal Co., Point Pleasant, W.V., to R. Andrew, junior engineer, Charleston, W.V., Jan. 31, 1917; RG 77, Entry 1348, File K1146/144 (Correspondence on Misc. Subjects Connected with Kanawha River Improvement), NARA—Philadelphia.

3. E. A. Burnside to E. O. Dana, Secretary, Great Kanawha River Improvement Association, Sept. 28, 1915; RG 77, Entry 1350, File K1232/10 (Correspondence Files, Kanawha River), NARA—Philadelphia.

4. Thomas E. Jeffries, Charleston, W.V., to District Engineer, Wheeling, W.V., Dec. 4, 1915; RG 77, Entry 1350, File K1233/13 (Correspondence Files, Kanawha River), NARA—Philadelphia.

5. Jeffries to Maj. George A. Zinn, Wheeling, W.V., Jan. 9, 1907; RG 77, Entry 1347 A, File K1158 (General Administrative Files, Kanawha River), NARA—Philadelphia; Jeffries to Capt. F. C. Boggs, Wheeling, W.V., Oct. 4, 1907; RG 77, Entry 1350, File K1233/4 (Correspondence Files, Kanawha River), NARA—Philadelphia.

6. Lt. Col. H. W. Stickle, Wheeling, W.V., to Division Engineer, Central Div., Cincinnati, Ohio, Dec. 15, 1917; RG 77, Entry 1350, File K1121/74 (Correspondence Files, Kanawha River), NARA—Philadelphia; F. B. Duis, Asst. Engineer, Wheeling, W.V., to Lt. Col. W. H. Stickle, Pittsburgh, Dec. 17, 1917; RG 77, Entry 1350, File K1121 (Correspondence Files, Kanawha River), NARA—Philadelphia; Stickle, Wheeling, W.V., to Warner-Klipstein Chemical Co., Charleston, W.V., Dec. 27, 1917; RG 77, Entry 1350, File K1121 (Correspondence Files, Kanawha River), NARA—Philadelphia; Warner-Klipstein Chemical Co. to Stickle, Dec. 31, 1917;

RG 77, Entry 1350, File K1121 (Correspondence Files, Kanawha River), NARA—Philadelphia.

7. Brig. Gen. William M. Black, Chief of Engineers, Washington, D.C., to Stickle, Dec. 13, 1917; RG 77, Entry 1350, File K1121 (Correspondence Files, Kanawha River), NARA—Philadelphia.

8. Ruffner to All Concerned, Nov. 26, 1901; RG 77, Entry 1350, File K1121/34 (Correspondence Files, Kanawha River), NARA—Philadelphia.

9. District Engineer, Wheeling, W.V., to Division Engineer, Cincinnati, Ohio, July 2, 1917; RG 77, Entry 1350, File K1121/70 (Correspondence Files, Kanawha River), NARA—Philadelphia; Assistant in Charge, Charleston, W.V., to District Engineer, Wheeling, W.V., July 13, 1914; RG 77, Entry 1350, File K1121/67 (Correspondence Files, Kanawha River), NARA—Philadelphia.

10. Secretary of War, *Kanawha River, W. Va.,* H.R. Doc. 41, 63d Cong., 1st sess., 1913, 3–9.

11. Scott to Capt. H. F. Hodges, Cincinnati, Ohio, Sept. 13, 1900; RG 77, Entry 1350, File K1116 (Correspondence Files, Kanawha River), NARA—Philadelphia.

12. Hodges to Scott, Sept. 14, 1900; RG 77, Entry 1350, File K1116 (Correspondence Files, Kanawha River), NARA—Philadelphia.

13. Hodges to Brig. Gen. John M. Wilson, Chief of Engineers, Washington, D.C., Sept. 15, 1900; RG 77, Entry 1350, File K28/2 (Survey, Kanawha River), NARA—Philadelphia.

14. Jeffries to Maj. George A. Zinn, Wheeling, W.V., July 10, 1903; RG 77, Entry 1350, File K1116/6 (Correspondence Files, Kanawha River), NARA—Philadelphia.

15. Ibid.

16. Jeffries to Zinn, Nov. 7, 1903; RG 77, Entry 1350, File K1116/25 (Correspondence Files, Kanawha River), NARA—Philadelphia.

17. U.S. Army Corps of Engineers, *History of the U.S. Army Corps of Engineers,* 122.

18. Johnson, *The Davis Island Lock and Dam,* 65–84.

19. Leland R. Johnson, *Men, Mountains and Rivers* (Washington, D.C.: Government Printing Office, 1977), 122.

20. *An Act Authorizing the Construction, Repair, and Preservation of Certain Public Works on Rivers and Harbors, and for Other Purposes,* chap. 427, Sept. 22, 1922, *Statutes at Large* 42 (April 1921–March 1923): pt. 1; *An Act Authorizing the Construction, Repair, and Preservation of Certain Public Works on Rivers and Harbors, And for Other Purposes,* chap. 47, Jan. 21, 1927, *Statutes at Large* 44 (Dec. 1925–March 1927): pt. 2.

21. Rice, *Charleston and the Kanawha Valley,* 57.

22. Secretary of War, *Kanawha River, W. VA., VA., and N.C.* H.R. Doc. 91, 74th Cong., 1st sess., 1935, 19–20, 29.

23. Johnson, *Men, Mountains and Rivers,* 137.

24. Rice, *Charleston and the Kanawha Valley,* 76–77.

25. Secretary of War, *Kanawha River, W. VA., VA., and N.C.,* 19.

Part 2: Roller Gated Dams and Locks

Introduction: The Prelude to a New Navigation System

1. Maj. Gen. Edgar Jadwin, Chief of Engineers, to Secretary of War, Feb. 17, 1928; RG 77, Entry 111, File 7245-10 (Kanawha R.), National Archives Building, Washington, D.C. (NAB).

2. Revised Estimates of Costs of Burning Springs Lock and Dam for 6 and 9-Foot Projects, Dec. 27, 1927; RG 77, Entry 111 Bulkies, File 7245-21/1 (Kanawha R.), NAB.

3. U.S. Congress, House, *Kanawha River W. Va.*, 70th Cong., 1st Sess., 1928, H. Doc. 190.

4. Ernest M. Merrill, President, Great Kanawha Valley Improvement Association, Charleston, W.V., to Congressman S. Wallace Dempsey, Chairman, Committee on Rivers and Harbors, Jan. 31, 1930; RG 77, Entry 111, File 7245-39 (Kanawha R.), NAB.

5. Gov. Conley to Gen. Brown, Jan. 31, 1930; RG 77, Entry 111, File 7245-38 (Kanawha R.), NAB.

6. George E. Sutherland to Lt. Col. E. D. Ardery, U.S. Engineer, Huntington, W.V., Jan. 30, 1930; RG 77, Entry 111, File 7245 (Kanawha R.), NAB.

7. Congressman J. A. Hughes, Committee on Military Affairs, Washington, to Brig. Gen. Deakyne, Feb. 27, 1930; RG 77, Entry 111, File 7245-42 (Kanawha R.), NAB.

8. Merrill to Brown, Feb. 22, 1930; RG 77, Entry 111, File 7245-41 (Kanawha R.), NAB.

9. Deakyne to Chief of Engineers, March 11, 1930; RG 77, Entry 111, File 7245-44 (Kanawha R.), NAB.

10. Brown to Senator David A. Reed, March 12, 1930; RG 77, Entry 111, File 7245-43 (Kanawha R.), NAB.

11. Spalding to District Engineer, March 24, 1930; RG 77, Entry 1355, File M736 (Budget and Estimate Files), NARA—Philadelphia.

12. Lt. Col. E. L. Daley, Office of the Chief of Engineers, to Division Engineer, Upper Mississippi Valley Division, St. Louis, Mo., April 23, 1930; RG 77, Entry 1355, File 3063 (Budget and Estimate Files), NARA—Philadelphia.

13. "Engineer Inspects Kanawha," *Montgomery News,* May 2, 1930.

14. *Rivers and Harbors Act, Statutes at Large* 46 (1930): 913–49.

15. Brown to Secretary of War, Nov. 1, 1930; RG 77, Entry 111, File 7245-46 (Kanawha R.), NAB.

16. "Work on Kanawha Will Begin Soon," *Montgomery News,* August 15, 1930, 1.

17. "Notice of Public Hearing," Aug. 27, 1930; RG 77, Entry 111, File 7245-19 (Kanawha R. L/D), NAB.

18. "Protests Are Heard on Kanawha Dams," *Montgomery News,* Sept. 12, 1930, 1.

19. *Montgomery News,* August 15, 1930.

20. C. Paul Heavener, Chairman, Drought Committee for Kanawha County,

Charleston, W.V., to President Herbert Hoover, Sept. 12, 1930; RG 77, Entry 111, File 7243-4 (Kanawha R.), NAB.

21. Herman to Chief of Engineers, Oct. 10, 1930; RG 77, Entry 111, File 7245-48 (Kanawha R.), NAB.

22. *Rivers and Harbors Act of 1927, Statutes at Large* 44 (1927), chap. 47, 1020.

23. Brown to Secretary of War, Oct. 10, 1930; RG 77, Entry 111, File 7245 (Kanawha R.), NAB.

24. *Kanawha River W. Va.* H. Doc. 190.

25. An 800-foot lock has been completed at Winfield to relieve the congestion experienced there. Studies have also been made for a similar lock to be constructed at Marmet. Brown to Secretary of War, Oct. 10, 1930; RG 77, Entry 111, File 7245 (Kanawha R.), NAB.

26. B. Byers, President, General Contracting Corporation, Pittsburgh, to A. G. Rothey, Elizabeth, Pa., Nov. 13, 1931; RG 77, Entry 111, File 3524 (Part 2), (Kanawha River–Marmet Locks and Dam [L/D]), NAB.

27. Herman to Chief of Engineers, Oct. 10, 1930; RG 77, Entry 111, File 7245-48 (Kanawha R.), NAB.

28. *Specifications Errata,* Jan. 26, 1931; RG 77, Entry 111, File 3524-7 (Kanawha R.–Marmet L/D), NAB.

6: DESIGN OF THE LOCKS AND DAMS

1. Nicholas J. Schnitter, *A History of Dams: The Useful Pyramids* (Rotterdam, Netherlands: A. A. Balkema, 1994), 217.

2. Hansell, *Josiah White: Quaker Entrepreneur,* 50, 52–53; Wegman, *Design and Construction of Dams,* 191–94.

3. William Patrick O'Brien, Mary Yeater Rathbun, and Patrick O'Bannon, *Gateways to Commerce* (Denver: National Park Service, 1992) 63–97.

4. Ibid.

5. Schnitter, *A History of Dams,* 218–19.

6. O'Brien, Rathbun, and O'Bannion, *Gateways to Commerce,* 78.

7. "Roller-Gate Dams for Kanawha River," *Engineering News-Record* 111, no. 12 (Sept. 21, 1933): 338.

8. O'Brien, Rathbun, and O'Bannion, *Gateways to Commerce,* 78–80.

9. Ibid., 79–80.

10. K. E. Hilgard, "Rolling Dams," *Transactions American Society of Civil Engineers* 54 (D),(1905): 439–48.

11. Ibid.

12. "Roller Gates on Dams Not Confined to Scandinavia and Germany," *Engineering News-Record* 101 (Nov. 29, 1928): 816.

13. "Advantages of the Rolling Dam," *Engineering Record* 68, no. 21 (Nov. 22, 1913): 564.

14. Ibid.

15. "Mississippi River Dam Has 11 Independent 100-Foot Steel Roller Gates,"

Steel 96 (April 15, 1935): 45–46; "Roller-Gate Dam Erection at Rock Island, Ill.," *Engineering News-Record* 112 (March 29, 1934): 410–14.

16. "Advantages of the Rolling Dam," 564.

17. "Winter Operation of Movable Dams," *Engineering Record* 69, no. 22 (May 30, 1914): 618; "Roller-Gate Dams for Kanawha River," 338.

18. "Roller-Gate Dams for Kanawha River," 338.

19. Harry Cole, "Design Analysis of Roller Gates for Movable Dams," *Engineering News-Record* 115 (Nov. 21, 1935): 718–22.

20. A. G. Hillberg, "Design of Rolling Dams," *Engineering Record* 68, no. 24 (Dec. 13, 1913): 656.

21. W. H. McAlpine, "Roller Gates in Navigation Dams," *Military Engineer* 26, no. 150 (Nov.–Dec. 1934): 423.

22. Hillberg, "Design of Rolling Dams," 656.

23. C. R. Martin, "New Design Cuts Costs of Roller Gates," *Engineering News-Record* 122, no. 21 (May 25, 1939): 66.

24. George Earl Troxell, Harmer E. Davis, and Joe E. Kelly, *Composition and Properties of Concrete*, 2d ed. (New York: McGraw Hill, New York, 1968), 157–58.

25. *Standard Government Form of Invitation for Bids*, Huntington, W.V., U.S. Engineer's Office, Jan. 7, 1931; RG 77, Entry 111 Bulkies, File 3524-10/1 (Kanawha R.–Marmet L/D), NAB.

26. *Standard Government Form of Invitation for Bids*, Huntington, W.V., U.S. Engineer's Office, Jan. 7, 1931; RG 77, Entry 111 Bulkies, File 3524-10/1 (Kanawha R.–Marmet L/D), NAB.

27. *Periodic Condition Inspection of Winfield Locks and Dams, Kanawha River, West Virginia*, Aug. 7, 1970, Huntington District, Corps of Engineers. *Periodic Inspection and Continuing Evaluation of Completed Civil Works Structures*, Department of the Army, Huntington District, Corps of Engineers, Huntington, W.V., May 14, 1970, boulins 023-L2-40/B, 40/A, 023-L2-53/2.

28. *Laboratory Tests on Hydraulic Models of Marmet Lock and Dam, Kanawha River, Due to Hydraulic Research*, State University of Iowa, Iowa City, July 1932, p. 3.

29. Henry M. Morris, *Applied Hydraulics and Engineering* (New York: Arnold Quest Company, 1963), 272–78.

30. *Laboratory Tests on Hydraulic Models at Marmet Lock and Dam*, 6.

31. Ibid., 3.

32. Ibid., 8.

33. *Report on Field Checks and Model Tests at Gallipolis Locks and Dam, Ohio River, and London Locks and Dam, Kanawha River*, Engineer Office, Huntington, W.V., Oct. 31, 1939, pp. 3–4.

34. Billy Joe Peyton, "History of the Mississippi Model Basin," U.S. Army Corps of Engineers, Vicksburg District, Vicksburg, Miss., 1996.

7. THE WORK AT LONDON AND MARMET BEGINS

1. Abstract of Bids, Marmet Lock, Feb. 6, 1931; RG 77, Entry 111 Bulkies, File 3524-10/1 (Kanawha R.–Marmet L/D), NAB.

2. Abstract of Bids, London Lock, March 17, 1931; RG 77, Entry 111 Bulkies, File 3524-10/1 (Kanawha R.–Marmet L/D), NAB.

3. Dravo to Brown, March 24, 1931; RG 77, Entry 111, File 3524-11 (Kanawha R.–London L/D), NAB.

4. Estimated Cost of Lock A, London Lock, March 16, 1931; RG 77, Entry 111, File 3524-16/1 (Kanawha R.–London L/D), NAB.

5. Herman to General Contracting Corporation, Aug. 15, 1931; RG 77, Entry 111, File 3524-42/1 (Kanawha R.–Marmet L/D), NAB.

6. Herman to Chief of Engineers, Aug. 22, 1931; RG 77, Entry 111, File 3524-20 (Kanawha R.–Marmet L/D), NAB.

7. "Delegates for River Meeting to Gather Here," *Montgomery News,* Oct. 9, 1931; "River Group is Feted Here," *Montgomery News,* Oct. 16, 1931.

8. Brown to Secretary of War, Sept. 5, 1931; RG 77, Entry 111, File 7245-88 (Kanawha R.), NAB.

9. Standard Government Form of Invitation for Bids, Marmet Lock B, Sept. 23, 1931; RG 77, Entry 111, Box 657, File 3524-22 (Kanawha R.–Marmet L/D), National Archives at Suitland, Md. (NARA—Suitland).

10. Herman to Chief of Engineers, Nov. 3, 1931; RG 77, Entry 111, File 3524-26 (Kanawha R.–Marmet L/D), NAB.

11. Congressman Clyde Kelly, Pa., to Brown, Nov. 12, 1931; RG 77, Entry 111, File 3524-28 (Kanawha R.–Marmet L/D), NAB.

12. B. Byers, President, General Contracting Corporation, Pittsburgh, to A. G. Rothey, Elizabeth, Pa., Nov. 13, 1931; RG 77, Entry 111, File 3524 (Part 2), (Kanawha R.–Marmet L/D), NAB.

13. H. W. Temple to Brown, Washington, D.C., Nov. 12, 1931; RG 77, Entry 111, File 3524-29 (Kanawha R.–Marmet L/D), NAB.

14. General Sales Manager, Green Bag Cement Company, Pittsburgh, to Lt. Casey, Washington, D.C., Nov. 12, 1931; RG 77, Entry 111, File 3524-30 (Kanawha R.–Marmet L/D), NAB.

15. Alexander Best, Secretary-Treasurer, Wheeling Structural Steel Co., Wheeling, W.V., to Major Fred W. Herman, District Engineer, Huntington, W.V., March 29, 1932; RG 77, Entry 111, File 3524-56 (Kanawha R.–Marmet L/D), NAB.

16. Standard Bid Invitation, Marmet Locks and Dam, June 23, 1932; RG 77, Entry 111, File 3524-75 (Kanawha R.–Marmet L/D), NAB.

17. J. Thomas Ward, Attorney-at-Law, Huntington, W.V., to Brig. Gen. George B. Pillsbury, Asst. Chief of Engineers, Aug. 7, 1932; RG 77, Entry 111, File 3524-90 (Kanawha R.–Marmet L/D), NAB.

18. Ward to Major Herman, Aug. 10, 1932; RG 77, Entry 111, File 3524-90/4 (Kanawha R.–Marmet L/D), NAB.

19. B. B. Byers, President, General Contracting Corporation, Pittsburgh, to Major Herman, May 28, 1932; RG 77, Entry 111 Bulkies, File 3524-100/6 (Kanawha R.–Marmet L/D), NAB.

20. Major Herman to Chief of Engineers, Aug. 25, 1932; RG 77, Entry 111, File 3524-97 (Kanawha R.–Marmet L/D), NAB.

21. "Notice of Public Hearing" by Major Herman, July 7, 1932; RG 77, Entry 111, File 7425-34 (Kanawha River L/D), NAB.

22. "List of Participants—Public Hearing," July 20, 1932; RG 77, Entry 111, Bulkies, File 7245-98/2 (Kanawha River L/D), NAB.

23. District Engineer, Huntington, W.V., to Division Engineer, St. Louis, Mo., "Report of Survey of Kanawha River, W.Va., Lock 5 to Mouth," Aug. 15, 1932; RG 77, Entry 111 Bulkies, File 7245-98 (Kanawha River), NARA—Suitland.

24. H. A. Zeller, Vice President and General Manager, West Virginia Rail Company, Huntington, W.V., to Senator H. D. Hatfield, Huntington, W.V., July 23, 1932, and Aug. 1, 1932; RG 77, Entry 111, File 3524 (Kanawha R.–Marmet L/D), NAB.

25. Col. George R. Spalding, Division Office, St. Louis, Mo., to Chief of Engineers, Oct. 3, 1932; RG 77, Entry 111, Box 655, File 3524-38 (Kanawha R.–London L/D), NARA—Suitland.

26. W. H. McAlpine, Head Engineer, Upper Mississippi Valley Division, to Gen. Pillsbury and Maj. Herman, Oct. 4, 1932; RG 77, Entry 111, File 3524-40 (Kanawha R.–London L/D), NAB.

27. V. B. Edwards, Vice President and General Manager, Dravo Contracting Company, Pittsburgh, to Major Herman, Oct. 14, 1932; RG 77, Entry 111, File 3524-46/9 (Kanawha R.–London L/D), NAB.

28. Maj. Gen. Brown to Dravo Contracting Company, Oct. 14, 1932, and William H. Fowler, Secretary, Dravo Contracting Co., Aug. 23, 1932; RG 77, Entry 111, File 3524-91 (Kanawha R.–Marmet L/D), NAB.

29. Circular No. 33-59, "Abstract of Proposals," London Locks and Dam, Oct. 17, 1932; RG 77, Entry 111, File 3524-44 (Kanawha R.–London L/D), NAB.

30. Major Herman to Chief of Engineers, Oct. 18, 1932; RG 77, Entry 111, File 3524-46 (Kanawha R.–London L/D), NAB.

31. *Emergency Relief and Construction Act of 1932, Statutes at Large* 47, part 1 (1932): 709.

32. F. H. Payne, Asst. Secy. of War, Washington, D.C., to W. H. White, United Brotherhood of Carpenters and Joiners of America, Charleston, W.V., Nov. 28, 1932; RG 77, Entry 111, File 3524-48 (Kanawha R.–London L/D), NAB.

33. Herman to Dravo, Feb. 21, 1933; RG 77, Entry 111, File 3524-58/1 (Kanawha R.–London L/D), NAB.

34. Bragdon to Brown, May 16, 1933; RG 77, Entry 111, File 3524-77 (Kanawha R.–London L/D), NAB.

35. King and King, attorneys for John L. Walsh, Northport Sand and Gravel Co., to Chief of Engineers, Dec. 22, 1932; RG 77, Entry 111, File 3524-51 (Kanawha R.–London L/D), NAB.

36. Herman to Division Engineer, May 25, 1933; RG 77, Entry 111, File 3524-51/1 Appendix A (Kanawha R.–London L/D), NAB.

37. Ibid., p. 5.

38. Ibid., p. 8.

39. Ibid., pp. 8–10.

40. Roy S. Taylor, Senior Inspector, Huntington District, to District Engineer, June 19, 1933; RG 77, Entry 111, File 3524-82/3 (Kanawha R.–London L/D), NAB.

41. Herman to Dravo, June 17, 1933; RG 77, Entry 111, File 3524 (Kanawha R.–London L/D), NAB.

42. Dravo to Herman, June 19, 1933; RG 77, Entry 111, File 3524-81/1 (Kanawha R.–London L/D), NAB.

43. Dravo to Herman, June 19, 1933; RG 77, Entry 111, File 3524-81 (Kanawha R.–London L/D), NAB.

44. Herman to Dravo, June 20, 1933; RG 77, Entry 111, File 3524 (Kanawha R.–London L/D), NAB.

45. Miller to Brown, July 11, 1933; RG 77, Entry 111, File 3524-82 (Kanawha R.–London L/D), NAB.

46. Herman to Chief of Engineers, Aug. 8, 1933; RG 77, Entry 111, File 3524-82 (Kanawha R.–London L/D), NAB.

47. Markham to Dravo, Feb. 14, 1934; RG 77, Entry 111, File 7245-94 (Kanawha R.–London L/D), NAB.

48. Markham to Dravo, May 10, 1934; RG 77, Entry 111, File 7245-100 (Kanawha R.–London L/D), NAB.

49. Herman to Chief of Engineers, Aug. 25, 1933; RG 77, Entry 111, File 7245-2 (Kanawha R. L/D 5), NAB.

50. Herman to Chief of Engineers, Sept. 13, 1933; RG 77, Entry 111, File 7245-108 (Kanawha R.–London L/D), NAB.

51. Chief of Engineers to Secretary of War, Oct. 4, 1933; RG 77, Entry 111, File 7245-110 (Kanawha R.), NAB.

52. President of the United States, Executive Order no. 6859 creating the National Industrial Recovery Fund, Sept. 27, 1934 (1 page).

53. Bragdon to District and Division Engineers, Nov. 29, 1933; RG 77, Entry 1349, File 3240 (National Industrial Recovery Act), NARA—Philadelphia.

54. Change order claims by Dravo, June 23, 1934, July 24, 1934, Aug. 2, 1934, Aug. 6, 1934, Aug. 9, 1934, Aug. 29, 1934, Oct. 19, 1934, Dec. 19, 1945; RG 77, Entry 111, File 3524 (Kanawha R.–London L/D), NAB.

55. Douglas MacArthur, Acting Secretary of War, to Dravo, Aug. 6, 1934; RG 77, Entry 111, File 3524-118 (Kanawha R.–London L/D), NAB.

56. Conklin to Chief of Engineers, Aug. 29, 1934; RG 77, Entry 111, File 3524-120 (Kanawha R.–London L/D), NAB.

57. Capt. Philip G. Bruton, Office of the Chief of Engineers to Dravo, Dec. 19, 1934; RG 77, Entry 111, File 3524-126 (Kanawha R.–London L/D), NAB.

58. Bragdon to Chief of Engineers, Feb. 25, 1935; RG 77, Entry 111, File 3524-123/9 (Kanawha R.–London L/D), NAB.

59. District Engineer to Chief of Engineers, June 18, 1934; RG 77, Entry 111, File 3524-111 (Kanawha R.–London L/D), NAB.

60. *Joint Resolution to Expand until April 1, 1936, Certain Provisions of the National Industrial Recovery Act, and for Other Purposes. Statutes at Large* 49 (1936): 375.

61. Conklin to Chief of Engineers, April 3, 1936; RG 77, Entry 111, File 3524-206 (Kanawha R.–Marmet L/D), NAB.

62. Division Engineer (Powell) to Chief of Engineers, March 18, 1935; RG 77, Entry 111, File 3524-203 (Kanawha R.–Marmet L/D), NAB.

8. GALLIPOLIS AND WINFIELD LOCKS AND DAMS

1. "Engineers to Ask Bids on New Dam Work This Month," *Huntington Advertiser*, Sept. 1, 1933, 1.

2. Herman to Chief of Engineers, Sept. 13, 1933; RG 77, Entry 111, File 7245-107 (Kanawha R.), NAB.

3. Chief of Engineers, *Annual Report 1934*, 967.

4. Neilson to Chief of Engineers, Oct. 5, 1933; RG 77, Entry 111, File 3524-6 (Kanawha R.–Winfield L/D), NAB.

5. Brown to Secretary of War, Oct. 10, 1933; RG 77, Entry 111, File 3524 (Kanawha R.–Winfield L/D), NAB.

6. Harry H. Woodring, Asst. Secretary of War, to Stephen B. Gibbons, Asst. Secretary of the Treasury, Oct. 17, 1933; RG 77, Entry 111, File 3524-12 (Kanawha R.–Winfield L/D), NAB.

7. Comptroller General of the United States to the Secretary of War, Nov. 17, 1933; RG 77, Entry 111, File 3524-19 (Kanawha R.–Winfield L/D), NAB.

8. Comptroller General to the Secretary of War, Jan. 17, 1934; RG 77, Entry 111, File 3524-26 1/2 (Kanawha R.–Winfield L/D), NAB.

9. Comptroller General to the Secretary of War, Jan. 17, 1934; RG 77, Entry 111, File 3524-26 1/2 (Kanawha R.–Winfield L/D), NAB.

10. Comptroller General to the Secretary of War, Feb. 14, 1934; RG 77, Entry 111, File 3524-39 (Kanawha R.–Winfield L/D), NAB.

11. Secretary of War to the Comptroller General, Feb. 16, 1934; RG 77, Entry 111, File 3524-41 (Kanawha River–Winfield L/D), NAB.

12. Herman to Chief of Engineers, Jan. 25, 1934; RG 77, Entry 111, File 3524 (Kanawha R.–Winfield L/D), NAB.

13. F. R. Dravo, President, Dravo Contracting Company, to Chief of Engineers, Feb. 19, 1934; RG 77, Entry 111, File 3524-42 (Kanawha R.–Winfield L/D), NAB.

14. Comptroller General to the Secretary of War, March 19, 1934; RG 77, Entry 111, Box 659, File 3524-50 (Kanawha R.–Winfield L/D), NARA—Suitland.

15. Maj. John F. Conklin, District Engineer, Huntington District, Huntington, W.V., to Chief of Engineers, Nov. 9, 1934; RG 77, Entry 111, File 3524-63 (Kanawha R.–Winfield L/D), NAB.

16. Data for final payment to Dravo for Winfield Locks and Dam, Contract No. W516eng.-726, Nov. 20, 1934; RG 77, Entry 111, File 3524-63/1 (Kanawha R.–Winfield L/D), NAB.

17. S. P. Puffer, Managing Director, Charleston Chamber of Commerce, to Major Herman, Oct. 26, 1934; RG 77, Entry 1349, File W12.2 (National Industrial Recovery Act), NARA—Philadelphia.

18. Herman to Puffer, Nov. 3, 1934; RG 77, Entry 1349, File W12.2 (National Industrial Recovery Act), NARA—Philadelphia.

19. William. H. Fowler, Secretary, Dravo, to Maj. Bragdon, Finance Division, Office of the Chief of Engineers, Feb. 5, 1934; RG 77, Entry 111, File 3524-43 (Kanawha R.–Winfield L/D), NAB.

20. Vinson to Brown, Feb. 3, 1934; RG 77, Entry 111, File 3524-36 (Kanawha R.–Winfield L/D), NAB.

21. Markham to Vinson, Feb. 7, 1934; RG 77, Entry 111, File 3524 (Kanawha R.–Winfield L/D), NAB.

22. Lt. C. T. Hunt, Huntington, W.V., to Chief of Engineers, Feb. 9, 1934; RG 77, Entry 111, File 3524-35 (Kanawha R.–Winfield L/D), NAB.

23. R. E. Plimpton, Asst. Deputy Administrator, National Recovery Administration, to Chief of Engineers, Feb. 21, 1934; RG 77, Entry 111, File 3524-44 (Kanawha R.–Winfield L/D), NAB.

24. Dravo to Bragdon, Feb. 22, 1934; RG 77, Entry 111, File 3524-44 (Kanawha R.–Winfield L/D), NAB.

25. Harold L. Ickes, Federal Emergency Administrator of Public Works, Washington, D.C., to the Secretary of War, July 20, 1934; and Ickes to Secretary of the Treasury, July 20, 1934; RG 77, Entry 111, File 7245 (Kanawha River), NAB.

26. Pillsbury to Fred E. Schnepfe, Director of Federal Projects, Federal Emergency Administrator of Public Works, Aug. 8, 1934; RG 77, Entry 111, File 7245 (Kanawha R.), NAB.

27. Proposed Expenditure of $2,200,000 Allotment for Lower Kanawha Project, Aug. 10, 1934; RG 77, Entry 111, File 7245-122/1 (Kanawha R.), NAB.

28. Schnepfe to Pillsbury, Aug. 14, 1934; RG 77, Entry 111, File 7245-123 (Kanawha R.), NAB.

29. Capt. John B. LaGuardia, Office of the Chief of Engineers, to District Engineer, Huntington, W.V., Aug. 27, 1934; RG 77, Entry 111, File 7245 (Kanawha R.), NAB.

30. Conklin to Chief of Engineers, Oct. 25, 1934; RG 77, Entry 111, File 7245-127 (Kanawha R.), NAB.

31. *Public Works and Construction Projects. Statutes at Large* 48 (1933): 200–205.

32. Secretary of War to Ickes, Dec. 18, 1934; RG 77, Entry 111, File 7245 (Kanawha R.), NAB.

33. Ickes to Secretary of War, Dec. 28, 1934; RG 77, Entry 111, File 7245-129 (Kanawha R.), NAB.

34. Secretary of War to Ickes, Jan. 7, 1935; RG 77, Entry 111, File 7245-130 (Kanawha R.), NAB.

35. Estimate of Lock 1 Building Machinery, March 14, 1935; RG 77, Entry 111, File 3524-83/3 (Kanawha R.–Winfield L/D), NAB; Bidding Abstract, Feb. 28, 1935; RG 77, Entry 111, File 3524-82/1 (Kanawha R.–Winfield L/D), NAB; Conklin to Chief of Engineers, Feb. 28, 1935; RG 77, Entry 111, File 3524-82 (Kanawha R.–Winfield L/D), NAB.

36. Conklin to Chief of Engineers, April 9, 1935; RG 77, Entry 111, File 3524-85 (Kanawha R.–Winfield L/D), NAB.

37. Conklin to Maj. D. O. Elliott, Cincinnati, May 28, 1935; RG 77, Entry 1348, File W12.2 (National Industrial Recovery Act), NARA—Philadelphia.

38. Advance Notice to Bidders on Construction of Dam No. 1 (Winfield), Kanawha River, June 15, 1935; RG 77, Entry 111, File 3524-91 (Kanawha R.–Winfield L/D), NAB.

39. Comparative Statement of Cost by Hired Labor Alterations, Winfield Locks and Dam, Aug. 1, 1935; RG 77, Entry 111, File 3524-98/2 (Kanawha R.–Winfield L/D), NAB; List of Bidders Invitations, Aug. 1, 1935; RG 77, Entry 111, File 3524-98/4 (Kanawha R.–Winfield L/D), NAB.

40. Walter King, Accountant-in-Charge, U.S. Treasury Department, to District Engineer, Huntington, W.V., Aug. 14, 1935; RG 77, Entry 1349, File W12.3/55.1 (National Industrial Recovery Act), NARA—Philadelphia.

41. Advice of Allotment (Construction of a Dam on the Ohio River, Gallipolis, Ohio), Aug. 27, 1934; RG 77, Entry 111, File 7245-653, NARA—Philadelphia.

42. Secretary of War to Ickes, Aug. 1, 1935; RG 77, Entry 111, File 7245-138 (Kanawha R.), NAB.

43. Conklin to *Manufacturers Record,* Baltimore, Md., June 8, 1935; RG 77, Entry 1348, File W12.2/256.1 (National Industrial Recovery Act), NARA—Philadelphia.

44. Capt. E. J. Bean, Finance Department, Office of the Chief of Engineers, Washington, D.C., to Chief of Engineers, Oct. 14, 1935; RG 77, Entry 111, File 7245-147 (Kanawha R.), NAB.

45. Pillsbury to Secretary of War, Dec. 3, 1936; RG 77, Entry 111, File 7245-63 (Kanawha River L/D), NAB.

46. Conklin to Ohio River Division Engineer, July 12, 1935; RG 77, Entry 111, Entry 3518-1 (Kanawha R.–Winfield L/D), NAB.

47. L. A. Mertz, Treasurer, Dravo Contracting Company, Pittsburgh, to Conklin, Nov. 11, 1936; RG 77, Entry 111, File 3524-139/1 (Kanawha R.–Winfield L/D), NAB.

48. Conklin to Chief of Engineers, March 2, 1937; RG 77, Entry 111, File 3346-8 (Kanawha R.–Winfield L/D), NAB.

49. Conklin to Chief of Engineers, Dec. 29, 1936; RG 77, Entry 111, File 2500-6 (Kanawha R.–L/D), NAB.

50. Conklin to Chief of Engineers, March 30, 1937; RG 77, Entry 111, File 7245-166 (Kanawha River), NAB.

51. Conklin to Division Engineer, Cincinnati, April 9, 1937; RG 77, Entry 111, File 7245-166/1 (Kanawha River), NAB.

52. Conklin to Chief of Engineers, Contract Modifications, April 19, 1937; RG 77, Entry 111, File 7245-168 (Kanawha River), NAB.

53. Lt. Col. J. D. Arthur, District Engineer, Huntington, W.V., to Chief of Engineers, Aug. 10, 1937; RG 77, Entry 111, File 3648-7 (Kanawha R.–Winfield L/D), NAB.

54. R. N. Elliott to Dravo Contracting Company, May 3, 1937; RG 77, Entry 111, File 3524-152 (Kanawha R.–London L/D), NAB.

55. Ibid.

56. Maj. F. F. Frech, Acting District Engineer, Huntington, W.V., to Mrs. Lois Ford, Chief, Department of Information, State Road Commission of West Virginia, Charleston, W.V., Aug. 25, 1937; RG 77, Entry 1349, File W12.3 (National Industrial Recovery Act), NAB.

57. Abstract of Proposals at Winfield project, June 8, 1937; RG 77, Entry 111, File 3648-5/1 (Kanawha R.–Winfield L/D), NAB.

58. Louis Johnson, Acting Secretary of War, Washington, D.C., to the Attorney General, Washington, D.C., ca. Jan. 1939, and General Contracting Corporation vs. The United States, in the Court of Claims of the United States No. 42796, Jan. 9, 1939; RG 77, Entry 111, File 3524-221 (Kanawha R.–Marmet L/D), NAB.

59. Chief of Engineers, *Annual Report,* 1945, 1571.

9. LABOR AND LAND

1. C. P. McKenna, Assistant State Director, State Reemployment Service, Charleston, W.V., to Conklin, Aug. 23, 1935; RG 77, Entry 1249, File W12.3/63.1 (National Industrial Recovery Act), NARA—Philadelphia.

2. "Drowned Man's Body Recovered," *Montgomery News,* March 30, 1933.

3. "Laborer Drowns Today at London," *Montgomery News,* Oct. 5, 1933.

4. U. S. Albertson, attorney, Charleston, W.V., to U.S. Engineering Department, Washington, D.C., Aug. 30, 1934; RG 77, Entry 111, File 3524-119 (Kanawha R.–London L/D), NAB.

5. *National Industrial Recovery Administration Act, Statutes at Large* 48 (1933), 195.

6. *New York Times,* Oct. 2, 1936.

7. Walter Burr, Associate Director for National Reemployment Service, July 17, 1933; RG 77, Entry 1349, File W12.2 (National Industrial Recovery Act), NARA—Philadelphia.

8. Herman to Colonel Long, *Huntington Advertiser,* Sept. 1, 1933; RG 77, Entry 1349, File W12.2 (National Industrial Recovery Act), NARA—Philadelphia.

9. Spalding to District Engineer, Sept. 9, 1933; RG 77, Entry 1349, File W12.2 (National Industrial Recovery Act), NARA—Philadelphia.

10. Miller, Dravo Contracting Company to Brown, Sept. 16, 1933; RG 77, Entry 111, File 3524-89 (Kanawha R.–London L/D), NAB; Miller to Herman, Sept. 18, 1933; RG 77, Entry 111, File 3524-89/1 (Kanawha R.–London L/D), NAB.

11. Herman to Harry White, Charleston Building Trades Council, Charleston, W.V., Oct. 10, 1933; RG 77, Entry 1349, File W12.2 (National Industrial Recovery Act), NARA—Philadelphia.

12. Isador Lubin, Commissioner of Labor Statistics, Labor Department, Washington, D.C., to U.S. Engineer, Huntington, W.V., Oct. 15, 1933; RG 77, Entry 1349, File W12.2 (National Industrial Recovery Act), NARA—Philadelphia.

13. *Public Works Administration Act of 1932, Statutes at Large* 49 (1935), 500–503.

14. Miller to Herman, Nov. 8, 1933; RG 77, Entry 1349, File W12.2 (National Industrial Recovery Act), NARA—Philadelphia.

15. D. P. Childress, Superintendent, Dravo, to C. T. Hunt, Aug. 28, 1934; RG 77, Entry 111, File 3524-58/1 (Kanawha R.–Winfield L/D), NAB.

16. Herman to Chief of Engineers, Feb. 19, 1934; RG 77, Entry 111, File 3524-97 (Kanawha R.–London L/D), NAB.

17. Childress to Hunt, Aug. 28, 1934; RG 77, Entry 111, File 3524-56/1 (Kanawha R.–Winfield L/D), NAB.

18. Conklin to Chief of Engineers, Sept. 10, 1934; RG 77, Entry 111, File 3524-56 (Kanawha R.–Winfield L/D), NAB.

19. J. B. Keenan, Asst. Attorney General, Washington, D.C., to Secretary of War, Nov. 6, 1934, Feb. 19, 1934, Aug. 28, 1934, Sept. 10, 1934, Oct. 1, 1934; RG 77, Entry 111, File 3524-61 (Kanawha R.–Winfield L/D), NAB.

20. Dravo to Hunt, July 3, 1935, and Hunt to Division Engineer, June 28, 1935; RG 77, Entry 1349, File W12.3 (National Industrial Recovery Act), NARA—Philadelphia.

21. "U.S. to Open Bids Monday on Building at Gallipolis Dam," *Herald-Dispatch*, Aug. 3, 1935, 1.

22. "Plans for Carrying out Work, Relief Program, Dec. 21, 1934"; RG 77, Entry 1348, File W12.2 (National Industrial Recovery Act), NARA—Philadelphia.

23. G. A. Sissons, Associate Engineer, Huntington District, to Chief of Engineers, Oct. 1, 1935; RG 77, Entry 1349, File W12.3.1/19 (National Industrial Recovery Act), NARA—Philadelphia.

24. Conklin to Chief of Engineers, Aug. 20, 1935; RG 77, Entry 111, File 7245-143 (Kanawha River), NAB.

25. Dravo to Conklin, July 2, 1935; RG 77, Entry 111, File 3524-96/2 (Kanawha R.–Winfield L/D), NAB.

26. Hunt to Dravo, July 8, 1935; RG 77, Entry 111, File 3524-96/1 (Kanawha R.–Winfield L/D), NAB.

27. Dravo to Markham, July 15, 1935; RG 77, Entry 111, File 3524-96 (Kanawha R.–Winfield L/D), NAB.

28. Thomas E. Jeffers, Clearance Officer, Department of Labor, to Conklin, Sept. 6, 1935; RG 77, Entry 1349, File W12.3/90 (National Industrial Recovery Act), NARA—Philadelphia.

29. C. B. Jansen, Asst. to the President, Dravo, to Conklin, Nov. 1, 1935; RG 77, Entry 111, File 3524-109/1 (Kanawha R.–Winfield L/D), NAB.

30. Hunt to Chief of Engineers, Nov. 4, 1935; RG 77, Entry 111, File 3524-109 (Kanawha R.–Winfield L/D), NAB.

31. Daley to Chief of Engineers, Sept. 16, 1933; RG 77, Entry 111, File 6495-6 (Kanawha River), NAB.

32. Brown to Neely, Aug. 29, 1933; RG 77, Entry 111, File 6495-6 (Kanawha River), NAB.

33. Markham to Neely, Dec. 13, 1933; RG 77, Entry 111, File 6495-7 (Kanawha River), NAB.

34. Herman to Chief of Engineers, Aug. 11, 1933; RG 77, Entry 111, File 6500-56 (Kanawha River), NAB.

35. "Public Notice" to all landowners affected by the flowage of the Marmet and London Pools, Nov. 21, 1933; RG 77, Entry 111, File 6500-76 (Kanawha River), NAB.

36. Attorney General to Secretary of War, Nov. 8, 1933; RG 77, Entry 111, File 6500-74 (Kanawha River), NAB.

37. Correspondence, United States vs. Quincy Coal Company, May 17, 1934, June 23, 1934, June 30, 1934, and July 5, 1934; RG 77, Entry 111, Files 6500-110 and 6500-144 (Kanawha River), NAB.

38. Herman to Chief of Engineers, April 10, 1933; RG 77, Entry 111, File 6500-42 (Kanawha River), NAB.

39. Herman to Chief of Engineers, Sept. 6, 1933; RG 77, Entry 111, File 6500-60 (Kanawha River), NAB.

40. The Chesapeake and Ohio Railway Company "Offer" to sell land to the United States, March 10, 1933; RG 77, Entry 111, File 6500-42/1 (Kanawha River), NAB.

41. "Hearings on Dam Land Progress at Charleston," *Montgomery News*, May 2, 1935.

42. United States Senate, *Land for Municipal Purposes, Marmet, W. Va.—Veto Message*, 76th Cong., 3d sess. (1940), Document No. 173.

43. Memorandum to Major Boatner pertaining to erosion at Winfield locks and dam, Nov. 30, 1940; RG 77, Entry 111, File 2500-5 (Kanawha R.–Winfield L/D), NAB.

44. Ibid., p. 3; emphasis in original.

45. Congressman Joe L. Smith, Washington, D.C., to Louis A. Johnson, June 2, 1939; RG 77, Entry 111, File 2500-5 (Kanawha R.–Winfield L/D), NAB.

46. Herman to Chief of Engineers, Sept. 8, 1933; RG 77, Entry 111, File 6500-62 (Kanawha River), NAB.

47. Lt. Col. J. D. Arthur, District Engineer, Huntington District, to Chief of Engineers, Aug. 25, 1937; RG 77, Entry 111, File 6500-626 (Kanawha River), NAB.

48. J. D. Londeree, Recorder, Town of South Charleston, to Senator Neely, June 1, 1939; RG 77, Entry 111, File 2500-6/1 (Kanawha R.–Winfield L/D), NAB.

49. W. M. Dickinson, General Contractor, South Charleston, W.V., to the President of the United States, July 9, 1940; RG 77, Entry 111, File 2500-18 (Kanawha R.–Winfield L/D), NAB.

50. Conklin to Chief of Engineers, Dec. 22, 1936; RG 77, Entry 111, File 7245-163 (Kanawha River), NAB.

10. HYDROELECTRIC POWER GENERATION

1. "Fayette County Has One of World's Greatest Hydroelectric Projects," *Montgomery News*, April 27, 1933, 1.

2. It began as early as the 1910 Dam Act, the Rivers and Harbors Act of 1912, the Federal Water Power Act of 1920, and the Rivers and Harbors Act of 1930.

3. "Memorandum Regarding Federal Regulations of the Operation of Power Developments in Connection with Two Navigation Dams at London and Marmet on the Kanawha River in West Virginia," March 19, 1932; RG 77, Entry 110, File 7495 Part 1, 1–45 (Kanawha Valley Power Co.), NAB.

4. Secretary of War, *Estimate of Cost of Examinations, Etc., of Streams Where Power Development Appears Feasible*, H.R. Doc. 308, 69th Cong., 1st sess., 1926, 1–6; *Division of Bookkeeping and Warrants*, H.R. Doc 309, 69th Cong., 1st sess., 1926.

5. Secretary of War, *Kanawha River, W. VA.*, H.R. Doc. 190, 70th Cong., 1st sess., 1928, 15.

6. Secretary of War, *Kanawha River, W. VA., VA., and N.C.* H.R. Doc. 91, 74th Cong., 1st sess., 1935, 74–75.

7. Kanawha Valley Power Company Application for License, Sept. 28, 1931; RG 77, Entry 110, File 7495 (Kanawha Valley Power Co.), NAB.

8. *Kanawha River, W. Va.*, H.R. Document 190, 70th Cong., 1st sess., 1928, 4, paragraph 11.

9. Spalding to Chief of Engineers, Feb. 24, 1932; RG 77, Entry 110, File 7495-4 (Kanawha Valley Power Co.), NAB. Lt. Col. John J. Kingman, Office of the Chief of Engineers, Washington, D.C., to Division Engineer, St. Louis, Mo., March 23, 1932; RG 77, Entry 110, File 7495-9 (Kanawha Valley Power Co.), NAB.

10. Gen. Brown to Chairman, Federal Power Commission, Washington, April 14, 1932; RG 77, Entry 110, File 7495-1 (Kanawha Valley Power Co.), NAB.

11. F. W. Scheidenhelm, Consulting Engineer, New York, to Gen. Pillsbury, Aug. 12, 1932; RG 77, Entry 110, File 7495 (Kanawha Valley Power Co.), NAB.

12. Kanawha Navigation Dam Power-Project No. 1175 at Marmet and London Navigation Dams on Kanawha River, W. Va. Economics of Power Development at One Dam, Oct. 30, 1933, and Estimate of Operating Costs for a Modern Kanawha Region Steam-Electric Station, Oct. 31, 1933, by Scheidenhelm; RG 77, Entry 110, File 7495 (Kanawha Valley Power Co.), NAB.

13. Federal Power Commission License on Navigable Waters, Project No. 1175, West Virginia, Kanawha Valley Power Company, Jan. 16, 1934; RG 77, Entry 110, File 7495-28 (Kanawha Valley Power Co.), NAB.

14. Frank R. McNinch, Chairman, Federal Power Commission, Washington, D.C., to Gen. Markham, Feb. 7, 1934; RG 77, Entry 110, File 7495-30 (Kanawha Valley Power Co.), NAB.

15. McNinch to Markham, May 29, 1934; RG 77, Entry 110, File 7495-38 (Kanawha Valley Power Co.), NAB.

16. Kanawha Valley Power Company Agreement with the United States of America, July 16, 1934; RG 77, Entry 110, File 7495-39/1 (Kanawha Valley Power Co.), NAB.

17. McNinch to Graham Clayter, Vice President, Kanawha Valley Power Co., New York, Sept. 18, 1934; RG 77, Entry 110, File 7495-43 (Kanawha Valley Power Co.), NAB.

18. Powell to Chief of Engineers, Dec. 22, 1934; RG 77, Entry 110, File 7495-44 (Kanawha Valley Power Co.), NAB.

19. "Marmet Lock to Be Open on May 10," *Montgomery News,* May 3, 1934.

20. "Power Projects to Be Let Soon," *Montgomery News,* May 24, 1934.

21. "100 Begin Work On Power Plants," *Montgomery News,* June 7, 1934.

22. C. L. Jarrett, Commissioner, West Virginia Department of Labor, Charleston, W.V., to Maj. John F. Conklin, District Engineer, Huntington, W.V., Dec. 6, 1934; RG 77, Entry 1349, File W12.2/179 (National Industrial Recovery Act), NARA— Philadelphia.

23. McNinch to Markham, Jan. 2, 1935, and Division Engineer, Ohio River Division, to Chief of Engineers, Jan. 15, 1935; RG 77, Entry 110, File 7495-45 (Kanawha Valley Power Co.), NAB.

24. Powell to Chief of Engineers, Feb. 12, 1935; RG 77, Entry 110, File 7495-7 (Kanawha Valley Power Co., Project 1290), NAB.

25. Memorandum from Scheidenhelm concerning Winfield Project, April 2 and April 4, 1935; RG 77, Entry 110, File 7495 (Kanawha Valley Power Co., Project 1290), NAB.

26. Powell to Federal Power Commission, Nov. 6, 1935; RG 77, Entry 110, File 7495-31/1 (Kanawha Valley Power Co.), NAB.

27. Federal Power Commission Order and Opinion No. 20, Feb. 4, 1936; RG 77, Entry 110, File 7495-54/1 (Kanawha Valley Power Co.), NAB.

28. Federal Power Commission License for Project No. 1290, March 31, 1936; RG 77, Entry 110, File 7495-31/2 (Kanawha Valley Power Co., Project 1290), NAB.

29. Scheidenhelm to Chief of Engineers, Sept. 9, 1937; RG 77, Entry 110, File 7495-35 (Kanawha Valley Power Co., Project 1290), NAB.

30. Powell to Chief of Engineers, Oct. 7, 1937; RG 77, Entry 110, File 7495-36 (Kanawha Valley Power Co., Project 1290), NAB.

31. Leon M. Fuquay, Secretary, Federal Power Commission, to Kanawha Valley Power Company, Nov. 6, 1937; RG 77, Entry 110, File 7495-37 (Kanawha Valley Power Co., Project 1290), NAB.

32. Scheidenhelm to Chief of Engineers, Nov. 8, 1937; RG 77, Entry 110, File 7495-38 (Kanawha Valley Power Co., Project 1290), NAB.

33. Federal Power Commission Order, Dec. 17, 1940; RG 77, Entry 110, File 7495-43/1 (Kanawha Valley Power Co., Project 1290), NAB.

34. Ibid.

35. Philip Sporn and E. L. Peterson, "Design Features of the London and Marmet Hydro Developments," *Power Plant Engineering* 44 (Feb. 1937): 81–87.

36. William P. Creager and Joel D. Justin, *Hydroelectric Handbook* (New York: John Wiley and Sons, 1950), 833.

37. Sporn and Peterson, "Design Features of the London and Marmet Hydro Developments," 81–87.

38. Ibid., 84.

39. Philip Sporn and E. L. Peterson, "Design and Operating Features of the Winfield Hydro-Development," *Power Plant Engineering* 44 (Feb. 1937): 36–42, 46.

40. Creager and Justin, *Hydroelectric Handbook*, 961.

41. Sporn and Peterson, "Design Features of the London and Marmet Hydro Developments," 86.

42. Sporn and Peterson, "Design and Operating Features of the Winfield Hydro-Development," 39.

Appendix B: District Engineers

1. Johnson, *An Illustrated History of the Huntington District*, 277.

Selected Bibliography

Addison Scott Collection. Special Collections Department, James E. Morrow Library, Marshall University, Huntington, W.V.

"Allot Six Million To Improve Kanawha." *Herald-Dispatch* (Huntington, W.V.), Sept. 1, 1933, 1–2.

American Society of Civil Engineers. *A Biographical Dictionary of American Civil Engineers*, vol. 2. Historical Publication No. 2. New York: ASCE, 1991.

Association of Graduates, United States Military Academy. *Register of Graduates and Former Cadets of the United States Military Academy*. West Point, N.Y.: Association of Graduates, 1990.

Baldwin, Leland D. *The Keelboat Age on Western Waters*. Pittsburgh, Pa.: University of Pittsburgh Press, 1941.

Belknap, J. H. "Electrical Equipment at Kanawha Dams." *Military Engineer* 27, no. 155 (September–October 1935):349–52.

Boulé, Auguste. "Nouvelle passe navigable." Memoires et Documents No. 42. *Annales des Ponts et Chaussées* (1873): 98–158.

———. "Un nouveau système de barrages mobiles." Memoires et Documents No. 15. *Annales des Ponts et Chaussées* (1876): 320–74.

Callahan, James Morton. *Semi-Centennial History of West Virginia*. Charleston: Centennial Commission of West Virginia, 1913.

Chanoine, Jacques. "Sur le barrage d'Epineau." *Annales des Ponts et Chaussées* 16 (1839): 238–80.

Cohen, Stan, and Richard Andre. *Kanawha County Images: A Bicentennial History 1788–1988*. Charleston, W.V.: Pictorial Histories Publishing Co., 1987.

Cole, Harry. "Design Analysis of Roller Gates for Movable Dams." *Engineering News-Record* 115 (Nov. 21, 1935): 718–22.

Conley, Phil. "Early Coal Development in the Kanawha Valley." *West Virginia History* 8 (Jan. 1947).

Craighill, William P. *Kanawha River Improvement: Proposals for the Iron Work of a Movable Dam on the Great Kanawha River.* Baltimore, Md.: U.S. Engineer Office, 1877.

Creager, William P., and Joel D. Justin. *Hydroelectric Handbook.* New York: John Wiley and Sons, 1950.

Dunaway, Wayland F. *History of the James River and Kanawha Company.* Ph.D. diss., Columbia University Studies in History, Economics and Public Law, vol. 104. New York: Columbia University Press, 1922.

Ellet, Charles, Jr. *The Mississippi and Ohio Rivers: Containing Plans for the Protection of the Delta from Inundation; and the Investigations of the Practicability and Cost of Improving the Navigation of the Ohio and Other Rivers by Means of Reservoirs.* Philadelphia: Lippincott, 1853.

———. *Report on the Improvement of the Kanawha and Incidentally of the Ohio River by Means of Artificial Lakes.* Philadelphia, 1858.

"Engineers To Ask Bids on New Dam Work This Month." *Huntington Advertiser,* Sept. 1, 1933, 1.

Every, Dale Van. *Ark of the Empire: The American Frontier, 1784–1803.* New York: Morrow, 1963.

Gamble, J. Mack. "Steamboats in West Virginia." *West Virginia History* 15 (Oct. 1953): 124–38.

Hahn, Thomas F., and Emory L. Kemp. *Cement Mills along the Potomac River.* Morgantown, W.V.: Institute for the History of Technology and Industrial Archaeology, 1994.

Hale, John P. "History of the Great Kanawha Slackwater Improvements." *West Virginia Historical Magazine* 1 (April 1901).

Hansel, Norris. *Josiah White: Quaker Entrepreneur.* Easton, Pa.: Canal History and Technology Press, 1992.

Harris, V. B. *Great Kanawha.* Charleston, W.V.: Jarrett Printing Company, 1974.

Hilgard, K. E. "Natural Waterways, Rolling Dams." *Transactions American Society of Civil Engineers* 54 (1905): 439–47, Part D, 905.

Hunter, Louis C. *Steamboats on the Western Rivers: An Economic and Technological History.* Cambridge, Mass.: Harvard University Press, 1949.

Hunter, Robert F., and Edwin L. Dooley, Jr. *Claudius Crozet: French Engineer in America, 1790–1864.* Charlottesville: University Press of Virginia, 1989.

Johnson, Leland R. *An Illustrated History of the Huntington District U.S. Army Corps of Engineers, 1754–1974.* Washington, D.C.: Government Printing Office, 1977.

———. *The Davis Island Lock and Dam: 1870–1922.* Pittsburgh: Pittsburgh District, U.S. Army Corps of Engineers, 1985.

"Kanawha River Is Key To Valley Progress." *Charleston Daily Mail,* May 22, 1927, sec. 3, p. 1.

Kirkwood, James L. *Waterways to the West.* Interpretive Series No. 1. N.p.: Eastern National Park and Monument Association, 1963.

Laing, James T. "The Early Development of the Coal Industry in the Western Counties of Virginia, 1800–1965." *West Virginia History* 27, no. 2 (Jan. 1966): 144–55.

"Lock and Dam No. 5, near Brownstown, WV, of Great Kanawha River Improvement." *The Virginias: A Mining, Industrial, and Scientific Journal* 2 (Aug. 1881).

Lorraine, Eduard. *The Central Water-Line from the Ohio River to the Virginia Capes.* Richmond, Va.: Gary, Clemmitt and Jones, 1869.

Loveland, P. W., and T. P. Bailey. "Navigation on the Ohio River." *Military Engineer* 41, no. 281 (May–June 1949): 171–75.

"Major Works Project Pushed: U.S. and State Act to Provide Jobs at Once." *Herald-Dispatch*, Oct. 18, 1933, 1–2.

Martin, C. R. "New Design Cuts Cost of Roller Gates." *Engineering News-Record* 122 (May 25, 1939): 716.

McAlpine, W. H. "Roller Gates in Navigation Dams." *Military Engineer* 150 (Nov.–Dec. 1934): 419.

Melhorn, Wilton N., and John P. Kempton, eds. "Geology and Hydrogeology of the Teays-Mahomet Bedrock Valley System." Special Paper 258. Boulder, Colo.: Geological Society of America, 1991.

"Modern Types of Movable Dams: Reports Read at the XVIth International Congress on Navigation, Brussels, 1935." *Engineer* 160 (Nov. 8, 1935): 471–73.

National Archives and Records Administration (NARA). Files of the Corps of Engineers. Record Group 77. Washington National Records Center, Washington, D.C. (Washington; College Park, Md.; Archives II.)

———. Files of the Corps of Engineers. Record Group 77. Mid-Atlantic Branch, Philadelphia, Pa.

O'Brien, William Patrick, Mary Yeater Rathbun, and Patrick O'Bannon. *Gateways to Commerce.* Denver: National Park Service, 1992.

Oxx, Francis H. "The Ohio River Movable Dams." *Military Engineer* 27, no. 151: 49–58.

"Protests Are Heard on Kanawha Dams." *Montgomery News*, Sept. 12, 1930, 1.

"Report States 2,034 Employed." *Montgomery News*, Aug. 15, 1935, 4.

Rice, Otis K. *Charleston and the Kanawha Valley.* Woodland Hills, Calif.: Windsor Publications, 1981.

"Roller-Gate Dam Erection at Rock Island, Ill." *Engineering News-Record* 112 (March 29, 1934): 410–14.

"Roller-Gate Dams for Kanawha River." *Engineering News-Record* 111 (Sept. 12, 1933): 337–42.

Rolt, L.T.C. *Navigable Waterways.* London: Arrow, 1973.

Scott, Addison M. *Coal: Commerce and Development on the Great Kanawha Valley, The Cheapest Transportation Known.* Charleston, W.V.: Daily Gazette, 1891.

———. "General Notes on the Great Kanawha Improvement." *Transactions of the American Society of Civil Engineers* 86 (1923): 132–33.

Spencer, Esther Adeline. "Transportation in the Kanawha Valley 1784–1890." M.A. thesis, Marshall College, 1941.

Sporn, Philip, and E. L. Peterson. "Design Features of the London and Marmet Hydro Developments." *Power Plant Engineering* 41, no. 2 (Feb. 1937): 80–87.

Sprague, John C. "Concrete for the Kanawha River Project." *Civil Engineering* 8, no. 12 (Dec. 1938): 797–800.

Sutphin, Gerald W., and Richard A. Andre. *Sternwheelers on the Great Kanawha River.* Charleston, W.V.: Pictorial Histories Publishing Co., 1991.

Thomas, B. F. "Movable Dams." *Transactions of the American Society of Civil Engineers* 39 (June 1898).

Thomas, Benjamin F., and D. A. Watt. *The Improvement of Rivers.* New York: John Wiley and Sons, 1913.

U.S. Army Corps of Engineers. *Annual Report.* Various years.

———. *The History of the U. S. Army Corps of Engineers.* Washington, D.C.: Government Printing Office, 1978.

U.S. Congress. House. *James River and Kanawha Canal.* 41st Cong., 3d sess., 1871. Ex. Doc. 110.

———. *James River and Kanawha Canal.* 43d Cong., 1st sess., 1874. Ex. Doc. 219.

———. *Plans for the Improvement of the Ohio River.* 46th Cong., 2d Sess., 1880. Misc. Doc. 33.

———. *Kanawha River, W. Va.* 63d Cong., 1st Sess., 1913. Doc. 41.

———. *Kanawha River W. Va.* 70th Cong., 1st Sess., 1928. H. Doc. 190.

———. *Kanawha River W. Va. from Lock 5 to Its Mouth.* 73d Cong., 1st Sess., 1933. H. Doc. 31.

———. *Kanawha River, W.VA., VA, and NC.* 74th Cong., 1st Sess., 1935. H.R. Doc. 91.

U.S. Congress. Senate. Committee on Appropriations. *Hearings on Public Works for Water and Power Resources.* 90th Cong., 2d Sess., 1969.

"U.S. Engineers Will Hire 200 More Men From Relief Rolls." *Herald-Dispatch*, Aug. 17, 1935, 14.

U.S. Statutes at Large 42 (1922): Part 1, Chapter 427, 1045. *An Act Authorizing the Construction, Repair, and Preservation of Certain Public Works on Rivers and Habrors, and for Other Purposes.*

U.S. Statutes at Large 44 (1927): Part 2, Chapter 47, 1020. *An Act Authorizing the Construction, Repair, and Preservarion of Certain Public Works on Rivers and Harbors, and for Other Purposes.*

Vernon-Harcourt, Leveson F. "Fixed and Movable Weirs." In *Minutes of Proceedings of the Institution of Civil Engineers.* Paper no. 1655 (Jan. 20, 1880): 28.

Watson, William. "River Improvements in France, Including A Description of Poiree's System of Movable Dams." *Van Nostrand's Engineering Magazine.* New York: D. Van Nostrand, 1878.

Wegmann, Edward. *The Design and Construction of Dams.* New York: John Wiley and Sons, 1900.

[West] Virginia. Legislature. "An Act to Amend and Re-enact the Act Passed May 15, 1862, Entitled 'An Act to Reorganize the Kanawha Board.'" *Ordinances and Acts of the Restored Government of Virginia, Prior to the Formation of the State of West Virginia, with the Constitution and Laws of the State of West Virginia, to March 2d, 1866.* Wheeling, W.V.: John Frew, 1866.

West Virginia. Legislature. "An Act in Relation to the Collection of Tolls on the Great Kanawha River and to Terminate the Existence of the Kanawha Board." *Acts of the Legislature*. Wheeling, W.V.: W. J. Johnston, 1881.

"Why Kanawha River Should Be Improved." *Huntington Advertiser*, Jan. 9, 1927, sec. 3, p. 1.

"Work on Kanawha Will Begin Soon." *Montgomery News*, Aug. 15, 1930, 1.

Yates, J. E. "Roller Gates Make Up the Major Portion of Powerdale Dam." *Engineering News-Record* 94, no. 12 (March 19, 1925): 482–83.

Zahlen, John V. "Roller Gates on Dams Not Confined to Scandinavia and Germany." *Engineering News-Record* 816 (Nov. 29, 1928).

Index

Engineers, 42–48. *See also specific engineers*

Erie Canal, 11, 13, 56

Erosion control, 127, 128, 219-20

Federal Employment Office, 215

Federal Power Commission (FPC), 226, 227, 231, 233

Federal Waterways Improvement Act (1824), 20

Fegle Construction Company, 140

Field vs. model tests, 137–39

Fisk, Charles B., 20

Flap-type drum, 117–18

Flap-type gate, 150–51, 200

Flash-lock system, 28, 86

Flood control, 205–6, 224, 252

Flooding, 13, 19, 154

Flowage easements, 217–22; erosion control and, 219–20

Frame/needle weirs, 28, 30

Francis (reaction type) turbine, 241

French movable dams, 22, 23, 26–27, 28, 30, 34–35

Froude, William, 127

Froudin discharge scale, 138

Funding, for locks and dams. *See under specific locks and dams*

Fuquay, Leon, 235

Gallatin, Albert, 5

Gallipolis and Winfield locks and dams, 132, 169–206, 189, 203, 251; construction materials for, 124–25, 186–87, 205, 206; contract bids for, 169–70, 172, 175–76, 181–82, 185–86, 195, 200–201; description of, 257–58; field tests of, 134, 137, 138; funds for, 190–91, 195, 199, 204; hydroelectric power at, 225, 243, 246–47; labor for, 213, 215–16; NIRA and, 210–12, 213–14; roller gates for, 105, 115, 250; siting of, 149, 150

Gate design, 102–6, 115–18, 137; bear trap, 25–27; flap-type, 150–51, 200; hydraulic loads and, 116–18; sector, 103–4; Tainter, 104–5, 109–10, 150. *See also* Roller gates; Weirs

Gauley River, 4

General Accounting Office, 204

General Construction Corporation, 167

General Contracting Corporation, 140, 143, 144, 146, 204

Geometric similarity, 127, 137

German roller-gate system, 99–100, 102, 106, 250

Gill, E. H., 20

Gillmore, Quincy Adams, 10, 58

Grant, Ulysses S., 8

Greenbag Cement Company, 143–44

Gustavburg Bridge Works, 106

Hains, 73

Harold and McDonald (contractors), 63

Harris and Black (contractors), 56

Harvey, R. W., 217

Hawk's Nest Dam, 223, 252

Hayes, Rutherford B., 47

Hazard and White (contractors), 25

Heath, George, 104

Heavener, C. Paul, 98

Hefright, Frank, 63

Herman, Fred W., Jr., 99, 153, 186, 218, 225; Marmet and, 141, 143, 144, 145, 157; NIRA and, 210–12

Hildreth, George, 104

Hilgard, K. E., 105

Hillberg, A. G., 117

Hodges, H. F., 87

House Document *190,* 99

Hughes, J. A., 96

Hunt, C. T., 215, 216

Hurters: Pasqueau, 60, 63; Scott, 65, 71; Thomas, 47, 52

Hutton, W. H., 47

Hutton, William R., 52–53

Hydration, heat of, 154
Hydraulic cement, 56, 57
Hydraulic loads, 116–18
Hydraulic model studies, 126–29, 132, 134, 137–39
Hydraulic pressure, 102, 103, 126
Hydraulics Laboratory at the Carnegie Institute of Technology, 132
Hydroelectric power, 102, 223–27, 232–33; construction of, 235, 236, 238–39; equipment, 239–45; federal government and, 223–24; private industry and, 225–27; stations, 88, 98, 206, 219, 256

Ice formation, on movable gates, 109–10
Ice piers, 63
Ickes, Harold L., 189, 196, 199, 209
Industry, 16–18; chemical production, 90; coal, 16, 18, 19, 21, 53; gas and oil, 16, 90; salt, 16, 17; sand and gravel, 96, 153, 186–87, 188; timber, 16, 17
Internal-improvements movement, 5–6
Iowa Institute of Hydraulic Research of the University of Iowa, 126
Iron and steel components, 59, 73, 150

Jacoby's method, 117
James River, 5, 6
James River and Kanawha Canal Company, 7, 8, 12, 13, 14; improvements and, 18, 20
James River Company, 6, 7, 17
Janicki, 28
Jarett, C. L., 228
Jeffries, Thomas E., 84–85, 87, 88, 216

Kanawha Board, 19, 21
Kanawha County Road Department, 98
Kanawha Improvement (1820–1870), 17–22

Kanawha Improvement (1875–1898), 48–81; Appropriations for, 54, 56; cofferdams and, 61–62, 77; completion of, 64–65, 68, 77–78, 80–81; construction materials for, 56–59; contractors for, 49–50; cost of, 78; delays in, 50–52, 72–74; engineering problems and, 60–61; estimated cost of, 49, 54; lock design and, 52–53; World's Columbian Expedition, 71
Kanawha Improvement (1930–1937): proposals for, 90–91, 95–100, 146, 149–50; surveys for, 86–88, 149. See also London and Marmet locks and dams; Gallipolis and Winfield locks and dams
Kanawha Valley Improvement Association, 89–90, 96
Kanawha Valley Power Company, 206, 226, 227, 231, 232, 233
Kaplan turbine, 241, 242, 243
Keenan, Joseph B., 212
Kelly, Clyde, 143
Kenova Works, 144
Keokuk Dam, 103
Keystone Sand and Gravel Company, 187
Kinematic similarity, 127
King, Walter, 201
King and King (attorneys), 153
Kingman, John J., 226
Krantz, 40
Krupp Corporation, 115, 151

Labor, 52, 207–16, 228, 230; eight-hour law and, 210–11, 212; operators and, 207–8; physical examinations and, 213–14; 90% rule for, 215–16; wage rates for, 8, 152, 208, 210, 211–12
Land acquisition, 217–22; condemnation proceedings for, 218, 220; easement claims for, 220–22
Landslide, 144–46
Lang, Robert A., 26

Latrobe, Benjamin Henry, Jr., 10–11
Leadership. *See* Engineers; *and specific engineers*
Lelia (ship), 203
Lewis, Marshall, 103
Livermore, Daniel, 7
Local 1207 of the Brotherhood of Carpenters and Joiners of America, 152
Local suppliers/subcontractors, 186–87, 189
Lock and dam: no. 1, 21; no. 11, 82–83, 86, 87; operational problems of, 82–86
Lock and dam improvements. *See* Kanahwa improvements; *specific locks and dams*
Lockwood, Daniel W., 88–89
London and Marmet locks and dams, 140–68, 151, 250; change orders for, 152–56, 160–61, 163–64, 167–68; contractors for, 140–44, 150, 152; description of, 253–56; hydroelectric power at, 226, 228, 231, 242, 244–46, 256–57; labor for, 210–11, 212–13; landslide at, 144–46; model/field tests at, 137–39
Long, Steven Harriman, 15
Lorraine, Eduard, 12, 20, 49
Loup Creek Shoals, 87
Lower Kanawha Project, 190–91, 195

McAlpine, William, 151
McDonald, C. I., 65, 72
McGafferty, Charles, and Company, 49–50
McNeill, 11
McNinch, Frank R., 227, 231
Markham, E. M., 156, 187, 212, 217
Marmet locks and dam. *See* London and Marmet locks and dams
Marshall, W. L., 71
Martin, C. R., 117–18
Maschinenfabrik Augsburg-Nurnberg (MAN), 99, 106, 115

Maury, James, 5
Mead and Scheidenhelm (consultants), 226
Meadow River, 20
Merchant, S. L., and Company, 58
Merrill, William E., 23, 44–46, 47, 96
Miller, J. S., 155, 210, 215
Mississippi Basin Model, 138–39
Mississippi Navigation, Upper, 104–5, 115, 126
Model, vs. field tests, 137–39
Monongahela River, 38, 39, 99
Monongahela-type locks, 99
Montgomery News (newspaper), 142, 219, 223
Movable dams, French, 22, 23, 28, 30, 34–35; bear-trap, 25–27. *See also* Chanoine wicket dams; Weirs
Muck, W. H., 212
Mumford and Reynolds (contractor), 65
Munford, Thomas, 74, 77
Mussel Shoals Canal, 26
Fred J. Myers Manufacturing Company, 73

National Industrial Recovery Act (NIRA, 1933), 176, 185, 187; allotments and, 160, 169, 189; labor and, 167, 207–11, 213–14, 231
National Relief Agency, 213
Navigation delays, 64, 82–86
Needle weirs, 28, 30
Neely, M. M., 217
Neilson, A. M., 169
Nelson, Martin E., 128
New Deal, 159, 187, 189, 228, 251; labor legislation, 152, 207–11, 214, 216. *See also* National Industrial Recovery Act (NIRA, 1933)
Newport News Shipbuilding and Drydock Company, 243–44, 257
New River, 3–4
New York Barge Canal, 13
90% rule, for labor, 215–16

Steam navigation, 16, 18
Steel/iron components, 59, 73, 144, 150
Stone, 58–59, 74, 77
Stoney, Francis G. G., 103
Stoney gates, 103, 109–10
Stoney valves, 103, 170, 185, 255
Strong and Son (contractor), 61, 63
Structural and hydraulic analysis, 126–
  29, 132, 134, 137–39
Suppliers/contractors, local, 186–87,
  189. *See also specific suppliers/contrac-
  tors*
Surveys, of Kanawha River, 86–88, 149
Sutherland, George E., 96
Synchronization, 245

Tainter, Jeremiah B., 104
Tainter gates, 104–5, 109–10, 150–51
Tanner, James A., 43
Taylor, Roy T., 154
Teichman, Frank, 106
Temple, A. W., 143
Ten Mile Island, 48
Thayer, O. A. and W. T., 63
Thirty-hour-week rule, 211–12
Thénard, 34
Thénard shutter, 34, 39
Thomas, Benjamin F., 28, 47, 52
Thomas Dam (Louisa, Kentucky), 28
Thomas hurters, 47, 52
308-309 Documents, 223–24
Timber industry, 16, 17
Traffic. *See* River traffic
Trippe, Harry M., 89
Turbines, hydroelectric, 240–43
Turtle, Thomas, 46, 47, 57, 60, 64–65
Tygart Dam, 225

U.S. Army Corps of Engineers, 15, 19,
  56, 71, 73, 199, 252; change orders
  and, 153–56; contracts and, 49, 54;
  flood control and, 225, 252; flowage
  easements and, 217–19; hydroelectric
  power and, 225, 226–27, 247; mov-

able dams and, 23, 35, 38–39, 40, 250;
  New Deal and, 159–60, 211; role of,
  102, 251; studies/surveys by, 89, 223–
  24
U.S. Bureau of Reclamation, 106
U.S. Congress, 9, 49, 88, 97

Vertical lift gate, 103
Vinson, Fred, 187
Virginia Assembly, 17–18

Wage rates, 8, 152, 208, 210, 211–12
Waite, H.M., 196
Ward, Thomas J., 144
War Department Appropriation Act
  (1930), 97
Warren, G. K., 42, 43
Washington, George, 6
Washington Water Power Company, 106
Water pressure, 40. *See also* Hydraulic
  loads
Waterways Experiment Station, 138
Weirs, 27–40; drum, 27, 38–39; frame/
  needle, 28, 30; movable shutter, 34–
  35; pontoon, 40
Weitzel, Godfrey, 10, 23, 45–46
Westinghouse (corporation), 254
West Virginia Rail Company, 150
West Virginia Sand and Gravel Com-
  pany, 96
Wheeling Steel Company, 144
White, Canvass, 56
Wicket dams. *See* Chanoine wicket dams
Wiley, Waitman T., 8
William Willson Aluminum Company,
  88
Willing, Wildurr, 126
Wilson, Clivy C., 208
Winfield dam, 135, 136; hydroelectric
  station for, 243, 246–47. *See also*
  Gallipolis and Winfield locks and
  dam
Winifrede Coal Company, 56
Woodring, Henry H., 175